IZAKAYA

Hideo Dekura

First published in 2015 by New Holland Publishers Pty Ltd
London • Sydney • Auckland

The Chandlery, Unit 9, 50 Westminster Bridge Road, London SE1 7QY, United Kingdom
1/66 Gibbes Street, Chatswood, NSW 2067, Australia
5/39 Woodside Avenue, Northcote, Auckland 0627, New Zealand

www.newhollandpublishers.com

Copyright © 2015 New Holland Publishers Pty Ltd
Copyright © 2015 in text: Hideo Dekura
Copyright © 2015 in images: Keiko Dekura

All rights reserved. No part of this publication may be reproduced, stored in a retrieval system or transmitted, in any form or by any means, electronic, mechanical, photocopying, recording or otherwise, without the prior written permission of the publishers and copyright holders.

A record of this book is held at the British Library and the National Library of Australia.

ISBN: 9781742575254

Managing Director: Fiona Schultz
Project Editor: Angela Sutherland
Designer: Thomas Casey
Proofreader: Jessica McNamara
Production Director: Olga Dementiev
Printer: Toppan Leefung Printing Limited

10 9 8 7 6 5 4 3 2 1

Keep up with New Holland Publishers on Facebook
www.facebook.com/NewHollandPublishers

IZAKAYA

Hideo Dekura

NEW HOLLAND

Contents

Acknowledgements 6
Foreword 7
Introduction 9

Drinks 13
Basics 19
Tsumami 27
Vegetables 59
Kushi-yaki 83
Oden 89
Deep-fried dishes 93
Poultry 109
Beef & Pork 125
Seafood 155
Rice 201
Dessert 217

Japanese groceries 232
Afterword 233
Index 235

Acknowledgements

Thanks to all those who have share their memories at Izakaya and helped me complete this book, especially Jill Elias and Keiko and Goutaro Dekura, Andrew Bishop, Emi Tanaka and Kanako Wada. Also thank you to the New Holland Publishers team who have patiently listened to my requests.

SPECIAL THANKS TO:
Claudio's Seafood
Ceramic Studio & Gallery En
Harris Farm Markets
Huon Salmon
Japan Food Corporation Australia
Kikkoman Australia
Sapporo Beer
Sun Masamune Pty Ltd

Foreword

In all the Australian capital cities, especially Sydney and Melbourne, the expansion of the "Izakaya" or "Izakaya restaurant" has been attracting a new trend.

Unlike the common format and image of Izakaya in Japan, here in Australia it is a casual Japanese tapas, serving Japanese fusion cuisine that celebrates fresh and seasonal local ingredients as well as Japanese food. Izakaya restaurants have gained a wider acceptance in Australia where multinational cuisine is well established and very popular with the Australian people.

Izakaya restaurants are where Australian brew Sake and imports can be enjoyed in a relaxed casual dining atmosphere, which is a long standing tradition in Japanese restaurants.

Allan Noble, Managing Director, Sun Masamune Pty Ltd

Introduction

Whenever I enter an Izakaya restaurant, nostalgic memories of my youth float to the surface. I'm not sure why, but I guess the relaxed atmosphere allowed us to talk freely together about our future, relationships, travel plans and lots of other things too. Those casual times with friends having a drink and a few nibbles make me feel good when I recall them even now.

I left Japan when I was in my late twenties, and back then, izakayas were not really what you would call restaurants. They were not particularly stylish, maybe even a bit shabby. Originally they were not much more than a counter bar-space in a Saka-ya (liquor shop) where the owner offered their customers a cup of sake with some nibbles. They became a place for men to drop in after work to have a few drinks, particularly sake, with a limited variety of food. Sometimes when you ordered sake you would also be served 'tsukidashi', a complimentary dish similar to hors d'oeuvre. At that time they were popular with males, and later females accompanied by men, but never girls' groups, or single women either. Since the late 1970s, Izakaya have slowly remodelled their image and atmosphere, developing the menu, moving away from the traditional counter bar, changing the furniture and interior design. In the '80s beer and Chuhai (shōchū mixed with soda water/citrus flavourings) were added to the menu, which was an attraction for younger people, in particular, women. The owners like to offer a personal touch to their menu choices and now some Izakaya are specialising in regional cuisine and sake and there is a greater variety of alcohol. Some Izakaya have catchy names such as the nickname of the owner with the friendly Japanese diminutive "chan", such as "Hide-chan", or other humorous varieties. The red lantern called an aka-chochin hanging outside the Izakaya is still used as a generic sign to indicate that sake is sold on the premises. Whatever their style, they all aim to make you feel welcome and relaxed, and it is easy for Izakaya to become an integral part of a person's lifestyle.

Although the evolution of the Izakaya has brought a lot of visual change, the foundation remains the same. Unlike a typical restaurant, an Izakayas' energy is very important. It is a place that brings people together (not dissimilar to a bar in western society). You can find yourself making new friends over good food and drink.

Izakaya continue to evolve, and more recently are becoming popular in countries outside of Japan. Some have become more upmarket and in a big city like Sydney, where I live, there is even one Izakaya that has a Sake Sommelier and is rather glamorous. They may be far from my image of the traditional Izakaya, but

I can still feel good energy from people enjoying food and alcohol. Regardless of changes, to me they will always be a relaxing, casual place where people can drop in after a busy day at work for a cheap drink and bite to eat.

Izakaya-ryouri

Unlike other Japanese restaurants, there is no predictable indicator of the style or type of food served at Izakaya restaurants. It always depends on the chef/owner. The chef's background may be quite unique and individual compared to other Japanese restaurants. Some may be from traditional restaurants, others trained overseas, regional areas, others from the fish markets. But they all work with the owners to produce good food at a budget price, and have a good nature and commitment to food and sake. Some specialise in particular ingredients or style, such as Oden (hot pot), Motsu (hotpot with entrails), or Yakitori. Yakitori Izakaya may serve only chicken, but others serve more unusual fowl such as Suzume (sparrow) or Uzura (quail). The chicken is grilled in front of the customers, and the pleasant aromas of the grilled chicken and soy sauce drift across the room in a tempting way.

Izakaya at home

In this book I would like to introduce the typical Izakaya menu, but also include some of the modern dishes. You can make your own choices to create an Izakaya atmosphere, enjoying good food and sake in your own home.

To add to the atmosphere, you can arrange the table in a more dramatic way, with the selection of earthy pottery dishes, both large and small. Pretty chopsticks and chopstick rests add to the effect. Various sake bottles and cups are available. Tall slender bottles are suitable for warm sake. For cold sake, small round glass or ceramic bottles with a narrow neck and pouring lip, called 'tokkuri' are just right.

Garnishes and decorations known as 'ashirai' can be made from a number of leaves in your garden, such as camellia, aspidistra, bamboo or maple.

As I have mentioned there are no set rules for Izakaya except to relax, enjoy sake with a delicious meal with friends and loved ones with the dim light of candles while listening to your favourite music.

Drinks

Sake has been synonymous with Izakaya since they were established but more recently other drinks have been introduced and become quite popular, particularly aerated drinks such as beer, and spirits mixed with soda. Chuhai, which is shōchū mixed with soda, is a typical example. Mixed drinks are often preferred by young people.

Starting with a glass or mug of beer while dining is quite common now, but if you are dining out in a group, sharing a bottle is a more economical way.

Of course there are many varieties of sake, and unless you have a particular favourite you are best guided by the Izakaya owner who has relevant knowledge about sake and food, which is the key to a good Izakaya. If you are buying sake for home consumption, and you have no particular preference, ask your sake retailer or check on the internet. Varieties of sake have increased since Japanese sake brewers have introduced their sake to the rest of the world and in some overseas countries it has been successfully produced for more than 20 years.

Typical Izakaya menu for drinks

BEER

SAKE: Japanese rice wine

SHŌCHŪ: Distilled shōchū spirits

AWAMORI: Okinawan spirits

SAWA: Sour cocktails

CHUHAI: Shōchū mixed with soda

HIGHBALL: Whisky and soda

COCKTAIL: Similar to those all over the world

UME SHU: Sweet plum wine as a dessert drink

WINE: Popular among young age group

SOFT DRINKS: Non-alcoholic beer is popular with women, especially pregnant women

RAMUNE: A unique lemonade in a special slender bottle with a marble ball inside the bottle neck to seal

Beer

Brands of beer may vary greatly from one Izakaya to another. More common beers include Dorai (dry), and Nama-bīru (draft, unpasteurised beer). Low calorie beer – which has recently been introduced – and non-alcoholic beer are also popular.

Sake

Sake is a Japanese alcoholic drink based on four ingredients: rice, yeast, koji mould and water. The alcohol content is generally between 14 percent and 15 percent, though it is possible to brew sake with 20 percent alcohol content. Sake is produced in many places throughout Japan. The different qualities of rice and water in each region contribute to the unique taste of each sake brand. Sake ranges from dry to fairly sweet. Dry sake is called Kara-kuchi and sweet is ama-kuchi.

You can order sake by the bottle, cup or glass. Amounts range from han-gou (half ichi-gou 90ml), ichi-gou (180ml), to ni-gou (360ml).

The four main varieties of sake are Honjo-shu, Junmai-shu, Ginjo-shu, and Kizake.

HONJO-SHU is mild flavoured sake with rice, rice koji, yeast and water, with added alcohol that must not exceed 25 percent of the total alcohol content. It is preferably served warm.

JUNMAI-SHU is made in the most traditional manner from rice, koji, yeast and water. It is quite rich and has a dominant rice flavour. It may be served cold or warm.

GINJO-SHU is considered the ultimate sake; it is expensive and hard to find, as it is made in very limited quantities. It uses 60 percent polished rice which gives it a distinctive, subtle, slightly sweet taste and a fruity aroma. It is best serve cold or slightly warm.

KIZAKE is a pure rice wine that does not involve any heat-treatment in its production process. Due to this it has a short shelf life. It has a natural mature, fruity aroma. Good to drink cold.

Sake can be enjoyed either warm or cold, depending on the season and sake's character.

Warm sake is known as atsukan, meaning 'hot sake', but it is never heated over 50°C (120°F). The term Hitohada-kan translates to body temperature, (35~40); jou-kan (45~50) means ordinary temperature.

To prepare hot sake:

一 Pour sake into a tokkuri (a small sake serving bottle), place the tokkuri in a pot of boiling water.

二 Depending on the type of bottle, heating times will vary. Heat to your preference, using a thermometer if available.

三 Using a cloth, remove the tokkuri from the pot and wipe away any excess water. Pour warm sake from tokkuri into ochoko (small sake cups).

Serve cold sake in small glasses or sakemasu which are small wooden box-like cups.

Shōchū:

Shōchū is called 'Hino-sake' meaning fiercely strong sake. Unlike most sake, which is brewed, shōchū is a distilled clear liquor. It is made from a combination of a number of raw ingredients such as rice, sweet potatoes, soba buckwheat, barley or black sugar. Each type tastes strongly of its source ingredient but its flavour is often described as nutty or earthy. The alcohol content is usually about 25 percent.

Shōchū production is mainly in the warmer areas of Japan, such as Kyushu, Okinawa and surrounding islands, which are suitable for growing particular sweet potatoes.

Shōchū is divided into two categories, depending on the ingredients and producing methods, Otsuri (or Honkaku) and Karui Shōchū.

OTSURUI OR HONKAKU SHŌCHŪ: Single distillation, produced by traditional manufacturing method and ingredients. Since it is made by single distillation, Honkaku Shōchū has the rich flavour and aroma of its main ingredients. It is preferable to drink straight, but may be taken with ice, or diluted with hot water or ice and cold water. Alcohol content may be as high as 45 percent.

To warm Honkaku Shōchū, heat water to about 60°C (140°F), pour into a glass and add shōchū. As the shōchū warms it gives off an evocative fragrance.

KORUI SHŌCHŪ: Made by consecutive distillation that produces a higher alcohol content, the shōchū is then diluted with water until it is 36 percent. This type of shōchū has a clear taste with less aroma. It is suitable for cocktail mixers and is often used for Chu-hai or Sawa (Sour), and cocktails.

You can order it by the bottle at an Izakaya restaurant which can be more economical in a big group, of course paying extra for mineral water, soda water, lemon, etc.

TO DRINK SHŌCHŪ: You may drink it straight, but it is also popular diluted with hot water or on the rocks. Pour hot water in a cup or glass and add shōchū. The popular ratio is 4:6 (water : shōchū).

Sawa-Sour:

Cocktail made of shōchū mixed with lemon, lime or other citrus juice to create varieties such as Fresh kiwi sour, lemon sour, grape fruit sour, orange sour.

Chuhai:

Shōchū mixed with soda/tonic water. There are many varieties of shōchū on the menu such as Uron hai (Oolong tea and shōchū), Umeboshi-hai (pickled plum, soda and shōchū), Ryokucha-hai (green tea and shōchū), Karupisu-hai (Japanese Karupisu drink, soda and shōchū), Yuzu-hai (yuzu citrus juice, soda and shōchū).
(The ratio of chuhai is 1:1 or 1:2).

TO MAKE OOLONG HAI: Mix shōchū and cold Oolong tea with ice cubes. Hot water is also good. Instead of Oolong tea, green tea or Jasmin tea can be substituted.

TO MAKE LEMON CHUHAI: Mix 100ml (3⅓ fl oz) shōchū and 100ml (3⅓ fl oz) tonic water or soda water, combine with ice and lemon juice.

UMEBOSHI-HAI: Mix shōchū and hot water added with umeboshi (a pickled salted plum).

Basics

Basic dashi: kelp and bonito stock

Awase-jyoyu (kaeshi)

Marinating sauce:
- Teriyaki sauce
- Wafu-marinating sauce

Ponzu: citrus dipping sauce

Dressings:
- Wasabi soy sauce dressing
- Mentaiko (salted Pollack roe) dressing
- White sesame dressing
- Shoga dare: ginger dressing
- Onion dressing
- Suri-goma dare: ground sesame seed dressing
- Umeboshi-dare: pickled plum dressing
- Hachimitsu-dare: honey dressing
- Ninniku dare: garlic dressing
- Sake-miso dare: sake and red miso dressing

Tama-miso: Miso with egg dressing

Tama-miso vinaigrette

Tama-miso mustard vinaigrette

Basic dashi: Kelp and bonito stock

1 litre (4 cups) water
15g or 8cm (½ oz) square kelp sheet
20g (¾ oz) Katsuo-bushi (bonito flakes)

一 Wipe kelp with dry cloth.
二 Put kelp in a pot of water and leave for half an hour.
三 Over low heat, bring it to the boil. Just as it boils, remove the kelp.
四 Add katsuo-bushi and remove from the heat.
五 Leave for 3 minutes and strain off over a bowl.
六 You may discard the katsuo-bushi or use for making miso dip.

Awase-jyoyu (kaeshi)

500 ml (2 cups) soy sauce
½ cup caster sugar
½ cup mirin

一 Place soy sauce and caster sugar in a pot and bring it to the boil, stiring occasionally.
二 Add mirin and remove from the heat.
三 Cool it down.
四 Store in a bottle and keep it for a month.

This sweet soy sauce can used as a dipping sauce for cold noodles with bonito stock.
For dipping sauce/ awase-jyoyu : dashi = 1:4
For hot soup with noodle/ awase-jyoyu : dashi= 1:8

Marinating sauce

TERIYAKI SAUCE

2 tbsp soy sauce
2 tbsp mirin
1 tsp caster sugar

— Simmer all ingredients together over low heat until it thickens.

WAFU-MARINATING SAUCE

FOR 500G (17½ OZ) BEEF, LAMB OR PORK

1 garlic clove
½ spring onion stem
1 small red chilli, halved, deseeded and chopped
1 tbsp sesame oil
1 tbsp mirin
1 tbsp honey
1 tbsp miso
1 tbsp grated apple
1½ tbsp soy sauce
2 tbsp sake
½ tbsp raw sugar
1 tsp ginger juice
1 kelp sheet, 4x4cm

— Place all ingredients in a pan and simmer for 5 minutes. Remove kelp and allow sauce to cool down.

Ponzu: Citrus dipping sauce

2 tbsp soy sauce or awase-jyoyu
2 tbsp citrus juice (Yuzu, lemon or lime)

— Ponzu is also used for Yu-dofu,(Tofu in hot pot) or Shabu-shabu with grated daikon and shichimi (Japanese seven spices).

Dressings:

All of these simple dressings are good with green salad. Simply combine the ingredients listed.

WASABI SOY SAUCE DRESSING

1 tsp soy sauce
1 or ½ tsp wasabi paste
1 tbsp rice vinegar
1 tsp vegetable oil

MENTAIKO (SALTED POLLACK ROE) DRESSING

30g (1 oz) mentaiko (salted Pollack roe)
2 tbsp Japanese mayo
2 tbsp plain yoghurt

WHITE SESAME DRESSING

15g Japanese mayo
1 tbsp milk
15g (½ oz) tahini
1 tbsp grounded white sesame seeds
½ tsp raw sugar
1 tsp ponzu or rice vinegar

This dressing is good for green salad with tofu.

SHOGA DARE: GINGER DRESSING

3 tbsp soy sauce
1 tbsp rice vinegar
1 tbsp vegetable oil
½ spring onion, trimmed and chopped
1 tsp ginger juice

ONION DRESSING

2 brown onions, peeled and grated or sliced
3 tbsp raw sugar or caster sugar
1 tsp salt
½ cup rice vinegar
½ cup vegetable oil
1 cup awase jyoyu

If you like hot and spicy dressing, add chopped fresh red chilli

SURI-GOMA DARE: GROUND SESAME SEED DRESSING

4 tbsp roasted white or black sesame seeds, ground
2 tbsp soy sauce
1 tbsp caster sugar
1 tbsp sake

Also goes well with steamed vegetables

UMEBOSHI-DARE: PICKLED PLUM DRESSING

8 umeboshi, pickled plums or 4 tbsp bainiku, pickled plum paste
2 tbsp mirin
2 tbsp sake
1 tsp roasted white sesame seeds

Also goes well with steamed vegetables and white flesh fish

HACHIMITSU-DARE: HONEY DRESSING

5 tbsp soy sauce
2 tbsp honey
2 tbsp grated onion
1 tbsp white wine vinegar or rice vinegar
Also use on steamed pork, vegetable sauté

NINNIKU DARE: GARLIC DRESSING

1 clove garlic, chopped
1 tsp chopped ginger
4 tbsp soy sauce
6 tbsp rice vinegar
2 tsp sesame oil
1 tsp raw sugar
Also use on steamed vegetables, steamed chicken

SAKE-MISO DARE: SAKE AND RED MISO DRESSING

5 tbsp red/Hachou miso
4 tbsp sake
1 tbsp mirin
1 tsp soy sauce
½ stem spring onion, chopped
1 clove garlic, grated
Good for steamed vegetables, especially steamed eggplant (aubergine)

Tama-miso: Miso with egg dressing

200g (7 oz) Saikyo miso
2 egg yolks
50ml (1½ fl oz) sake
20g (¾ oz) caster sugar
10 ml (⅓ fl oz) mirin

— Place all the ingredients in a pan and cook over moderate heat stirring with a wooden spoon.

二 Cook to evaporate water until it the texture resembles miso-paste.

Tama-miso can be used in various ways. It can add a delightful flavour to plain boiled or steamed vegetables. Other suggestions are as follows:

Tama-miso vinaigrette

50g (1¾ oz) tama-miso
1 tbsp rice vinegar
1 tsp Yuzu-kosho, Yuzu flavoured paste

— Combine all the ingredients. Serve with simple chicken dishes.

Tama-miso mustard vinaigrette

50g (1¾ oz) Tama-miso
40g (1½ oz) cashew nuts, roasted
½ tsp karashi or English mustard
½ tsp caster sugar
1 tbsp rice vinegar

— Combine all the ingredients. It is suitable to combine with steamed or grilled scallops or vegetables.

Tsumami

Tsumami is a simple appetiser to have with sake or other alcoholic drinks. Here are some easy recipes.

Tsukemono: Pickles:
- Celery sticks in salt and kelp
- Pickle cabbage in salt
- Carrot and daikon in shio-kombu

In vinaigrette:
- Sliced lotus roots and mandarin orange pickled in sweet rice vinegar
- Vegetable pickles in soy sauce

Edamame: Young green soy beans
- Yaki-edamame: Scorched edamame served with shichimi

Varieties of dips
- Cream cheese with bainiku (pickled plum puree) or yukari (salted red shiso flakes)
- Cream cheese with wasabi
- Cream cheese with miso or saikyo miso
- Sardine cream cheese dip
- Avocado tofu dip
- Tofu-cream dip

Miso dips with vegetable sticks
- Sesame miso
- Namban miso
- Karashi miso
- Negi miso cream cheese

Yaki miso: Grilled miso on wooden rice spoon
Deep-fried garlic
Soba age: Crispy buck wheat noodle
Crispy nori
Boiled egg in miso
Satsuma-imo (Japanese sweet potato) chips with sweet soy sauce
Renkon chips: Lotus roots chips
Quick tsumami spicy sardines in a can
Spicy konnyaku
Hiyayakko: Tofu with toppings
Nori ribbon
Deep-fried mochi cubes
Diced rice cake with sweet soy sauce
Tofu steak
Shiro-ae: Tofu salad
Tofu salad
Tofu-dengaku with sansho miso
Grilled abura-age
Agedashi-dofu
Mizore-nabe: Hot pot with grated daikon with tofu
Tofu in hot pot

Tsukemono: Pickles

Pickles are convenient dishes as a Tsumami, as they can be prepared in advance and stored in the refrigerator.

Salted pickles:

CELERY STICKS IN SALT AND KELP

2 celery stems
A pinch salt
2 strips kelp, approx. 1 x 3 cm (⅓ x 1 inch)
Fresh red chilli (optional)

一 Peel the celery and cut into sticks.
二 Place celery sticks in a snap-lock plastic bag.
三 Add salt and kelp (and chilli), and then zip.
四 Rub celery with salt and kelp while in the bag.
五 Leave for more than 30 minutes before serving.

Other vegetables such as cucumber or daikon can be used.

PICKLE CABBAGE IN SALT

100g (3½ oz) cabbage or Chinese cabbage, chopped
A pinch salt
1 red chilli, chopped
1 tsp grated ginger
Soy sauce for serving

一 Place cabbage in a snap plastic bag.
二 Add salt and chilli, and then zip.
三 Rub cabbage with salt through the plastic bag for 1 minute.
四 Leave for at least 30 minutes.
五 Take out cabbage and squeeze out excess water.
六 Arrange in a bowl and top with ginger.
七 Serve with soy sauce

Kelp or chilli can also be included. Instead of ginger, try a little nob of wasabi.

CARROT AND DAIKON IN SHIO-KOMBU

1 small carrot, peeled and cut into sticks
¼ daikon, peeled and cut into sticks
1 Lebanese cucumber, cut in quarter lengthways and deseeded, then cut into sticks
1 tsp shio-kombu*

一 In a container, place carrot, daikon, cucumber and shio-kombu.
二 Put a lid on and shake the container.
三 Leave for 30 minutes before serving.

*Shio-kombu (dried salted kelp strips) is eaten in 'chazuke' or 'ochazuke' – cooked rice with green tea in a bowl. But shio-kombu is also used in stir-fries with vegetables, pickles or soup.

In vinaigrette:

SLICED LOTUS ROOTS AND MANDARIN ORANGE PICKLED IN SWEET RICE VINEGAR

100g (3½ oz) renkon, lotus root, peeled and thinly sliced
1 tbsp rice vinegar
4 mandarin oranges
4 tbsp raw sugar
¼ cup rice vinegar

— In a pan add water and 1 tbsp rice vinegar and bring it to the boil. Add renkon slices and cook for 2–3 minutes, and then drain.

二 To prepare mandarin oranges, peel off skin and separate segments by hands. Then open the inside layer and remove seeds and skin.

三 Combine mandarins, sugar and vinegar in a container or a bowl, then add the renkon. Marinate for more than 1 hour.

VEGETABLE PICKLES IN SOY SAUCE

Vegetables (such as kabu (radish), carrot, cucumber, celery, daikon)
2 tbsp awase-jyoyu or soy sauce

— Cut vegetables into mouth size pieces and place in a zip-lock plastic bag.

二 Lightly squeeze and leave for 2–3 hours in refrigerator.

Option: You may add sliced red chilli for spicy pickles.

Edamame: Young green soy beans

Edamame may be steamed, boiled or grilled. As fresh edamame are difficult to obtain outside of Japan, frozen edamame are the usual way to buy. Cook according to the instructions on the packet. They are eaten warm or cold, straight from the pod.

YAKI-EDAMAME: SCORCHED EDAMAME SERVED WITH SHICHIMI

40 edamame
1 tsp shichimi

— Arrange edamame on a tray and grill until slightly scorched.

二 Sprinkle with shichimi before serving.

Varieties of dips

CREAM CHEESE WITH BAINIKU (PICKLED PLUM PUREE) OR YUKARI (SALTED RED SHISO FLAKES)

50g (1¾ oz) cream cheese

10g (⅓ oz) bainiku (salted pickled plum puree) or 15g (½ oz) Umeboshi (salted pickled plum), deseeded and chopped

— Spread bainiku over cream cheese. Rest for more than one hour before serving.

If you do not have time, just arrange bainiku next to cream cheese. Serve with vegetable sticks or unsalted crackers, such as wafer crackers.

CREAM CHEESE WITH WASABI

50g (1¾ oz) cream cheese

10g (⅓ oz) wasabi paste

— Same as bainiku.

CREAM CHEESE WITH MISO OR SAIKYO MISO

50g (1¾ oz) cream cheese

10g (⅓ oz) miso

— Same as bainiku.

SARDINE CREAM CHEESE DIP

50g (1¾ oz) can of sardines, oil drained

3 tbsp cream cheese

Salt and pepper to taste

— With a fork, break up sardines into flakes.

二 Add cream cheese, add with salt and pepper.

AVOCADO TOFU DIP

50g (1¾ oz) momen tofu, hard tofu, drained on a rack

½ avocado, peeled and deseeded

A drop of usukuchi (light colour) soy sauce or fish sauce

1 tsp lemon juice

Coriander

Slice of lemon or lime

— Place tofu on the kitchen paper and drain excess liquid.

二 In a bowl, place avocado and tofu.

三 With a fork combine them and taste with usukuchi-shoyu or fish sauce.

四 Garnished with slice of lemon and coriander.

TOFU-CREAM DIP

½ momen tofu, hard tofu, drained on a rack
1 tsp white sesame paste
1 tsp olive oil
1 tsp lemon juice
A pinch salt
1 tsp chopped basil

— In a food processor, add all ingredients except basil and combine until smooth.
二 Add salt and lemon juice to taste.
三 Serve in a bowl and top with basil.

Miso dips with vegetable sticks

SESAME MISO

30g (1 oz) miso
1 tbsp raw sugar
1 tsp mirin
1 tsp ground roasted white or black sesame seeds
1½ tbsp sour cream

— In a small saucepan combine all ingredients and cook over low heat until combined well. Serve in a small bowl with vegetable sticks.

NAMBAN MISO

30g (1 oz) miso
1 tbsp raw sugar
1 tsp mirin
½ fresh chill, deseeded and chopped
1½ tbsp plain yogurt
1 tbsp katsuobushi, bonito flakes

— In a small sauce pan, add miso, sugar and mirin and combine well over low heat. Add chilli and bonito flakes and stir for 30 seconds. Serve in a small bowl with vegetable sticks.

KARASHI MISO

5 tbsp Saikyo miso
1 tbsp rice vinegar
1 tsp English mustard

— Combine all ingredients and serve with fresh or steamed vegetable sticks.

NEGI MISO CREAM CHEESE

30g cream cheese
½ tbsp miso
5 spring onion stems, trimmed and chopped
A few drops olive oil
Nori strips for garnishing
Soy sauce, to taste

— Place cream cheese and miso in a bowl and mix well.
二 Add chopped spring onion and combine.
三 Combine soy sauce and olive oil in a spoon and mix into the cream cheese.
四 Serve with crackers.

Yaki miso: Grilled miso on wooden rice spoon

1 tbsp sesame oil
1 spring onion stem, trimmed and finely chopped
10 g (⅓ oz) ginger, finely chopped
1 tsp finely chopped green capsicum
5 shiso (Japanese basil) leaves, julienned
1 tbsp ground soba (buckwheat)*
60g (2 oz) miso
1 tsp mirin
½ tbsp sake
1 wooden rice spoon
1 lime wedge

一 Drop sesame oil in a pan and heat it over a moderate heat. Add spring onion and ginger, cooking for 1 minute. Add capsicum and cook for 2 minutes or until cooked through.

二 Add shiso and soba and stir for 10 seconds, add miso, mirin and sake and simmer stirring the pan continually without burning for 6 minutes. Allow to cool down slightly.

三 Spread miso paste over the wooden spoon except the handle.

四 Make a criss-cross pattern over the miso with a knife.

五 Grill the miso until slightly scorched.

六 Serve with a lime wedge.

*Instead of soba, grounded walnuts, almonds or sesame may be used.

IZAKAYA • TSUMAMI

Deep-fried garlic

2 red chilli, deseeded and chopped
1 tbsp mirin
1 tbsp caster sugar
1 tbsp soy sauce
12 cloves garlic, husked
Vegetable oil for deep frying

— To prepare marinating sauce, combine chilli, mirin, sugar and soy sauce in a plastic zip bag.

二 Place garlic in the sauce and marinate for 1 hour.

三 Prepare oil in a deep pan and heat to 180°C (355°F).

四 Deep fry garlic until it floats to the surface. Drain off oil on kitchen paper.

Soba age: Crispy buck wheat noodle

45g (1½ oz) soba noodles, break in half
Vegetable oil for deep frying
½ tsp salt for serving
½ tsp shichimi, Japanese seven spices for serving

— Prepare oil and heat it up to 150°C (300°F).

二 Deep-fry soba noodles over low heat until crispy.

三 Serve with shichimi and salt.

Crispy nori

8 ajitsuke nori (flavoured nori) sheets, approx. 3 x 10 cm (1 x 4 inches) each
Tempura batter
2 tbsp tempura flour
2 tbsp water
Vegetable oil

— Prepare tempura batter in a bowl, lightly mixing flour and water.

二 Dip ½ nori strip into the tempura batter and deep fry in the prepared oil. Drain oil off well.

Boiled egg in miso

4 medium boiled eggs, shelled
⅓ cup miso
1½ tbsp mirin
A pinch of daikon sprouts or sprouts

— Put eggs, miso and mirin in a zipped plastic bag and gently massage eggs with miso inside the bag.

二 Leave for more than 3 hours in the refrigerator.

三 Slice in half lengthways or into wedges and top with sprouts.

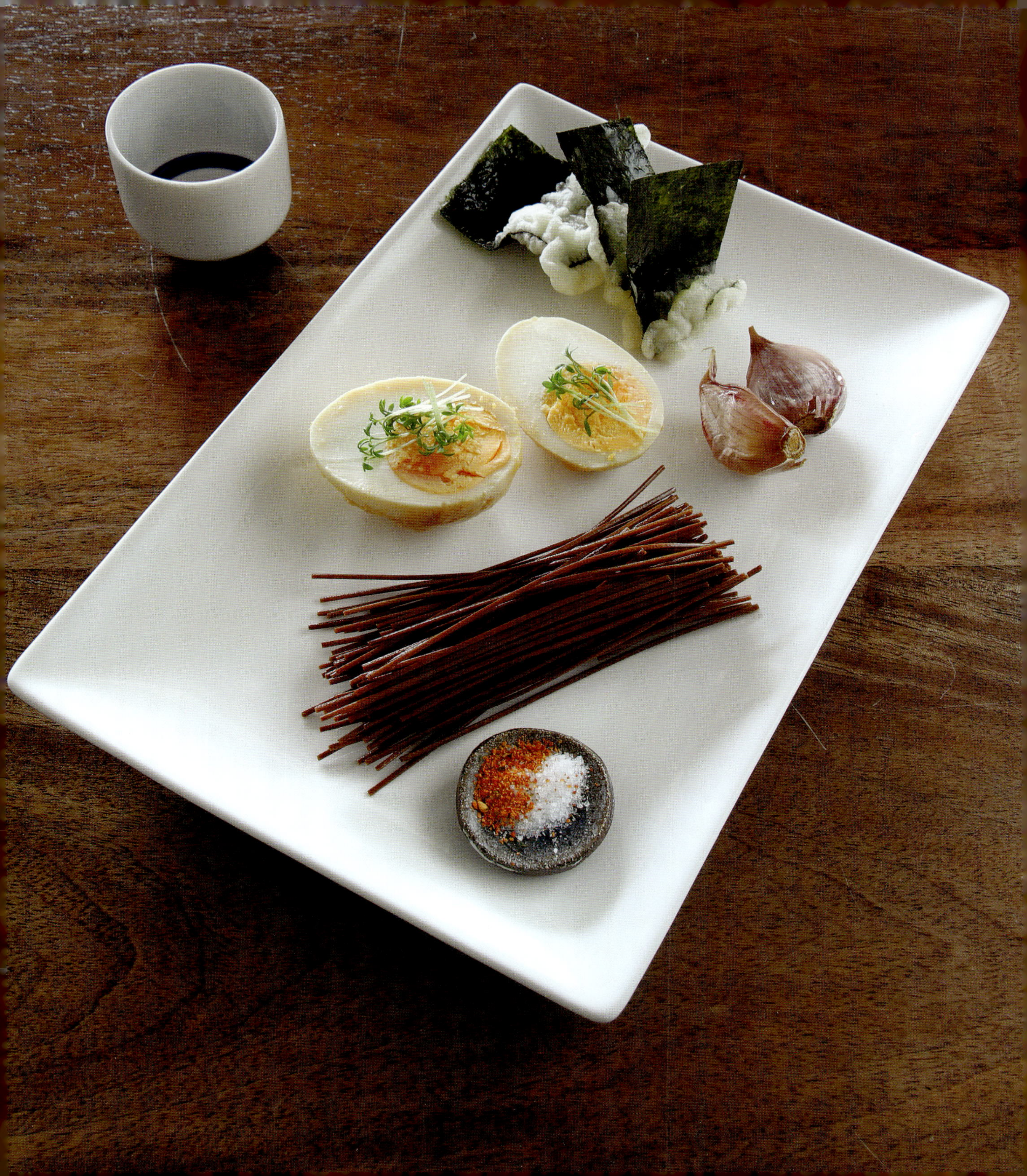

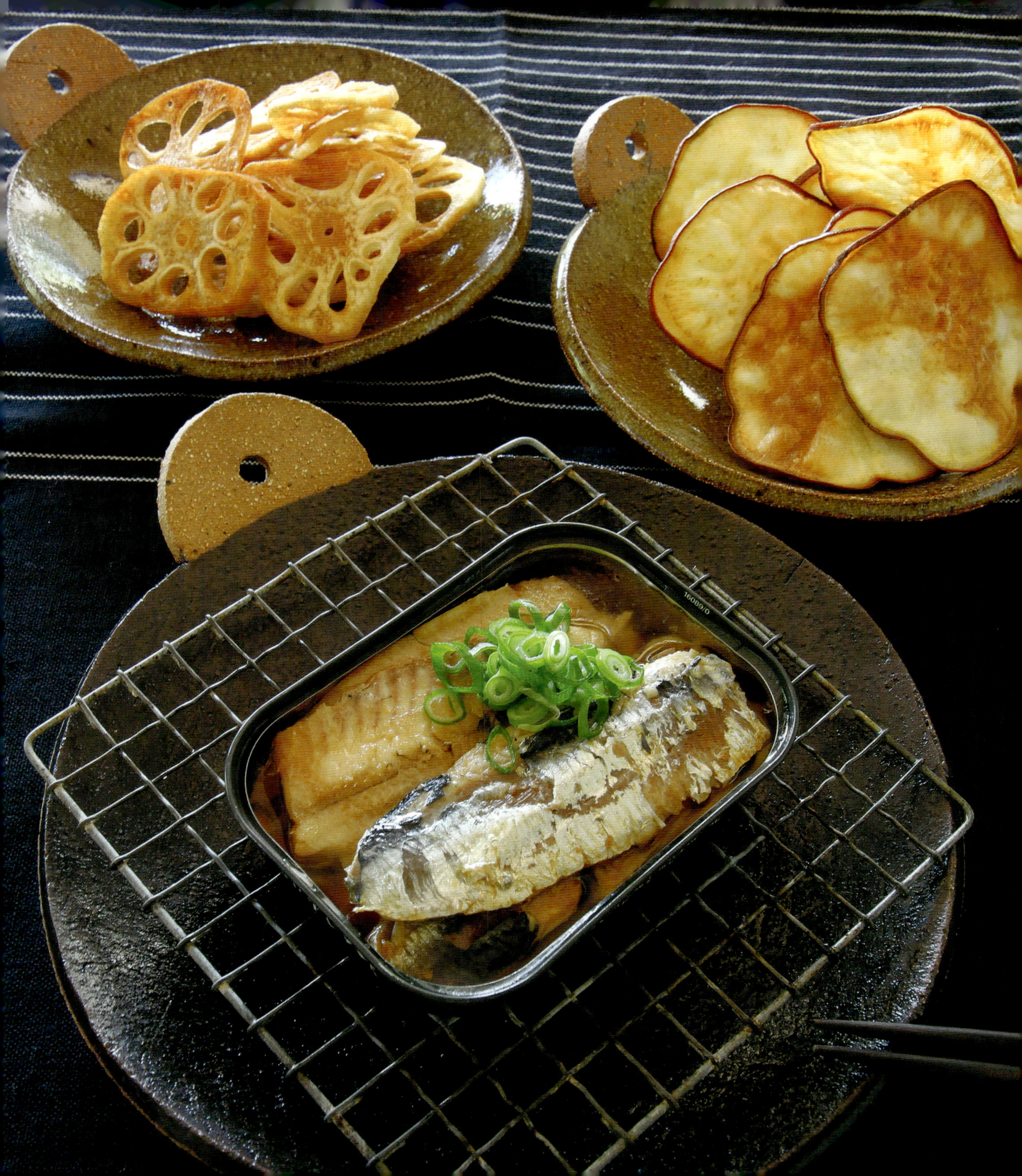

Satsuma-imo (Japanese sweet potato) chips with honey soy sauce

400g (14 oz) satsuma-imo, Japanese sweet potato
Vegetable oil for deep frying
Salt for seasoning
1 tsp soy sauce
1 tbsp honey
Sweet chilli is another option.

一 With slicer, slice the Satsuma-imo.
二 Prepare oil and heat it up to 170°C (340°F).
三 Over low heat, deep-fry satsuma-imo until crispy.
四 Drain off oil on a rack or kitchen paper.
五 Sprinkle on salt.
六 To make honey soy sauce combine soy sauce and honey.
七 Drizzle the sweet honey soy over the chips.

Renkon chips: Lotus roots chips

100g (3½ oz) fresh lotus roots, peeled and sliced or frozen sliced lotus roots (available from Japanese or Asian groceries)
Vegetable oil for deep frying
Salt or yukari for seasoning

一 If you use frozen lotus roots, defrost and pat with kitchen paper to wipe off excess liquid.
二 Prepare oil and heat up to 170°C (340°F).
三 Deep fry lotus roots over low heat until crispy.
四 Drain off oil well, sprinkle with salt or yukari while still hot and serve on a plate.

Quick tsumami spicy sardines in a can

1 can sardines in spring water
½ tbsp grated ginger
A pinch of shichimi (Japanese seven spices)
1 tbsp awase jyoyu

一 Remove outer paper from the sardine can.
二 Open the can of sardines and tip out one-third of the liquid.
三 Add awase jyoyu.
四 Arrange a wire rack on the gas and place tin on top (or put tin in the griller).
五 Bring it to boil over low heat and simmer for 2 minutes.
六 Carefully transfer the tin wire onto the plate.
七 Top with ginger and shichimi before serving.

Spicy konnyaku

SERVES 2

Approx. 125g (4½ oz) konnyaku
2 cups dashi stock
2 tbsp soy sauce
2 tbsp sake
2 tbsp mirin
2 tbsp caster sugar
Vegetable oil
Karashi (Japanese mustard) or English mustard to serve

一 Precook konnyaku in boiling water.

二 Drain and cool it down under running water.

三 Using a sharp knife, score over the surface in a criss-cross pattern.

四 Place dashi stock, soy sauce, sake, mirin and sugar in a pan.

五 Bring it to the boil.

六 Add konnyaku and simmer for about 30 minutes over a low heat.

七 Set aside and allow it to cool.

八 Take out konnyaku and wipe off the excess liquid with paper towel.

九 Drop oil into the frying pan and heat it up.

十 Cook until the surface is scorched both sides.

十一 Slice into bite-sized pieces.

十二 Serve with mustard.

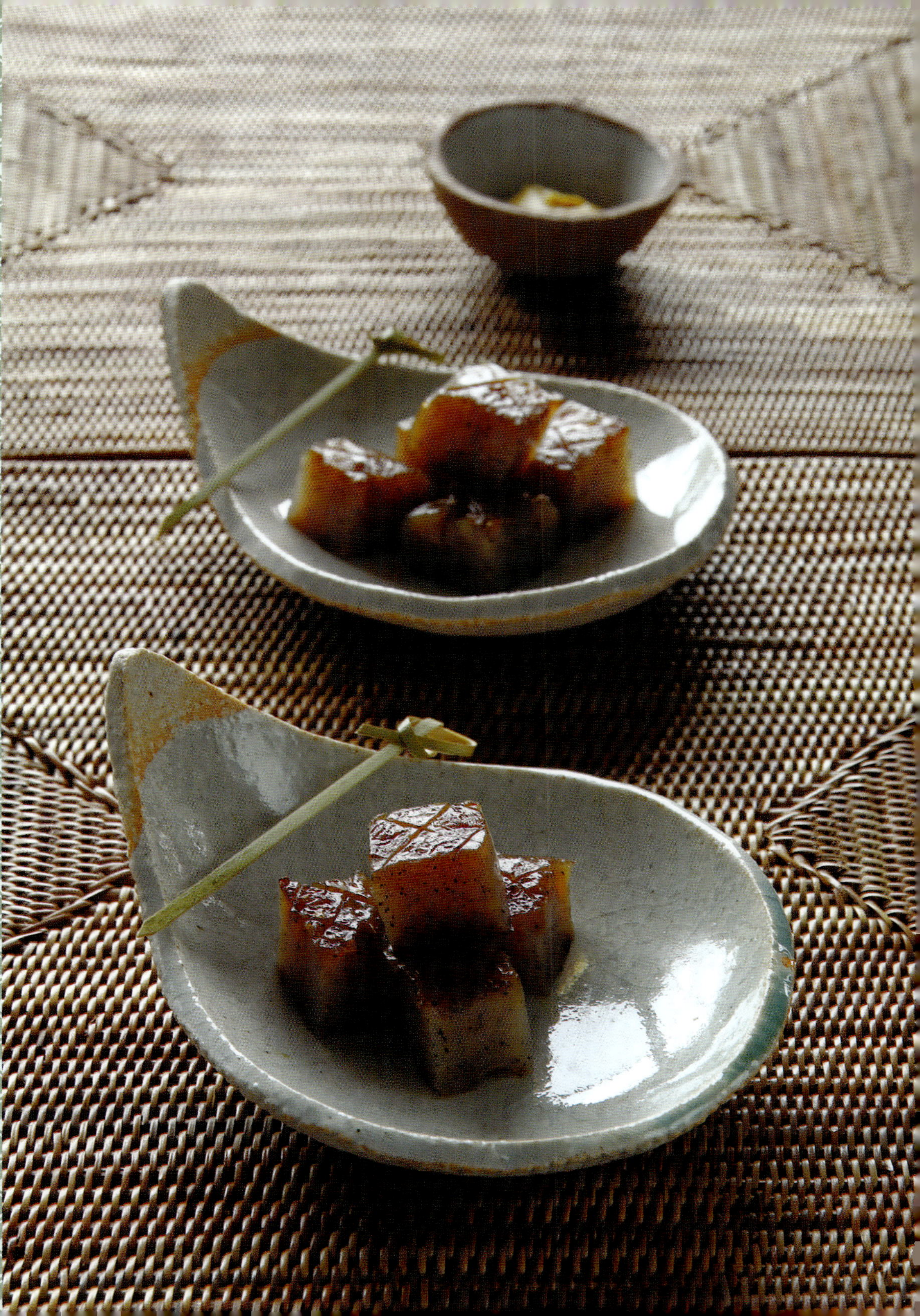

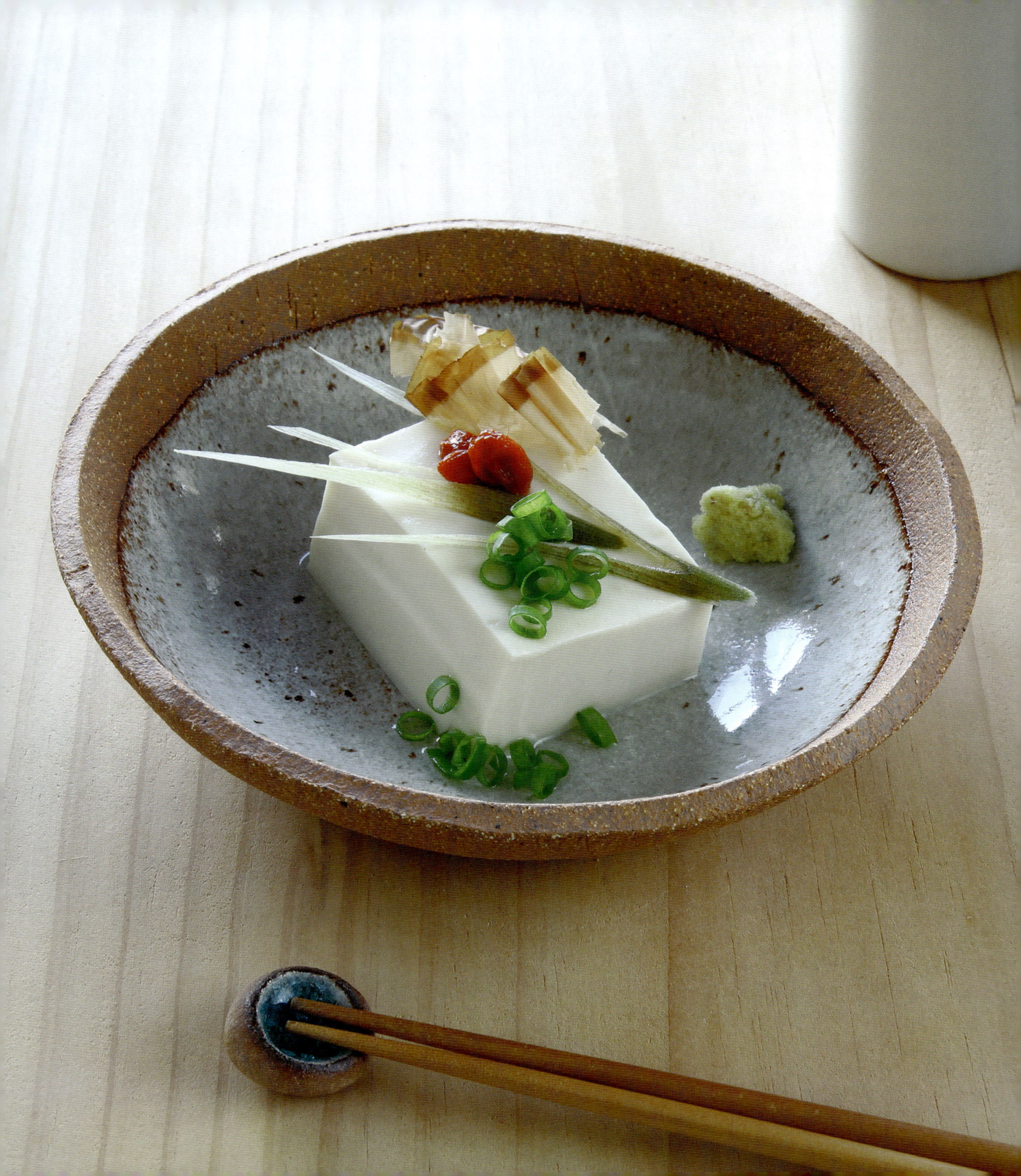

Hiyayakko: Tofu with toppings

SERVES 2

200g (7 oz) silken tofu
1 myoga ginger bud, sliced diagonally
2 tsp grated ginger
1 spring onion, trimmed and chopped
2 pinches bonito flakes
6 goji, soaked in hot water
Soy sauce or awase-jyoyu for serving

一 Arrange tofu in individual bowls.
二 Top with myoga, ginger, spring onion, goji and bonito flakes.
三 Serve with soy sauce or awase-jyoyu.

Myoga is a seasonal vegetable available from Japanese supermarkets. Other options for toppings: tomato, shiso (Japanese green basil), bainiku (pickled ume-boshi plum puree), etc

IZAKAYA • TSUMAMI

Nori ribbon

15 RIBBONS
1 pastry sheet
Sweet chilli sauce
1 sheet nori

一 Preheat oven 180°C (355°F).

二 Place pastry sheet on a dry board.

三 Spread sweet chilli sauce on pastry sheet, and top with nori.

四 Cut into 15 strings and gently tie each string.

五 Arrange the strings on a tray and bake for 8 minutes.

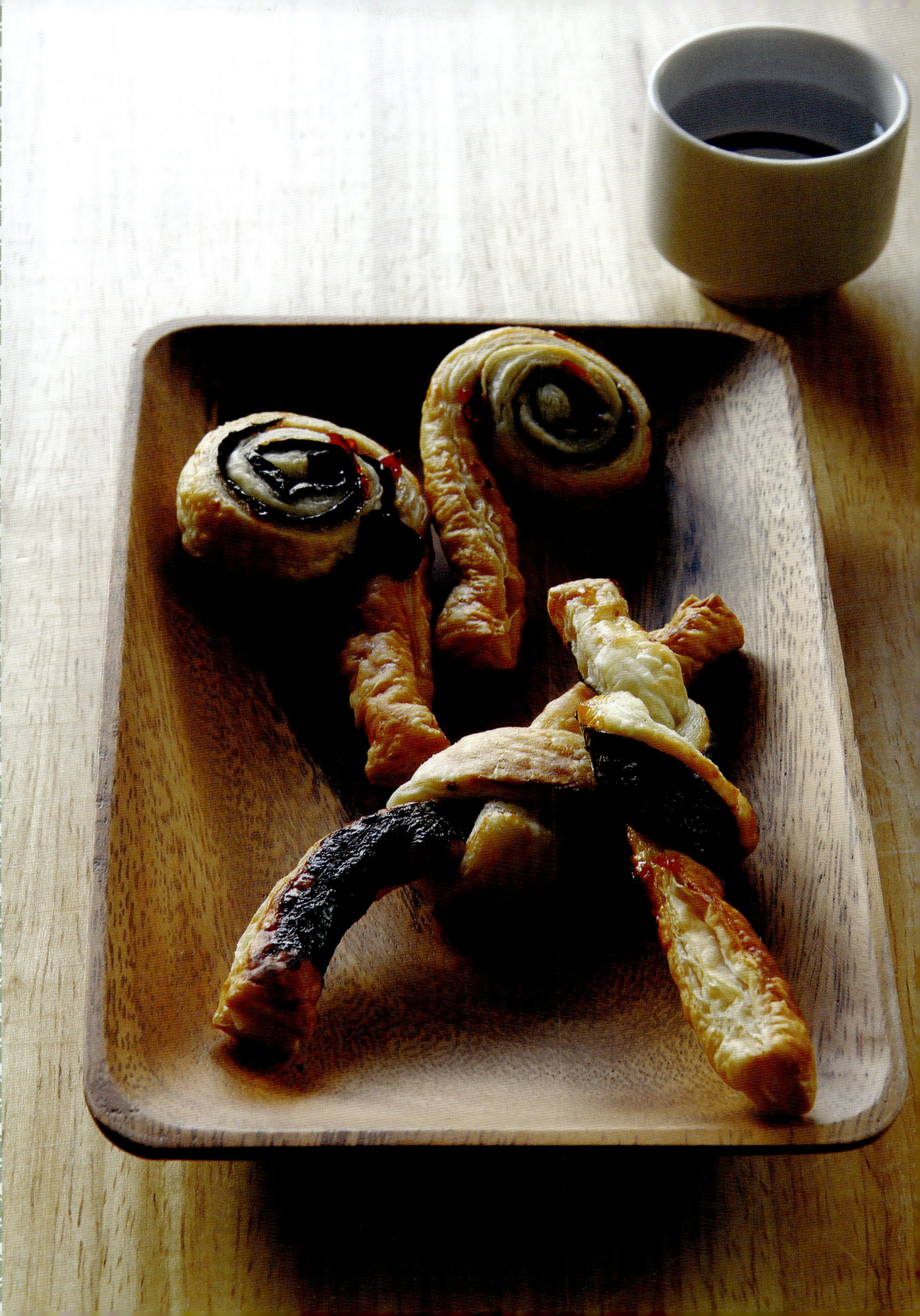

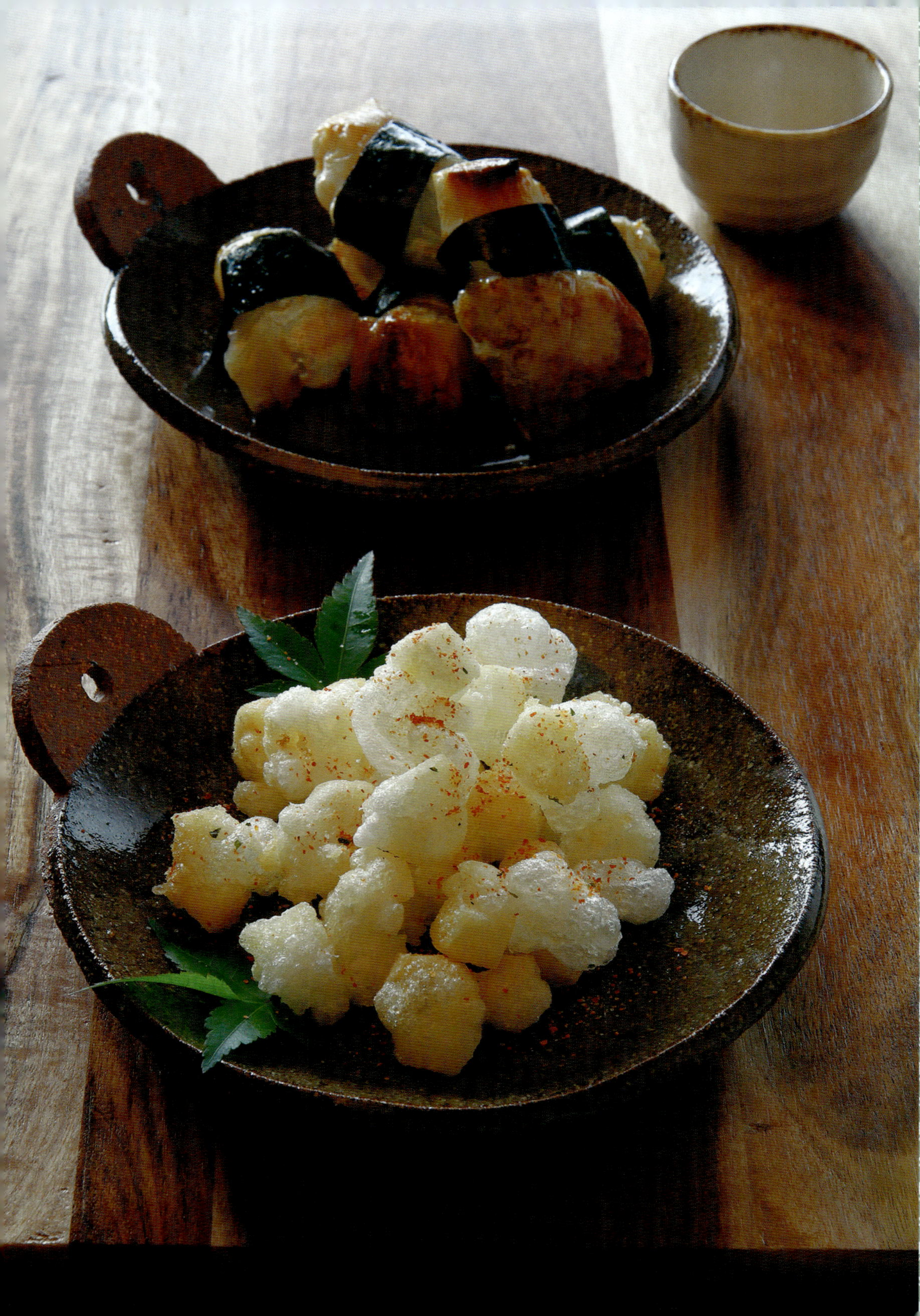

Deep-fried mochi cubes

1 mochi (rice cake)
Salt to serve
Shichimi (Japanese seven spices) to serve
Vegetable oil for deep frying
Note: It takes two days to dry rice cakes.

一 Cut mochi into 0.5 cm (¼ inch) cubes and lay on a baking tray to dry for 2 days.
二 Warm oil to 160°C (320°F). Deep fry mochi until golden.
三 Drain off oil and sprinkle with salt.

Diced rice cake with sweet soy sauce

TO MAKE 12 PIECES
2 mochi (rice cake)
2 tbsp caster sugar
2 tbsp soy sauce
8 nori strips, 2 cm x 5 cm (¾ x 2 inch)

一 Cut mochi into 2 cm (¾ inch) cubes.
二 Combine sugar and soy sauce.
三 Grill mochi under the griller until it starts to puff over the surface.
四 With chopsticks or tongs, dip into the soy sauce.
五 Wrap nori sheet around mochi.

Tofu steak

100g (3½ oz) momen (hard) tofu
Plain flour for coating
1 tsp olive oil
20g (¾ oz) butter
1 tsp grated garlic
1 tbsp awase-jyoyu (see Basics page)
Freshly grounded black berry pepper to taste

一 Pat the tofu with kitchen paper.
二 Coat the tofu with flour.
三 Heat olive oil in a frying pan, and add butter.
四 When butter has melted, add tofu and cook until both sides are brown.
五 Remove from the heat and transfer tofu onto a plate.
六 Add garlic and awase-jyoyu to the pan and cook until combined.
七 Pour the sauce over the tofu.
八 Crack pepper over the top.

Shiro-ae: Tofu salad

SERVES 2
100g (3½ oz) momen tofu
80g (2¾ oz) bunch English spinach, discard root and rinse
1 tsp ground roasted white sesame seeds
½ tsp caster sugar
A drop of soy sauce
2 tbsp bonito flakes
Sesame seeds for decoration
Awase-jyoyu (see Basics page) for serving

一 Wrap tofu with kitchen paper or muslin and place on a rack on a plate. Put weight on top and stand for 15-20 minutes in refrigerator.
二 Blanch spinach in salted boiling water and refresh under running water. Squeeze out excess water with hands. Transfer spinach onto a chopping board and cut into 2cm (¾ inch) pieces.
三 Place tofu and spinach in a bowl and stir with fork or chopsticks.
四 Add sesame seeds, sugar, soy sauce and bonito flakes, and combine well.
五 Serve in individual bowls and top with sesame seeds.

Other combinations with tofu are: kaki persimmon, shungiku (edible chrysanthemum leaves), raisin, carrot

Tofu salad

SERVES 2

100g (3½ oz) hard-momen tofu, diced

50g (1¾ oz) salad leaves, soaked in water and drained

2 cherry tomatoes

50g (1¾ oz) Lebanese cucumber, sliced diagonally

1 red radish, trimmed and sliced

1 tsp dried wakame seaweed, soaked in water and drained

GOMA-MAYO DRESSING

15g (½ oz) Japanese mayonnaise

1 tbsp milk

15g (½ oz) tahini

1 tbsp ground roasted white sesame

½ tsp raw sugar

½ tsp soy sauce

— To make the goma-dressing combine all ingredients in a bowl and mix well.

二 Place the tofu, salad leaves, tomato, cucumber, red radish and wakame in a bowl and toss.

三 Drizzle the goma-dressing over before serving.

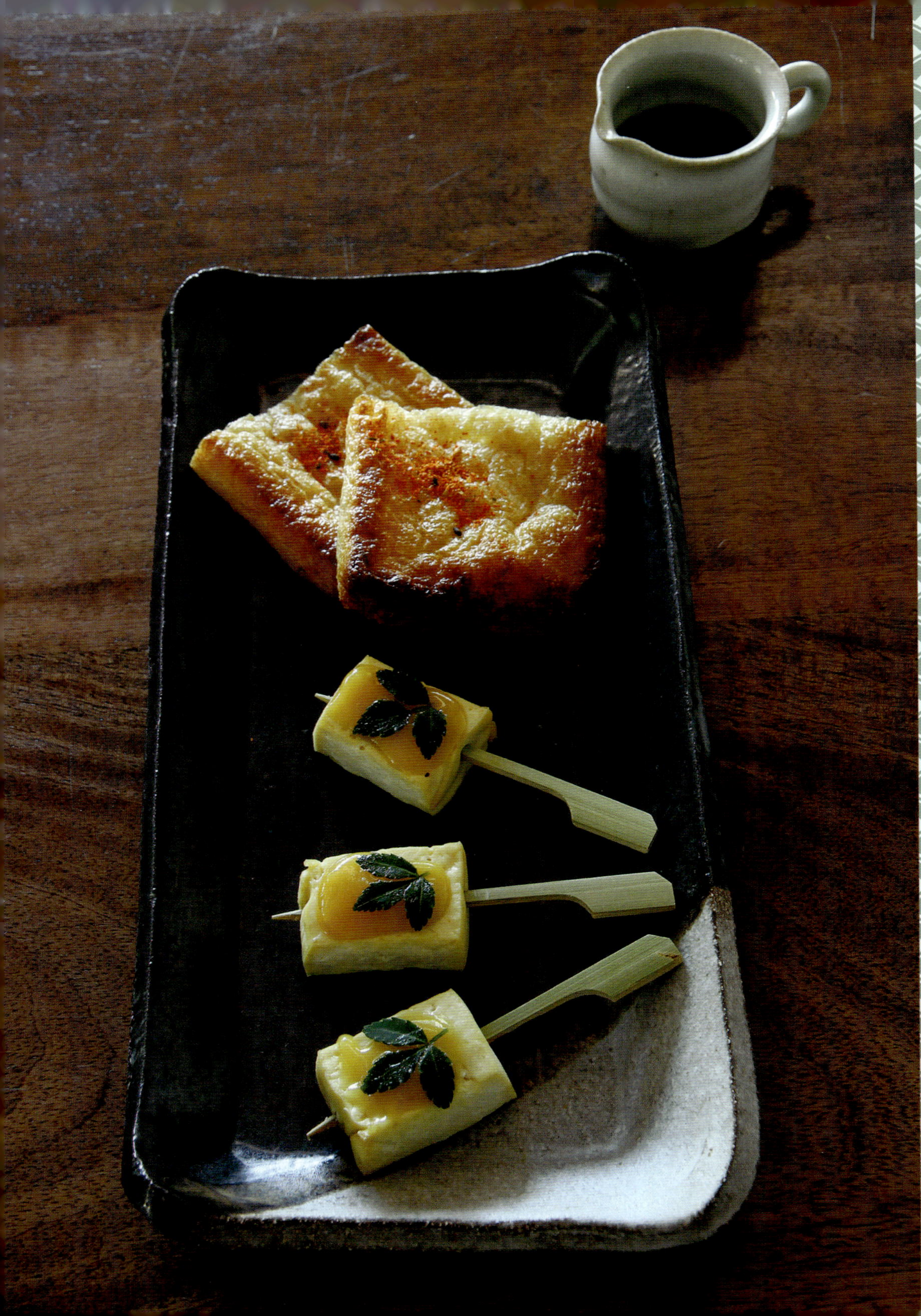

Tofu-dengaku with sansho miso

100g (3½ oz) momen-dofu (hard tofu)
4 tbsp saikyo miso
1 tbsp mirin
1 tsp caster sugar
1 tbsp sake
1 tbsp dashi (see Basics page)
¼ tsp sansho powder
2 strings kinome (Japanese mountain pepper)
6 wide bamboo sticks are preferable

一 Slice tofu into 6 pieces, wrap each slice with kitchen paper or muslin and place tofu on a rack on a plate. Put weight on top and stand for 15-20 minutes in refrigerator.

二 To make sansho miso paste, add miso, mirin, sugar, sake and dashi in a small pot and simmer over low heat until well combined, stirring with wooden spoon continuously, taking care not to burn. Remove from heat and add sansho powder, then mix.

三 Skewer each tofu with a bamboo stick and grill both sides occasionally turning over until lightly golden. Spread miso over the tofu, put it back under the griller and lightly bake.

四 Top with kinome sting. Serve on plates and sprinkle with extra sansho powder if you like.

Grilled abura-age

1 abura-age (deep-fried sliced tofu)
2 sliced cheese slices
1 tsp chopped spring onion
A pinch bonito flakes
Awase-jyoyu (see Basics page) for serving
Shichimi (Japanese seven spices) for serving

一 Cut the abura-age in half. Insert the cheese slices into each pouch.

二 Grill the abura-age until cheese has melted about 2-3 minutes.

三 Serve on a plate and sprinkle the spring onion and bonito flakes over the top.

四 Serve with awase-jyoyu and shichimi.

IZAKAYA • TSUMAMI

Agedashi-dofu

100g (3½ oz) silken tofu
SAUCE:
½ cup dashi (see Basics page)
1 tbsp usukuchi-shoyu (light colour soy sauce)
1 tbsp mirin
1 tbsp grated daikon radish
Potato starch for coating
Vegetable oil for deep-fry
 Grated ginger
1 tsp chopped spring onion

一 Press and drain tofu for 15 minutes. Cut into squares, approx. 2cm (¾ inch) thick 5x5cm (2 inches) square. Pat tofu dry with kitchen paper.

二 Meanwhile, prepare sauce by simmering dashi, soy sauce and mirin in a saucepan for 3 minutes.

三 Squeeze grated daikon lightly with hands to remove liquid and set aside.

四 Dip tofu in potato starch and coat on all sides.

五 Prepare oil in a tempura pan or heavy frying pan such as a wok. Heat to 170°C (340°F) over high heat.

六 Carefully slide tofu into the oil and deep-fry over a medium heat until the surface becomes crispy and golden brown. Drain on a rack or kitchen paper.

七 Pour sauce into bowls and add tofu. Top with the grated daikon and ginger, then spring onion.

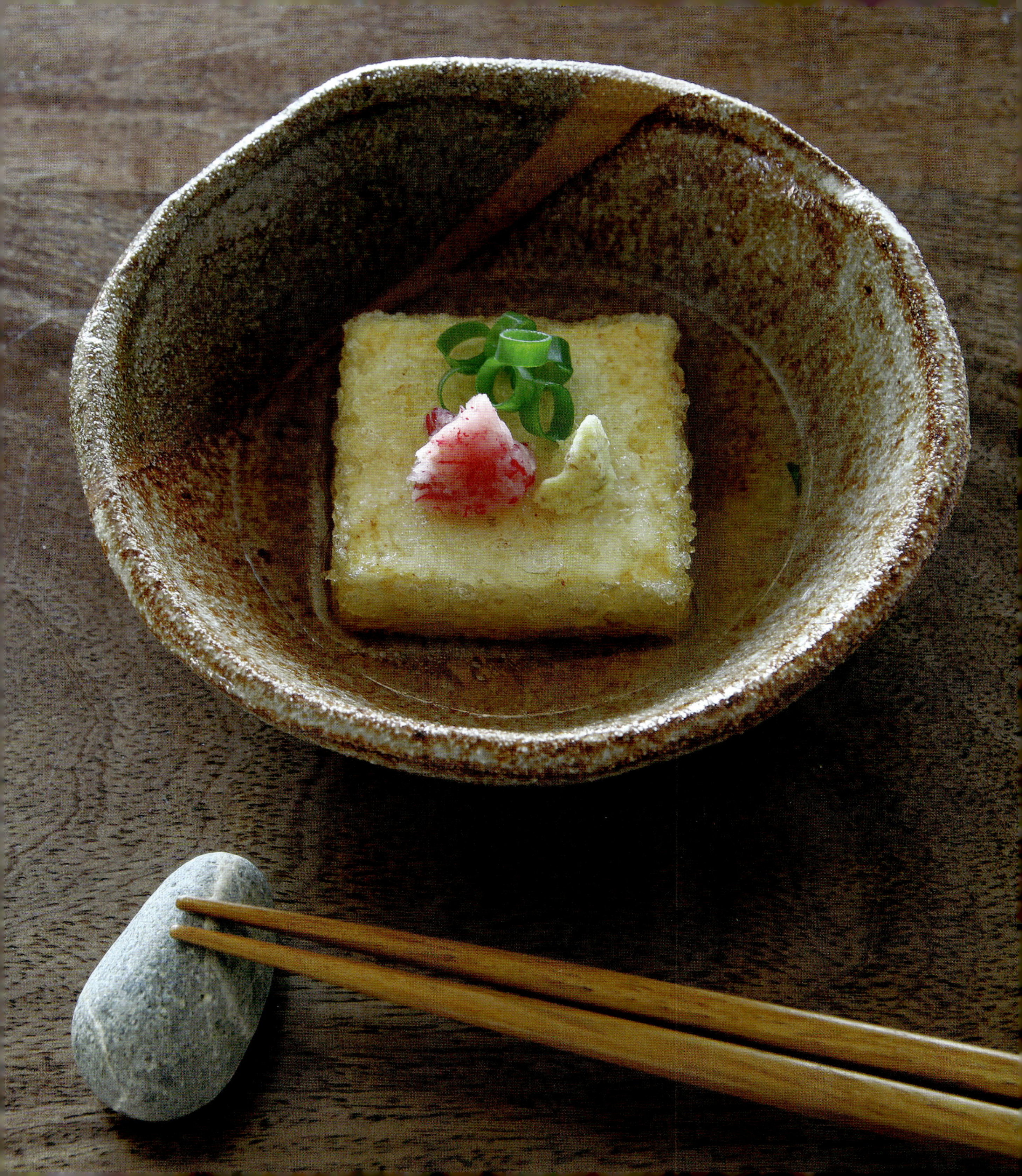

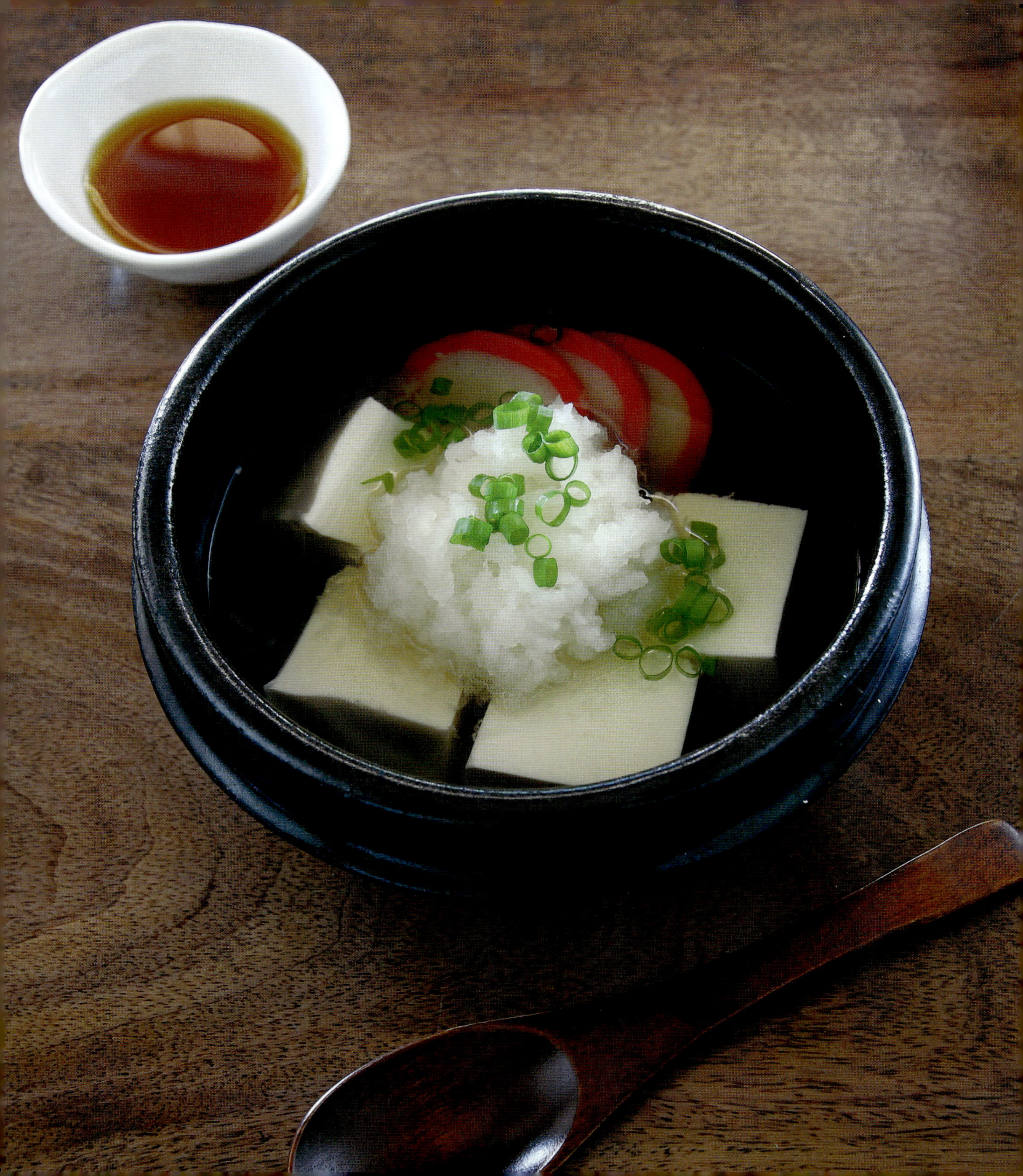

Mizore-nabe: Hot pot with grated daikon with tofu

1 cup water
150g (5¼ oz) silken tofu
30g (1 oz) kamaboko (fish cake), sliced
100g (3½ oz) daikon-oroshi (grated daikon)
1 tbsp chopped spring onion
Yuzu-su (yuzu citrus vinegar) or ponzu (see Basics page) for serving
Soy sauce for serving

一 Bring the water to the boil in an earthen pot.
二 Add the tofu and kamaboko, simmer over a moderate heat for 1 minute.
三 Add the daikon oroshi and sprinkle in the spring onion.
四 Cover with a lid and cook another 2 minutes.
五 Serve with yuzu-su and soy sauce.

Tofu in hot pot

SERVE 1
½ momen tofu
1 4x4cm (1½ x 1½ inch) kelp sheet, wiped
2 tbsp ponzu (see Basics page) to serve
2 tbsp soy sauce
Shichimi (Japanese seven spice) to serve

一 Place kelp in an earthen pot and fill one-third with water. Leave for 15 minutes.
二 Meanwhile, mix ponzu and soy sauce in a dipping bowl.
三 Add tofu and bring it to the boil, simmer for 1 minute with a lid.
四 Serve in the pot with the ponzu mixture and shichimi.

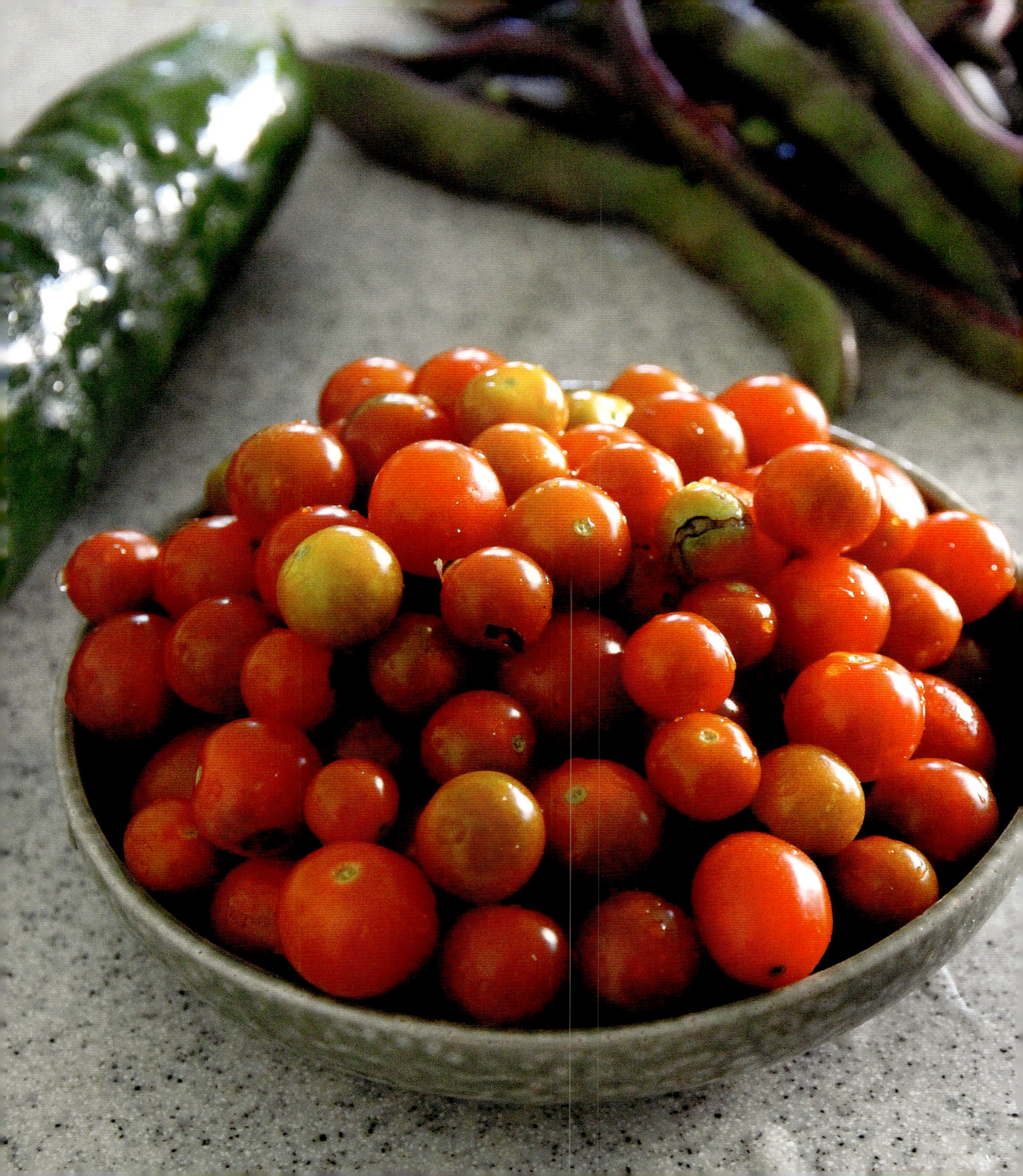

Vegetables

Rice noodle salad drizzled with lemon dressing

Agedashi mochi: Deep-fried rice cake in broth

Hijiki-seaweed and soy bean salad

Edamame harumaki: Edamame spring roll

Deep-fried Brussels sprouts

Cabbage and bacon with soy sauce butter

Steamed iceberg lettuce

Steamed vegetables with ponzu and sesame dip

Kyuri no Ume-ae: Cucumber ume salad

Tomato salad with red onion

Deep-fried lotus roots in olive oil, grilled with parmesan cheese

Grated daikon salad with Shimeji and enoki mushrooms

Stirred potato and carrot with salt and shichimi

Deep-fried gyoza sheet with cheese and nori sheet

Eggplant marinated in lemon vinaigrette

Yaki shiitake: Grilled shiitake tossed with bonito flakes and soy sauce

Grilled eggplant with various sauce

Furofuki daikon: Simmered daikon with miso paste

Braised sliced eggplant topped with red miso

Daikon salad

Diced avocado and julienned cucumber tossed with wasabi mayonnaise

Tossed chrysanthemum and enoki mushrooms with Japanese mustard

Bari-Bari salad

Summer salad with plum gellée

Rice noodle salad drizzled with lemon dressing

SERVES 4

100g (3½ oz) cooked harusame (thin rice noodle)

10g (⅓ oz) garlic chives, trimmed and cut into 5cm (2 inch) lengths

50g (1¾ oz) moyashi (bean sprouts), discard roots

½ Lebanese cucumber, deseeded and sliced thinly diagonally

1 tsp caster sugar

1 tsp soy sauce

A drop sesame oil

1 tbsp lemon juice

一 Cook harusame according to the packet instructions and refresh under running water, then cut into 5cm (2 inch) lengths.

二 Blanch garlic chives and moyashi in salted boiling water, then refresh under running water.

三 Place harusame in a bowl, add garlic chives, moyashi and cucumber, then combine together.

四 To make dressing: combine sugar, soy sauce, and sesame oil and lemon juice.

五 Drizzle the lemon dressing over the salad.

Agedashi mochi: Deep-fried rice cake in broth

4 mochi – rice cake – approx. 2x2cm (¾ x ¾ inch)

Vegetable oil for deep-frying

1 cup bonito and kelp dashi (see Basics page)

1 tbsp awase-jyoyu (see Basics page)

100g (3½ oz) grated daikon

1 tbsp chopped spring onion

一 Prepare oil in a deep pan and heat to 180°C (355°F).

二 Deep fry mochi until puffy and crispy and drain oil well.

三 Heat dashi and awase-jyoyu in a small pan.

四 Serve mochi in a bowl and pour on dashi.

五 Top with grated daikon and spring onion.

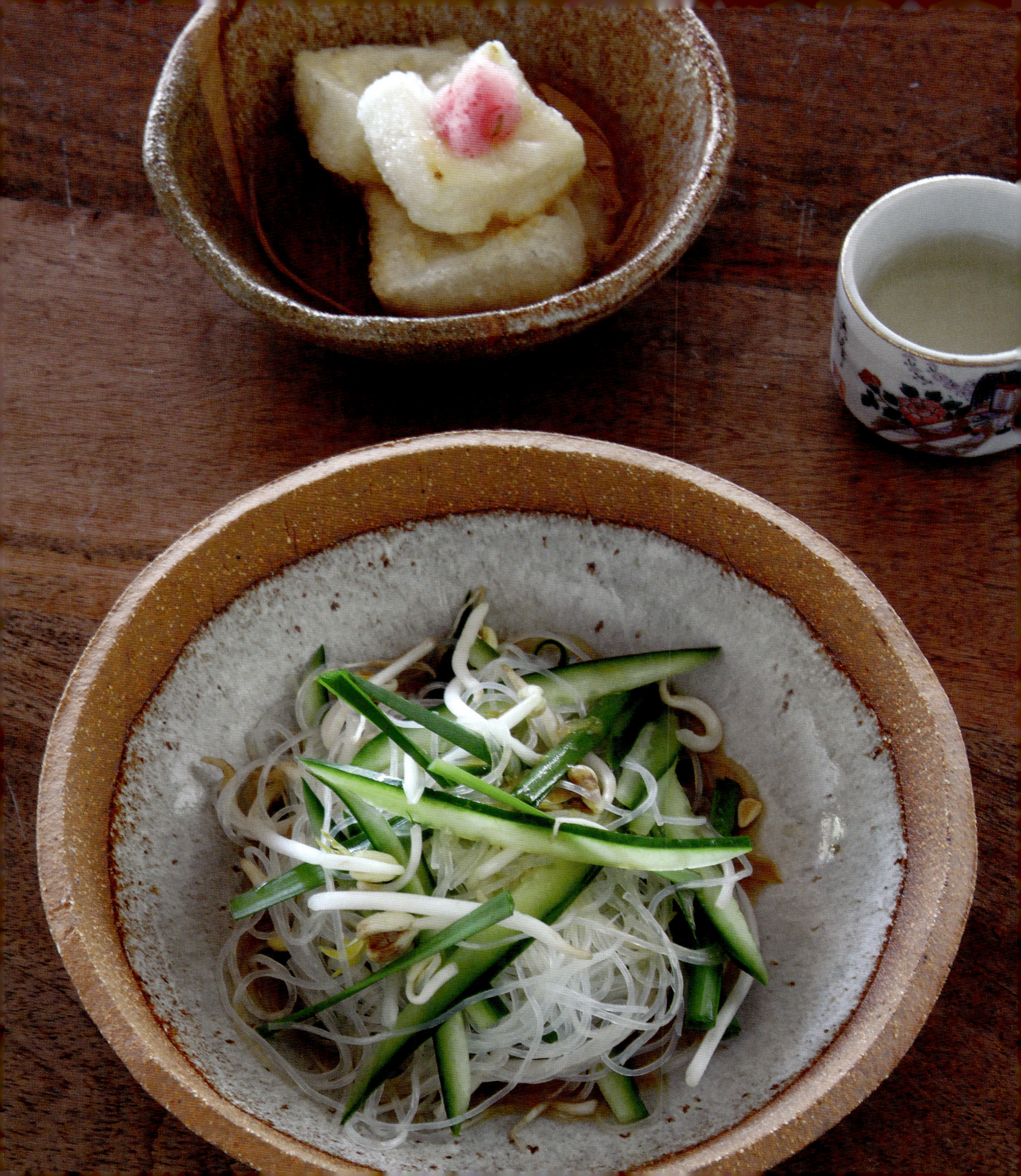

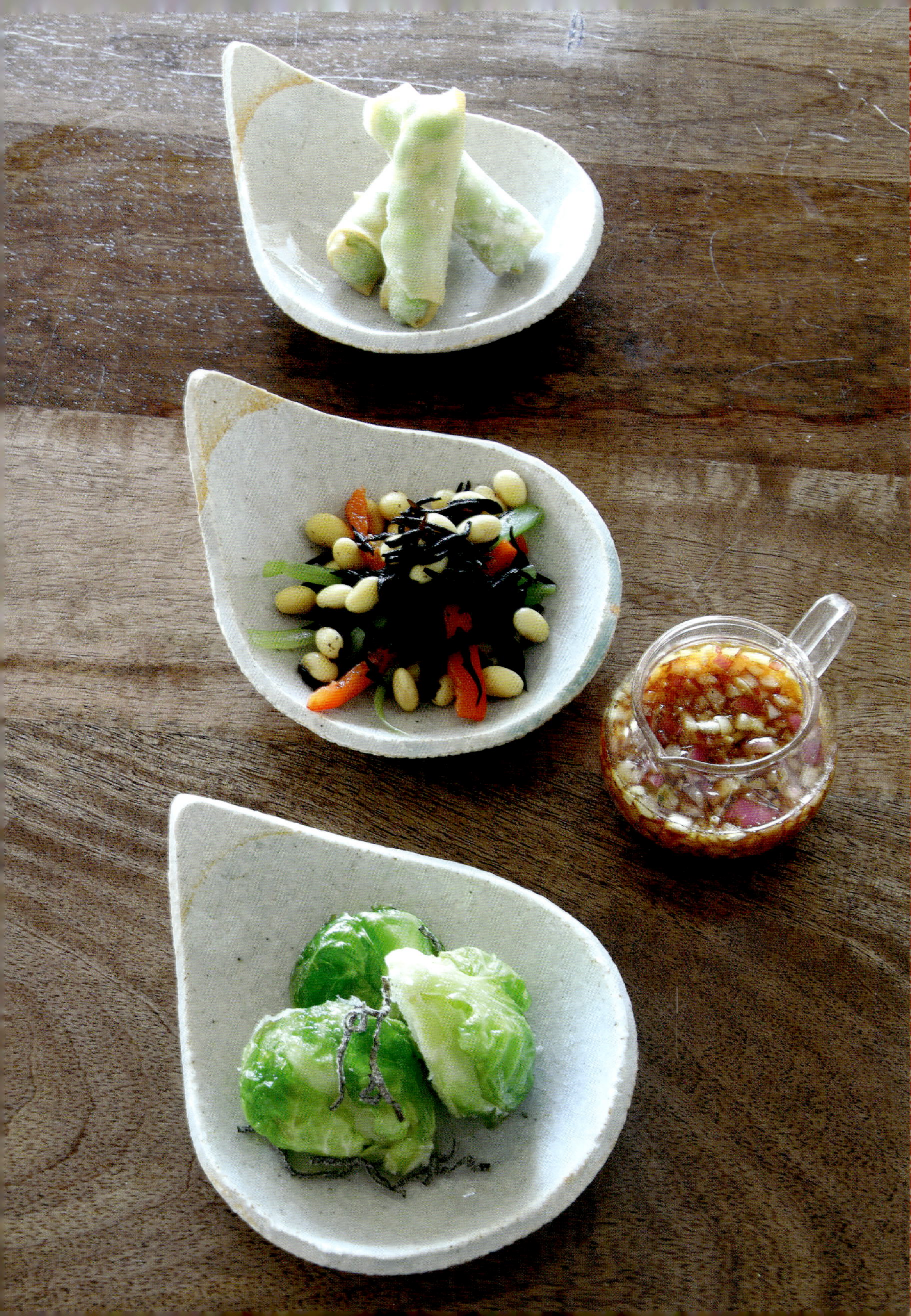

Hijiki-seaweed and soy bean salad

10g (⅓ oz) hijiki seaweed, soaked in water
10cm (4 inch) celery stork, chopped
¼ small red capsicum, julienned
100g (⅓ oz) cooked soy beans, drained
Salt to taste
A few drops of sesame oil

DRESSING
1 tbsp chopped Spanish onion
2 tbsp rice vinegar
1 tsp sesame oil
2 tsp soy sauce
1 tsp caster sugar
Freshly ground salt and black pepper to taste

一 To prepare dressing, put all the ingredients in a bowl or bottle and mix well.

二 Place hijiki seaweed in a pan with water and bring to the boil, then strain.

三 Blanch celery and capsicum in salted boiled water and drain.

四 Heat sesame oil in a frying pan, then add soy beans and stir fry over moderate heat until cooked through.

五 Add hijiki, celery, and capsicum to the pan and stir lightly.

六 Serve on a plate and drizzle over with dressing.

Edamame harumaki: Edamame spring roll

TO MAKE 12 ROLLS
100g (3½ oz) edamame, frozen or fresh green soy beans
12 spring roll sheets, 125x125mm (5 x 5 inches)
Vegetable oil for deep frying
1 tsp green tea powder
1 tsp salt

一 Remove edamame from the husks.

二 Place spring roll sheet on a dry plate and wrap up edamame like a parcel.

三 Prepare oil in a deep pan and heat to 170°C (340°F).

四 In the meanwhile, combine green tea and salt.

五 Deep-fry wrapped parcels until crispy and drain oil over a rack or paper towel.

六 Serve with green tea salt.

Deep-fried Brussel sprouts

SERVES 2
10 Brussel sprouts, cut in half
Potato starch for coating
Vegetable oil
Shio-kobu or cracked salt

一 With a knife make a slit across the Brussel sprouts.

二 Coat sprouts with potato starch.

三 Heat oil to 160°C (320°F) and deep-fry sprouts until lightly brown.

四 Drain and crack salt over top.

Cabbage and bacon with soy sauce butter

SERVES 2

¼ cabbage
2 rashers bacon, sliced
¼ cup water
1 tsp sake
1 tsp soy sauce
1 tbsp butter
Shichimi (Japanese seven spices) for serving

一 Cut cabbage into four.

二 In a pot, arrange cabbage.

三 Insert bacon among cabbage.

四 Add water, sake and soy sauce.

五 Top with butter.

六 Put a lid on and bring it to the boil, and then simmer for 10 minutes.

七 Serve with shichimi.

Steamed iceberg lettuce

¼ iceberg lettuce (about 150g/5¼ oz)
1 tbsp lemon juice
1 tbsp vegetable oil
½ spring onion stalk, sliced diagonally
½ tbsp ginger, sliced julienne
1 tsp soy sauce
1 tsp fish sauce
½ tsp caster sugar
1 tbsp sesame oil

一 Separate lettuce leaves.

二 Mix the lemon juice and vegetable oil in a bowl. Brush with the lemon oil over the lettuce leaves.

三 Prepare a steamer and steam the lettuce over high heat for 1 minute.

四 Arrange the lettuce leaves on a plate and top with spring onion and ginger.

五 Combine soy sauce, fish sauce, and sugar and drizzle over the lettuce.

六 Heat up oil and pour over the salad.

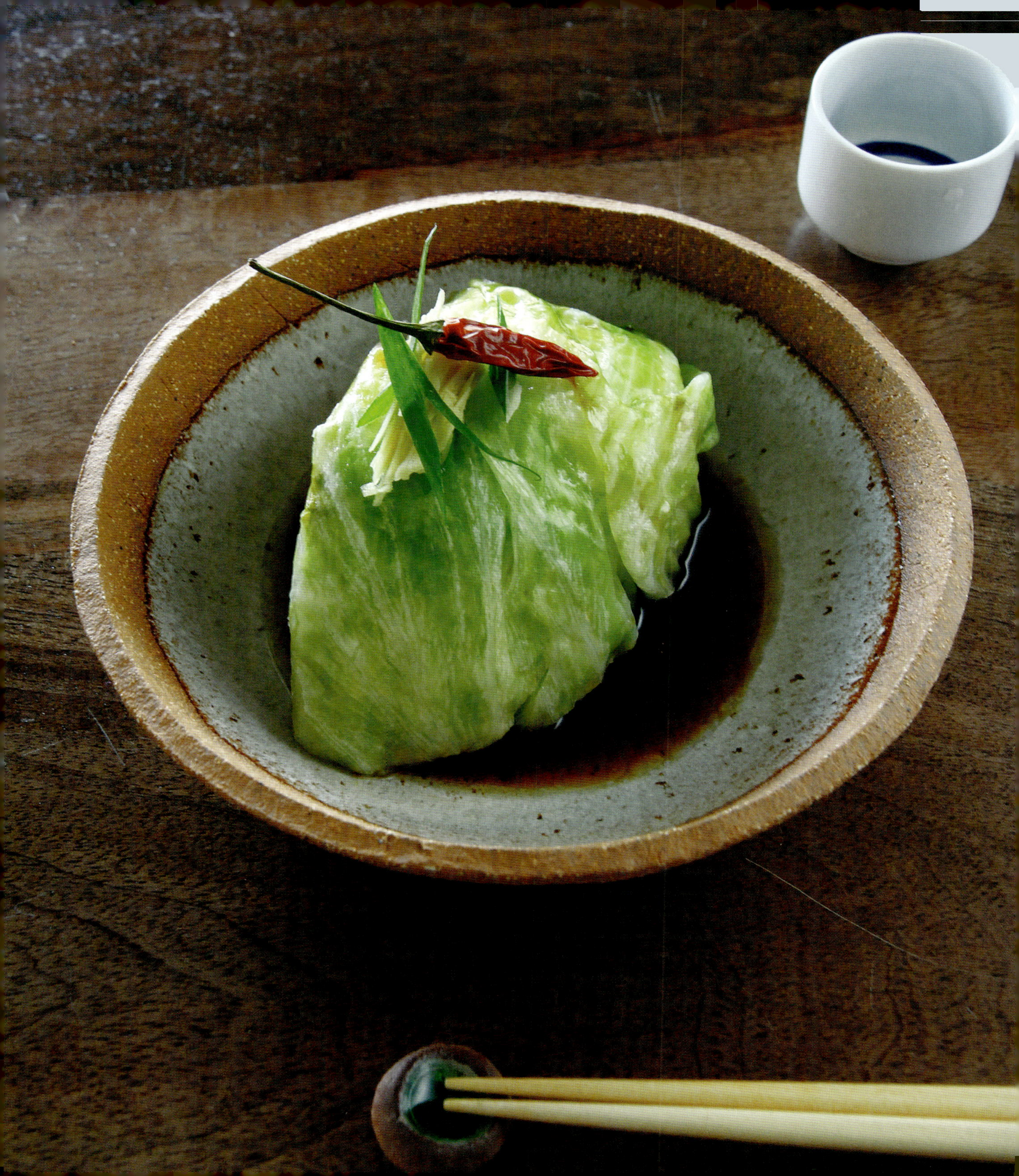

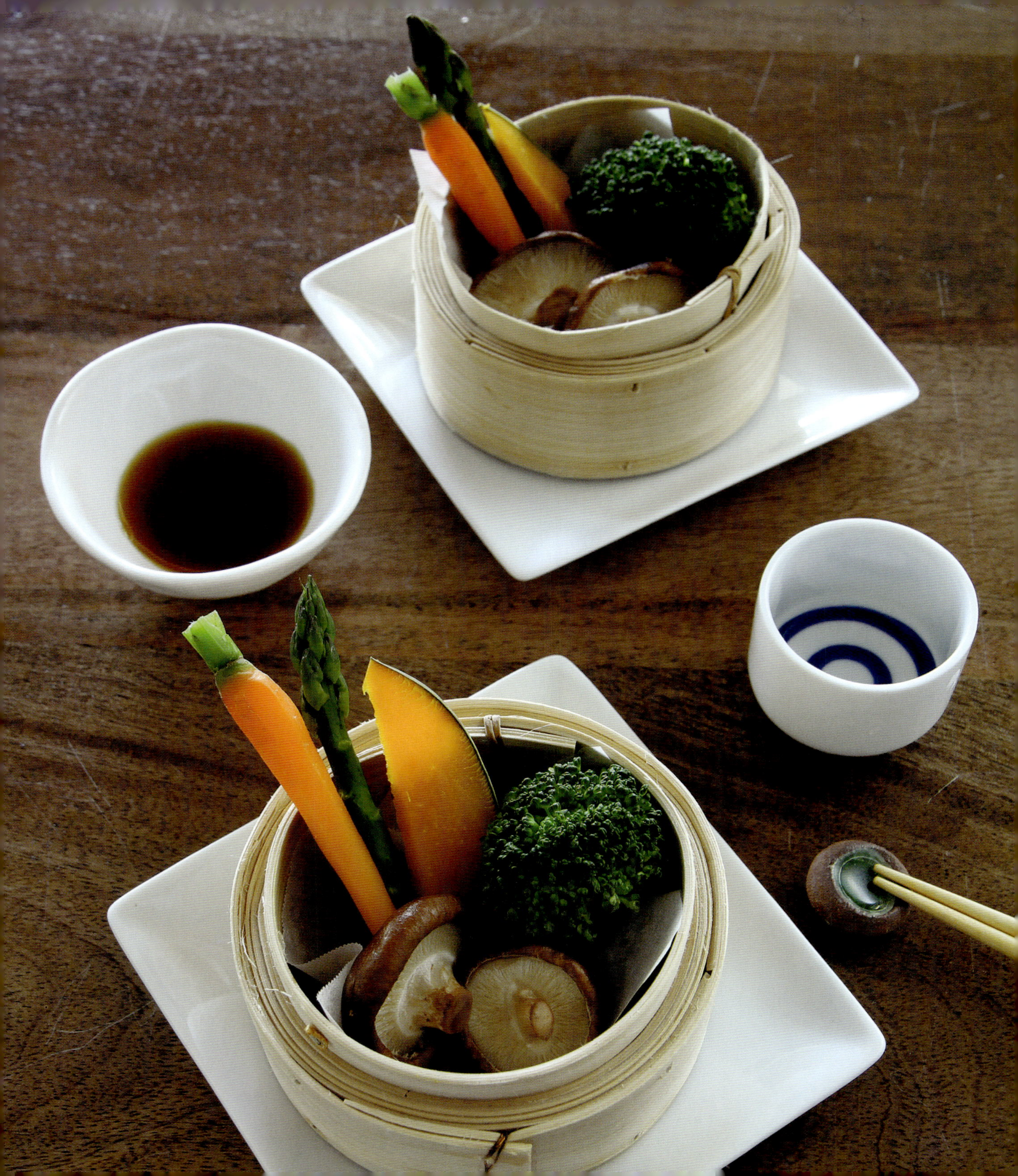

Steamed vegetables with ponzu and sesame dip

SERVES 2

30g (1 oz) Japanese pumpkin, deseeded and sliced
2 Dutch carrots, cut lengthways
30g (1 oz) broccoli, cut into bunches
2 fresh shimeji or shiitake mushrooms, trimmed
2 asparagus, trimmed
Ponzu (see Basics page) for serving,
Sesame-mayo dipping or ground sesame seed dressing (see Basics page) for serving
Other seasonal vegetables: spinach, cauliflower, turnip

一 Lay baking paper over steam-baskets and place the vegetables.
二 Steam over high heat for 5 minutes or until cooked.
三 Serve with ponzu or sesame dip.

Kyuri no ume-ae: Cucumber ume salad

1 Lebanese cucumber
1 shiso (Japanese green basil), sliced
1 tsp bainiku (Japanese pickled plum paste)
A pinch of roasted white sesame seeds
Nori strips for decoration

一 Trim off the sides of cucumber.
二 Lightly bash cucumber with something like a rolling pin.
三 Chop into 3–4cm (1–1½ inch) pieces.
四 Toss cucumber with shiso and bainiku.
五 Serve in a bowl and top with sesame seeds, bonito flakes, and nori strips.

Tomato salad with red onion

1 vine tomato
1 small red/Spanish onion, peeled and sliced, then soaked in water
2 green shiso leaves, sliced
1 tsp soy sauce
1 tsp sesame oil
1 tsp rice vinegar
A pinch of caster sugar

一 To make dressing, combine soy sauce, sesame oil, vinegar and sugar and mix well.
二 Arrange tomato and onion in a bowl and drizzle dressing over top.
三 Top with shiso leaves.

Deep-fried lotus root in olive oil, grilled with parmesan cheese

150g (5¼ oz) lotus root
1½ tbsp olive oil
50g (1¾ oz) grated parmesan cheese
Salt to taste

一 Using slicer or knife, slice lotus root into 5mm–1cm (¼–½ inch) pieces.
二 Heat olive oil in a pan.
三 Add sliced lotus root and cook over moderate heat until lightly scorched both surfaces about 3-4 minutes.
四 Add salt and place in a bowl.
五 Sprinkle with cheese before serving.

Grated daikon salad with shimeji and enoki mushrooms

50g (1¾ oz) daikon, peeled and grated
100g (3½ oz) shimeji mushroom, trimmed
100g (3½ oz) enoki mushroom, trimmed
1 tbsp Yuzu-su or lime or lemon juice
1 tbsp usukuchi-shoyu, light colour soy sauce

一 Boil water in a pan and blanch shimeji and enoki mushrooms, and then strain and refresh under running water. Drain well.
二 Transfer the mushrooms into a serving bowl and add grated daikon.
三 Mix yuzu-su and usukuchi-shoyu and drizzle over the daikon.

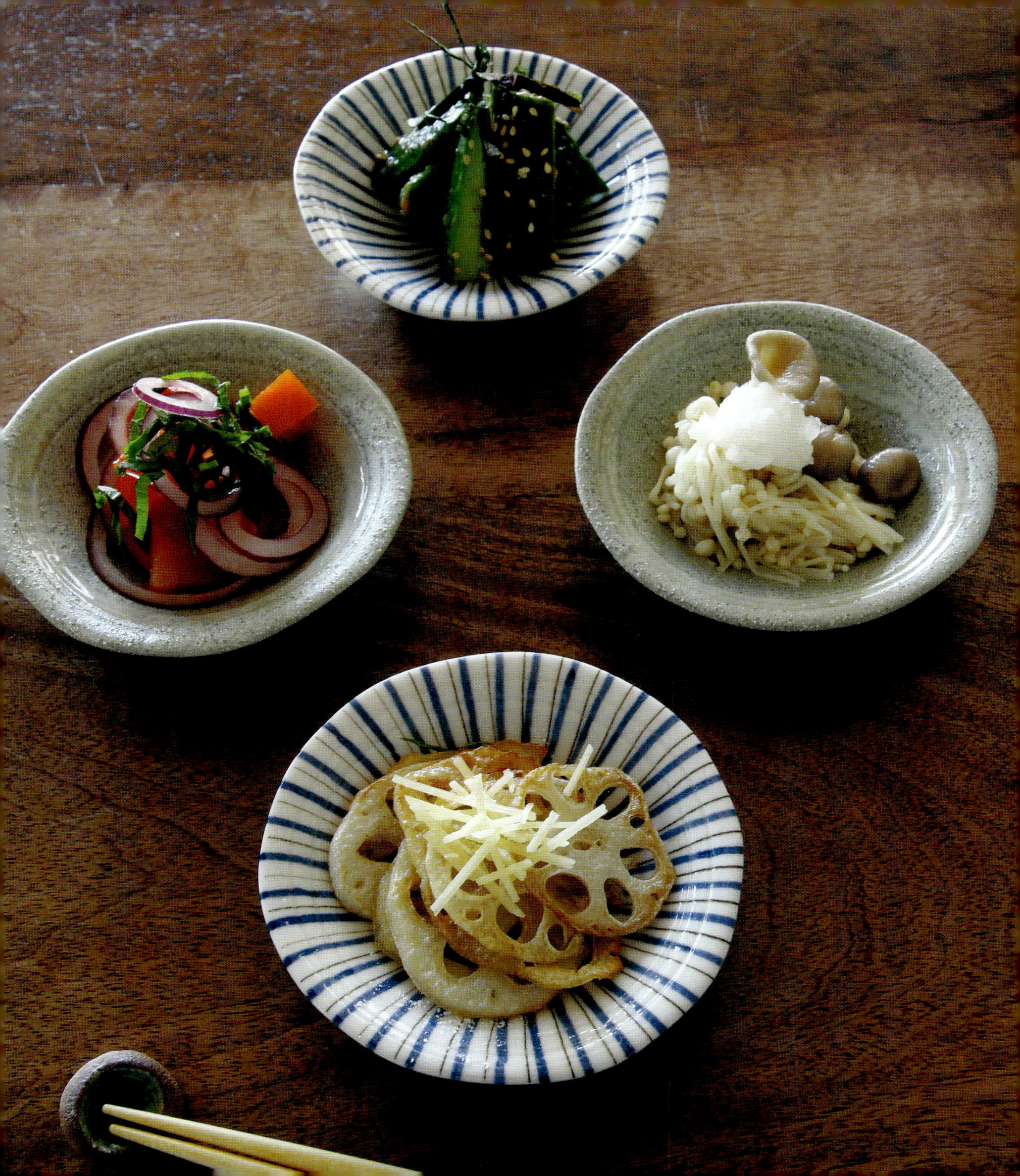

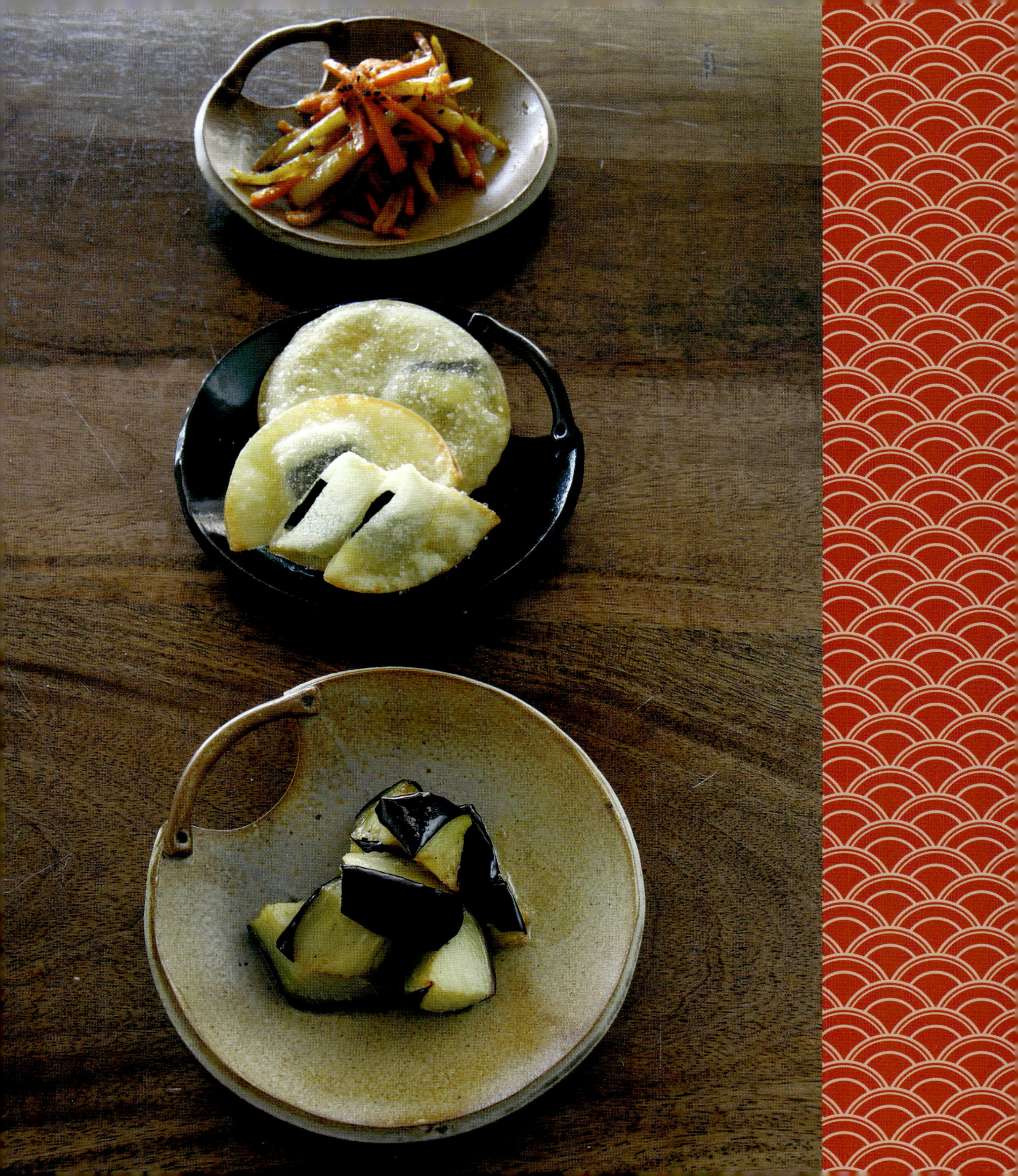

Stirred potato and carrot with salt and shichimi

2 tbsp potato starch
2 medium size waxy potato, peeled and julienned
2 carrots, peeled and julienned
A drop of vegetable oil
Freshly ground salt to taste
1 tsp shichimi

一 Coat the potato and carrot with the potato starch.

二 Put the oil in a frying pan and braise carrot and potato over moderate heat until crispy. Sprinkle the salt and shichimi, and then serve.

Deep-fried gyoza sheet with cheese and nori sheet

12 gyoza sheets
6 sliced cheese, sliced into 2 x 2cm (¾ x ¾ inch)
6 nori sheets, 2x 2cm each (¾ x ¾ inch)
Salt to taste
Vegetable oil for deep frying

一 Sandwich cheese and nori between 2 gyoza sheets.

二 Dampen a finger with water and trace the corner of gyoza to seal.

三 Prepare oil in a deep pan and heat to 170°C (340°F).

四 Deep fry gyoza until crispy and drain oil.

五 Serve on a plate and sprinkle with salt.

Alternatively, place cheese and nori, and then fold in half. Water the corner of gyoza sheet to seal.

Eggplant marinated in lemon vinaigrette

4 nasu (Japanese) eggplant or small eggplant
Vegetable oil for deep-frying
MARINADE DRESSING
1 tbsp rice vinegar
½ tbsp olive oil
½ tsp lemon juice,
Salt and pepper to taste

一 Trim eggplant and chop into chunks.

二 To make dressing, combine all ingredients in a bowl.

三 Heat oil in a deep pan.

四 Deep fry eggplant for 2–3 minutes or until cooked, then drain well.

五 Transfer eggplant into the dressing while hot.

Yaki shiitake: Grilled shiitake tossed with bonito flakes and soy sauce

8 fresh shiitake mushrooms
1 tbsp mirin
¼ cup bonito flakes
2 tbsp awase jyoyu (see Basics page)

一 Set shiitake on a tray for grilling.
二 Drizzle mirin over the shiitake.
三 Grill shiitake for about 3 minutes or until lightly scorched.
四 Place shiitake in a bowl and top with bonito flakes.
五 Serve with awase-jyoyu.

Instead of mirin, butter sweet soy sauce is tasty alternative. Top with a little butter, drizzle awase-jyoyu, and then grill.

Grilled eggplant with various sauce

300g (10½ oz) eggplant, cut into 2cm (¾ inch) rounds

一 Grill eggplant and serve with a sauce.

BAINIKU-SAUCE: 1 chopped umeboshi, 2 sliced shiso leaves, a pinch white roasted sesame seeds, ½ tsp honey. Combine all the ingredients.

GOMA SAUCE: 1 tbsp sesame paste, 1 tbsp honey and ½ tbsp soy sauce.

NIKU-MISO: Stir 100g (3½ oz) minced pork with tbsp caster sugar, 1 tbsp miso, 1 tbsp sake, 1 tbsp soy sauce and a pinch shichimi for 5 minutes. Serve with grilled eggplant.

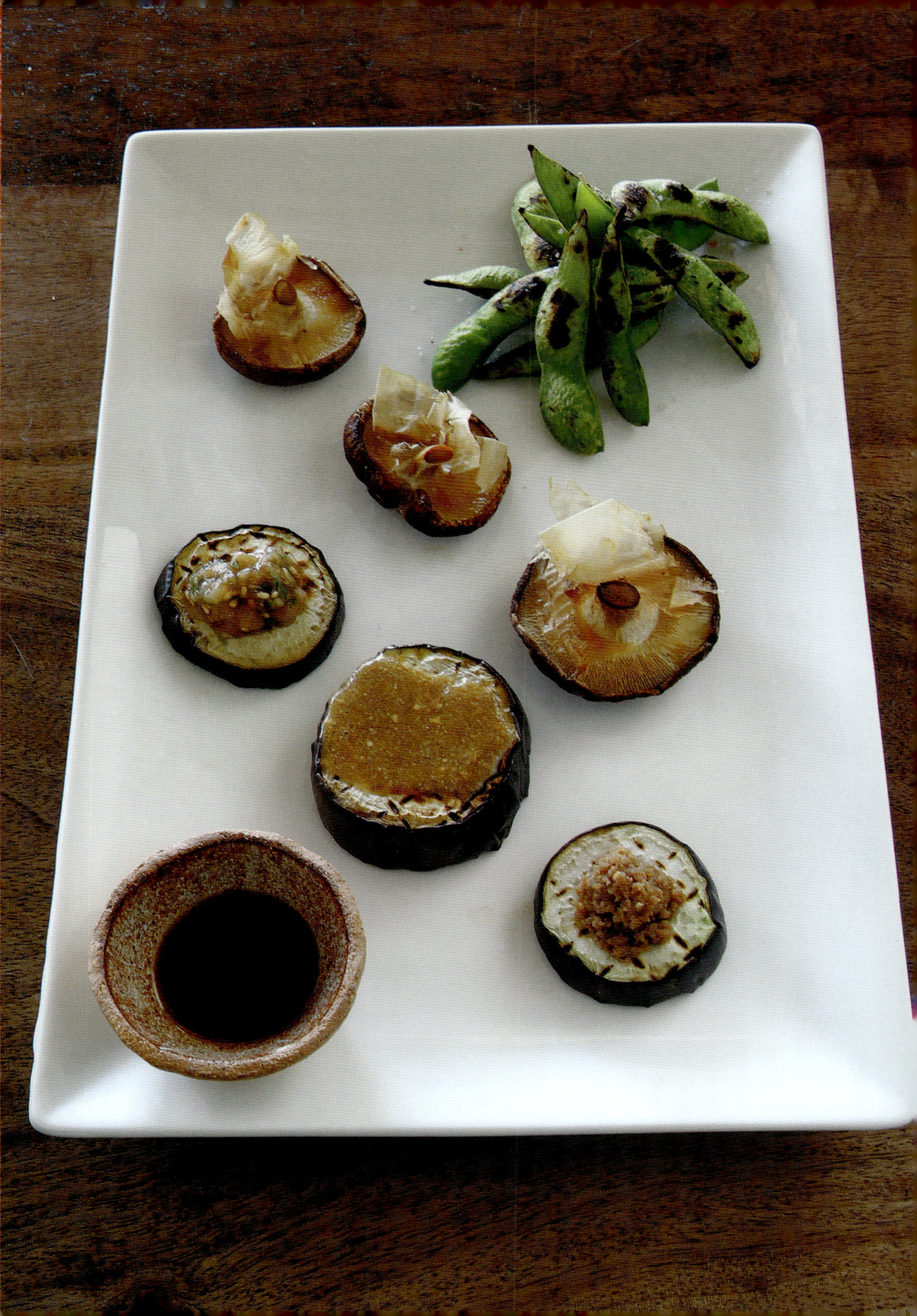

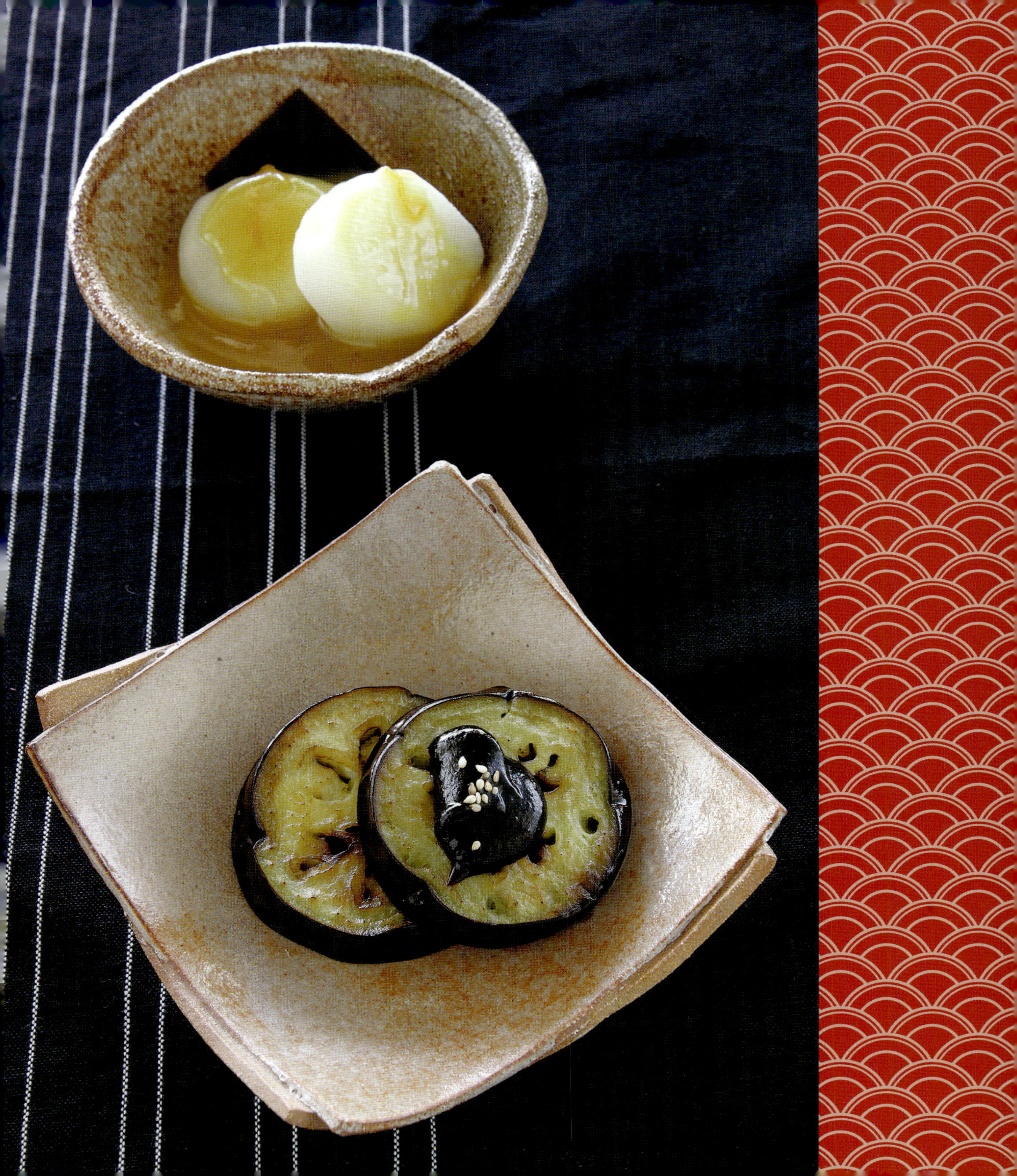

Furofuki daikon, Simmered daikon with miso paste

SERVES 4

4 daikon slices (4–5cm/1½ –2 inches thick), peeled
1 tsp raw shot grain rice
⅓ cup Saikyo miso, white miso
⅓ cup mirin
2 tbsp caster sugar
Yuzu or lemon zest for topping
1 (5x5cm/2 x 2 inch) kelp sheet, wiped and soaked in 2 cups water in a pan

一 To prepare the daikon, peel and round off the edges and make criss-cross scoring over the surface to allow the flavour to penetrate.

二 Place daikon and rice in the pan, and add extra water to about 10cm (4 inches) above the daikon. Simmer until soft or about 30 minutes over low heat. Strain and discard the water. Transfer daikon in the pan with kelp. Bring it to boil and simmer over low heat until tender.

三 In the meantime, in a pan, add miso, mirin and caster sugar and combine well with a wooden spatula over low heat until sauce thickens and becomes slightly glossy. Remove from the heat and add yuzu zest.

四 Arrange daikon in a bowl with miso paste.

Braised sliced eggplant topped with red miso

1 eggplant
¼ cup Hatcho miso
¼ cup caster sugar
1 tbsp mirin
Vegetable oil
1 tsp roasted white sesame seeds

一 Slice eggplant into 2cm (¾ inch) thick round shape.

二 Combine miso, caster sugar, and mirin in a pan and stir over low heat until sugar has dissolved.

三 Put oil in a frying pan and stir eggplant over moderate heat until cooked.

四 Transfer the eggplant onto a plate and spoon the miso mixture on top of eggplant.

五 Sprinkle with sesame seeds.

Daikon salad

100g (3½ oz) daikon, peeled and julienned
DRESSING
2 tbsp mayo
1 tbsp sesame paste
1 tsp soy sauce
Salt to taste

一 To make the dressing, mix all the ingredients and combine well.

二 Serve the daikon with the dressing in a bowl.

Diced avocado and julienned cucumber tossed with wasabi mayonnaise

1 avocado
1 Lebanese cucumber
1 tsp wasabi
1 tbsp Japanese mayonnaise
1 tbsp plain yoghurt or milk
Salt to taste

一 Cut avocado in half lengthways. Remove seed. Cut into approx. 3 cm (1 inch) cubes.

二 Cut cucumber lengthways, cut off the seeds and cut into julienne.

三 Toss avocado and cucumber in a bowl and serve in a salad bowl.

四 Mix wasabi, mayonnaise and yoghurt.

六 Drizzle wasabi mayonnaise over the salad.

Tossed chrysanthemum and enoki mushrooms with Japanese mustard

4 stems shungiku, edible chrysanthemum leaves or rocket salad leaves
1 bunch enoki mushroom
1 tsp wagarashi, Japanese mustard or English mustard
1 tsp mirin
1 tbsp soy sauce

一 Bring water to the boil in a pan and blanch shungiku and enoki mushrooms.

二 Drain and leave under the running water until cool.

三 Slightly squeeze out water.

四 Combine wagarashi, mirin and soy sauce in a bowl and toss shungiku and mushrooms.

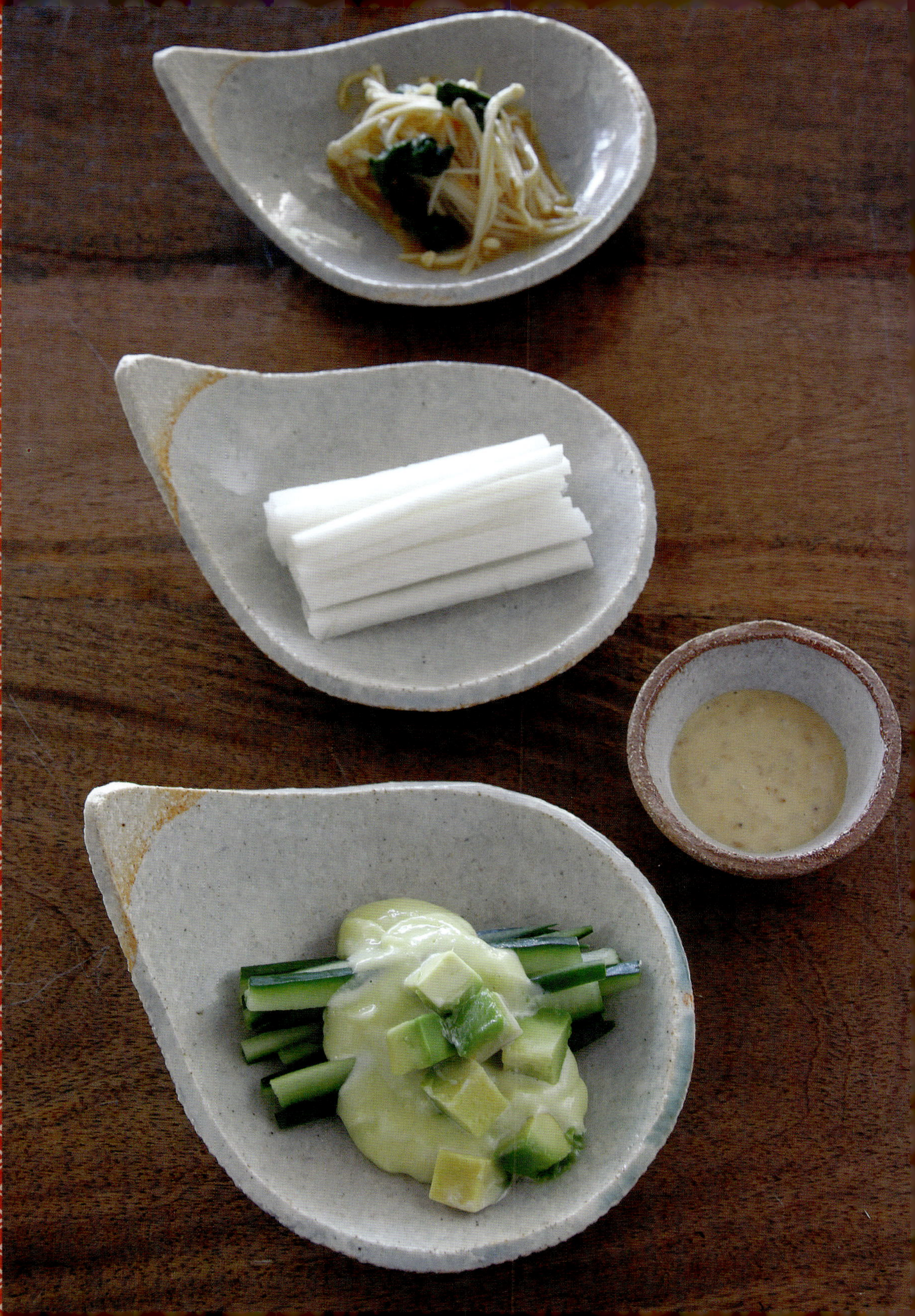

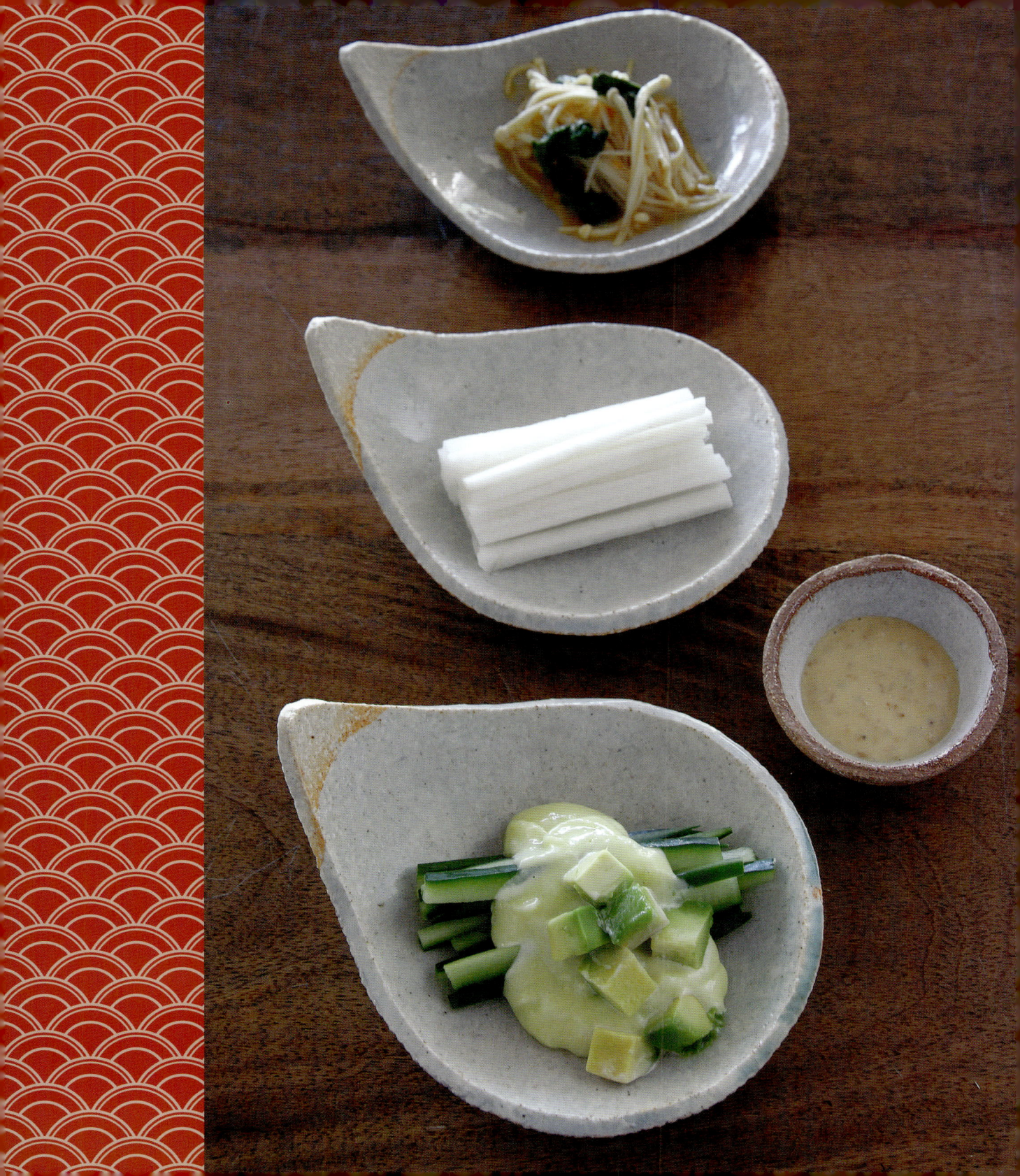

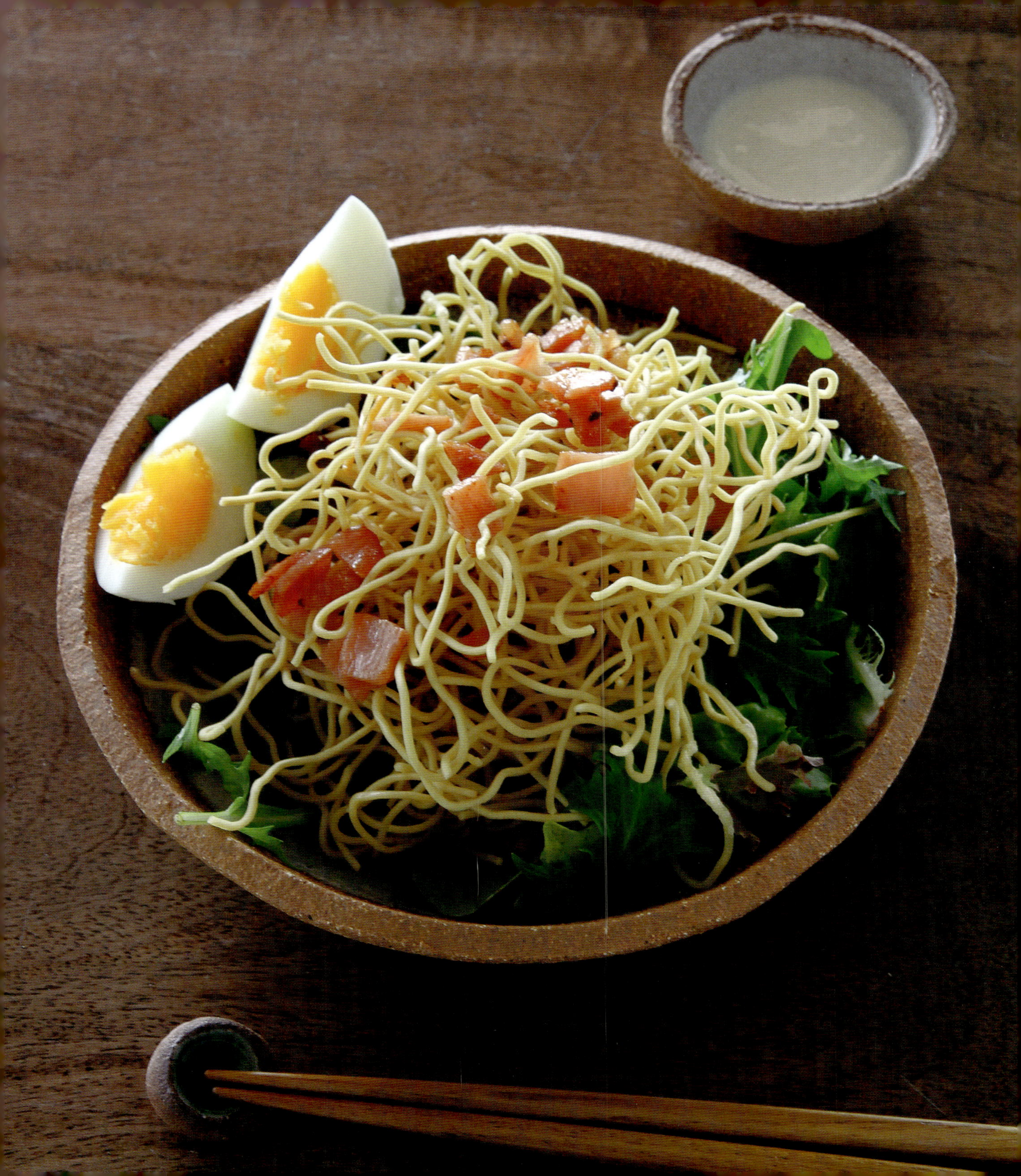

Bari-Bari salad

SERVES 2

50g (1¾ oz) semi-dried egg noodles or fried egg noodles, available from Asian groceries

Green salad leaves

1 hard-boiled egg, shell removed and halved lengthways

1 rasher bacon, chopped and stir-fried

Vegetable oil for deep-frying

DRESSING

20g (¾ oz) Japanese mayo

1 tsp caster sugar

1 tbsp milk

A pinch salt

— Heeat oil in a heavy deep pan or wok to around 170°C (340°F). Deep fry noodles until crispy and drain well.

二 Serve the noodles in a salad bowl and add the green salad leaves, egg and bacon.

三 Mix mayo, caster sugar and milk to make dressing. Salt to taste.

四 Drizzle the dressing over the salad.

Summer salad with plum gellee

SERVES FOR 4

6 umeboshi (picked plum), pitted or 40g (1½ oz) bainiku (pickled plum puree)
1 tbsp mirin
150ml (5 fl oz) water
5g (⅕ oz) gelatine combined with 1 tbsp water
1 tsp raw sugar
1 Lebanese cucumber, sliced or decorative cut (see below)
8 daikon flower shaped petals
Green salad leaves
20g (¾ oz) rice vermicelli

DRESSING

a few drops rice bran oil or vegetable oil
1 tbsp soy sauce
1 tbsp yuzu-vinegar
1 tbsp raw sugar

一 To make plum gellee, using a stick mixer or mixer, add umeboshi, mirin and water to a bowl and blend until smooth. Transfer into a pan and bring it to the boil. Remove from the heat and add the gelatine mixture. Bring back to the heat and cook until dissolved. Transfer the mixture into the mould can/tin and set in refrigerator.

二 To prepare dressing, combine all ingredients.

三 Prepare daikon and cucumber.

四 Prepare vermicelli according to the packet.

五 Transfer the moulded gellée onto the chopping board and chop finely.

六 In a glass bowl, spoon umeboshi gellee and place cucumber, daikon petals and salad leaves.

七 Sprinkle yukari.

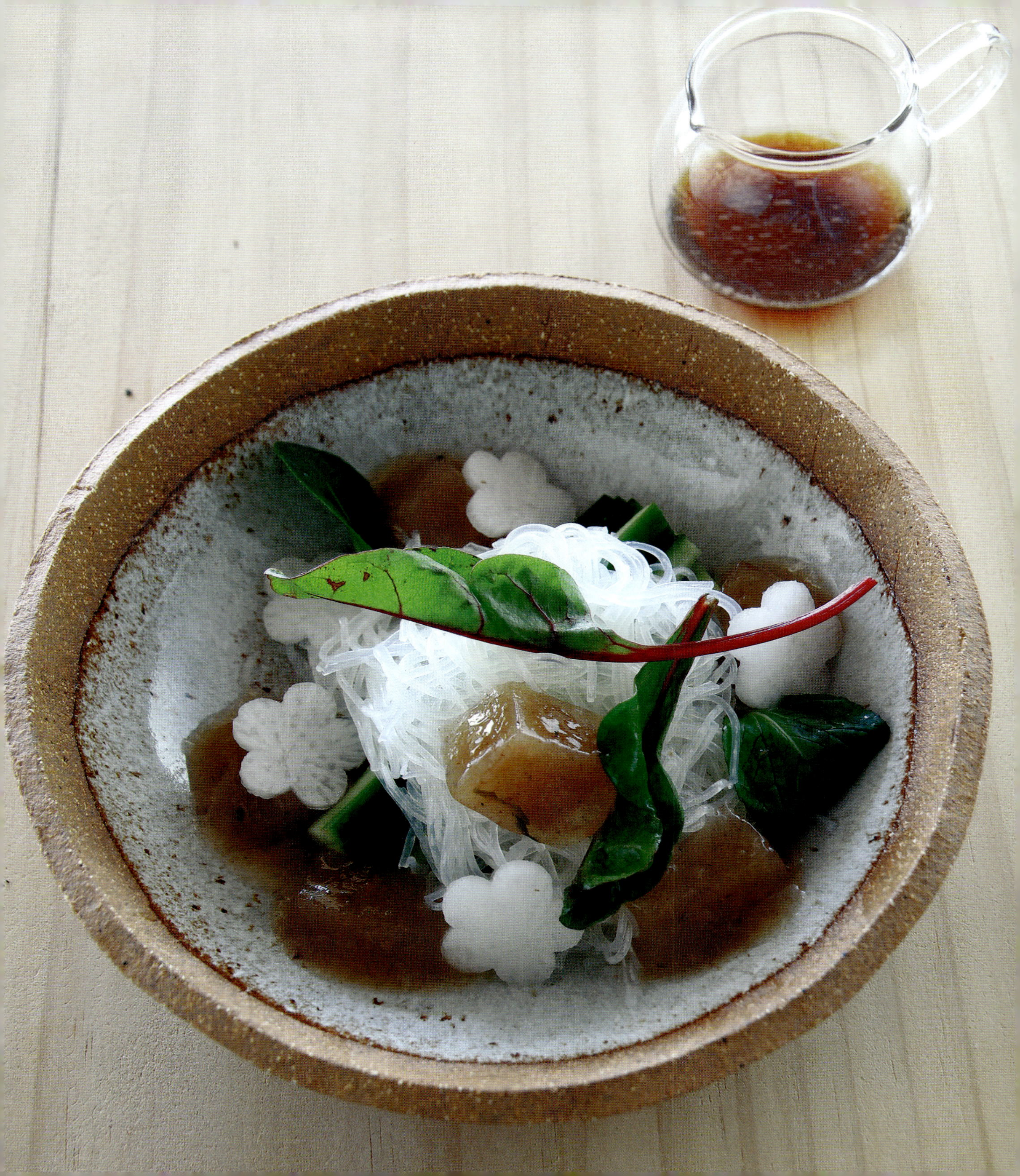

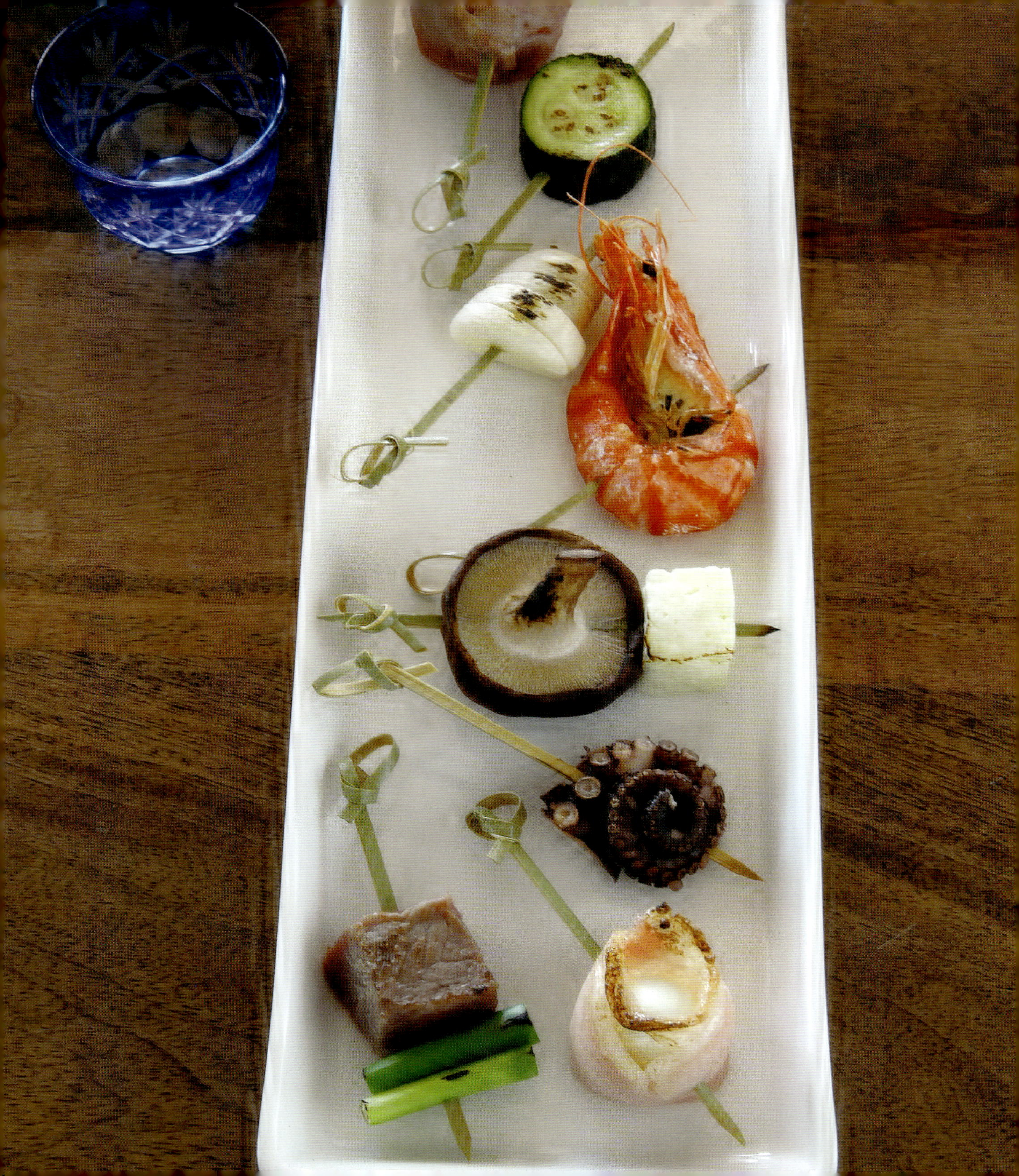

Kushi-yaki

Barbecued chicken yakitori
Kushi-age, Skewered pork in breadcrumbs

Skewered dishes are suitable for nibbling without the need of cutlery. These days quite a few varieties of skewers are available at shops.

Varieties of grilled skewered dishes:

Octopus
Prawns
Mini tomato wrapped with bacon
Shiitake mushroom with cheese (haloumi)
Spring onion and beef
Beef: diced steak served with grated daikon and ponzu

Mushroom: shiitake mushroom, Engiri mushroom, Zucchini or Japanese eggplant

Topping: Oroshi-daikon (grated daikon) and ponzu, mayonnaise, chopped spring onion

Barbecued chicken yakitori

Yakitori is skewered chicken, flavoured with sauce or salt, grilled over a charcoal fire. In specialised small shops throughout Japan known as Yakitori-ya, barbecued titbits of chicken meat, livers, hearts, intestines and skin are served with alcohol. Yakitori-ya are always crowded with people on their way home after work.

MAKES 4 SKEWERS

200g (7 oz) chicken breast or thighs, cut into bite-sized cubes

200g (7 oz) chicken livers, trimmed and cut into bite-sized cubes

200g (7 oz) chicken hearts, cut into bite-sized cubes

3 spring onion stems, cut into 3cm (1 inch) lengths

YAKITORI TERIYAKI-SAUCE

½ cup water

½ cup soy sauce

1 tbsp caster sugar

1 tbsp mirin

1 tbsp sake

½ tbsp potato starch, mixed with 1 tbsp water

Salt

— To make teriyaki sauce. Combine water, soy sauce and sugar in a pan and bring to the boil. Add mirin and sake. Pour in potato starch mixture and stir until combined well. Remove from the heat.

二 Thread chicken and spring onion onto bamboo skewers. Repeat with liver and hearts.

三 Cook skewers in a frying pan, grill, or barbeque, in the sauce.

*You may create yakitori without spring onion.
*You may sprinkle chicken with salt before grilling.

Instead of using teriyaki sauce, seasoning with salt is popular.

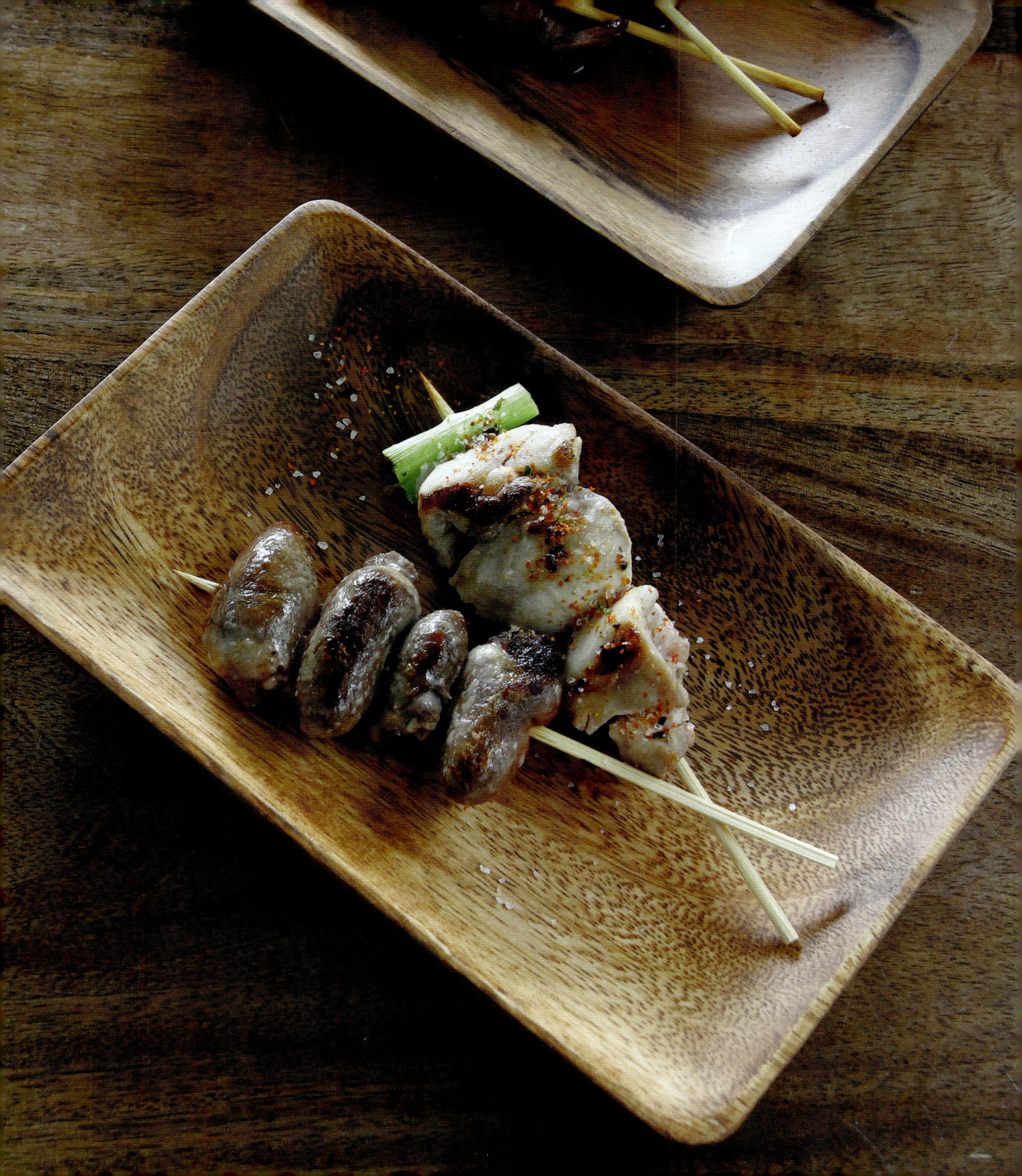

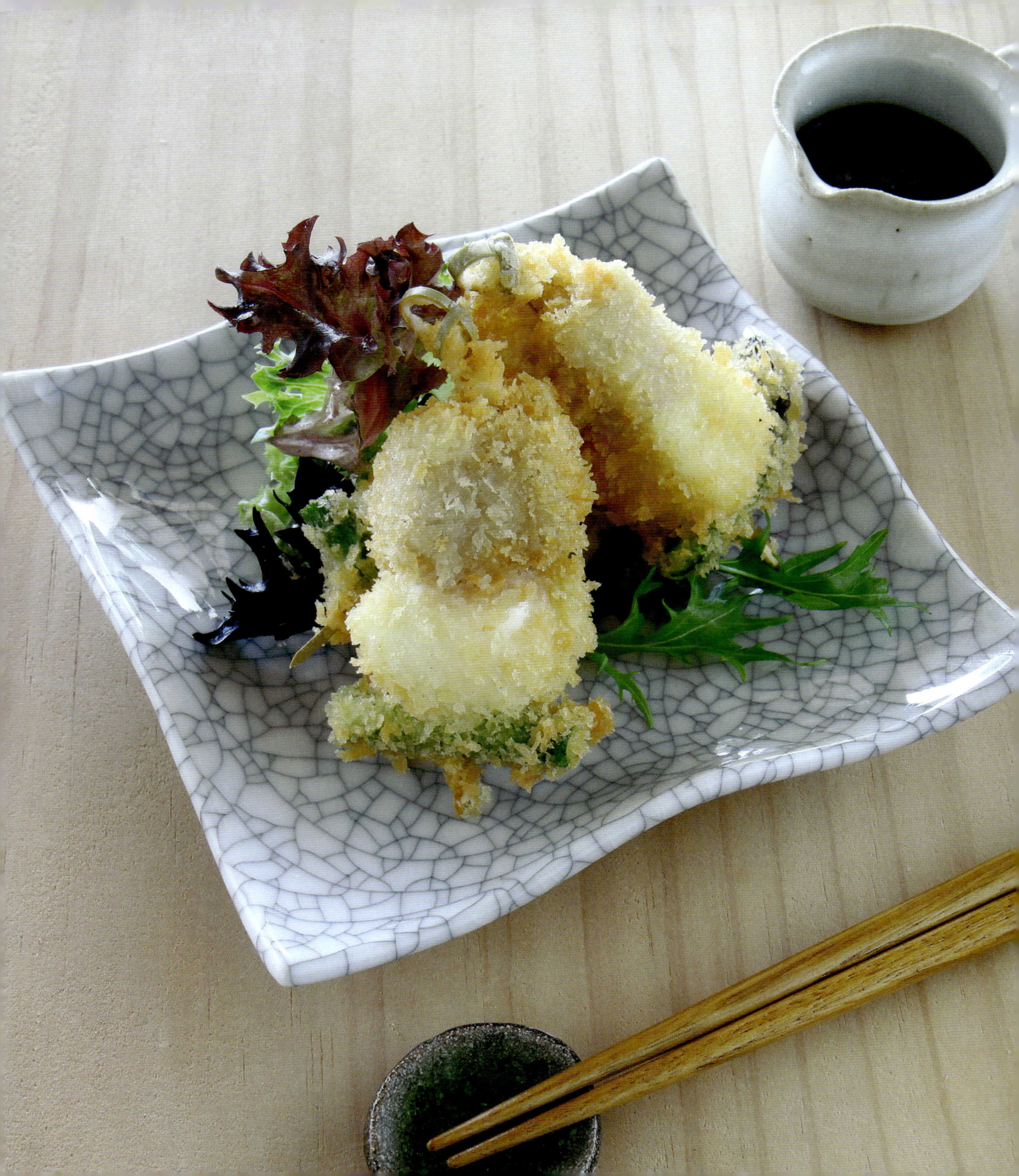

Kushi-age: Skewered pork in breadcrumbs

16 bamboo skewers: 3 pieces of each ingredient to be put on each skewer
4 asparagus stems or 8 French beans, cut into 5cm (2 inch) lengths
12 quail eggs, boiled and shells removed
12 x 1.5 cm (½ inch) cubes pork loin, skewered 3 pieces to each bamboo stick
12 x 1.5 cm (½ inch) cubes haloumi cheese, skewered 3 pieces to each bamboo stick
Salt for seasoning
Black pepper for seasoning
Plain flour for coating
1 egg, lightly beaten
Japanese breadcrumbs, slightly coarser than Western ones for coating
Also you may make kushi-age in tempura batter.
Vegetable oil for deep-frying
Tonkatsu sauce for serving

一 Prepare ingredients and attach to skewers.

二 Salt and pepper over the skewered pork.

三 Prepare flour, egg and breadcrumbs in separate bowls in a line. First coat with flour, then egg, then breadcrumbs for all the skewered ingredients.

四 Prepare oil in a deep frying pan and heat to 180°C (355°F) or test for readiness by dropping in a sprinkle of breadcrumbs, if they float the oil is hot enough.

五 Deep fry until golden brown. Drain well on a rack or kitchen paper.

六 Serve with tonkatsu sauce.

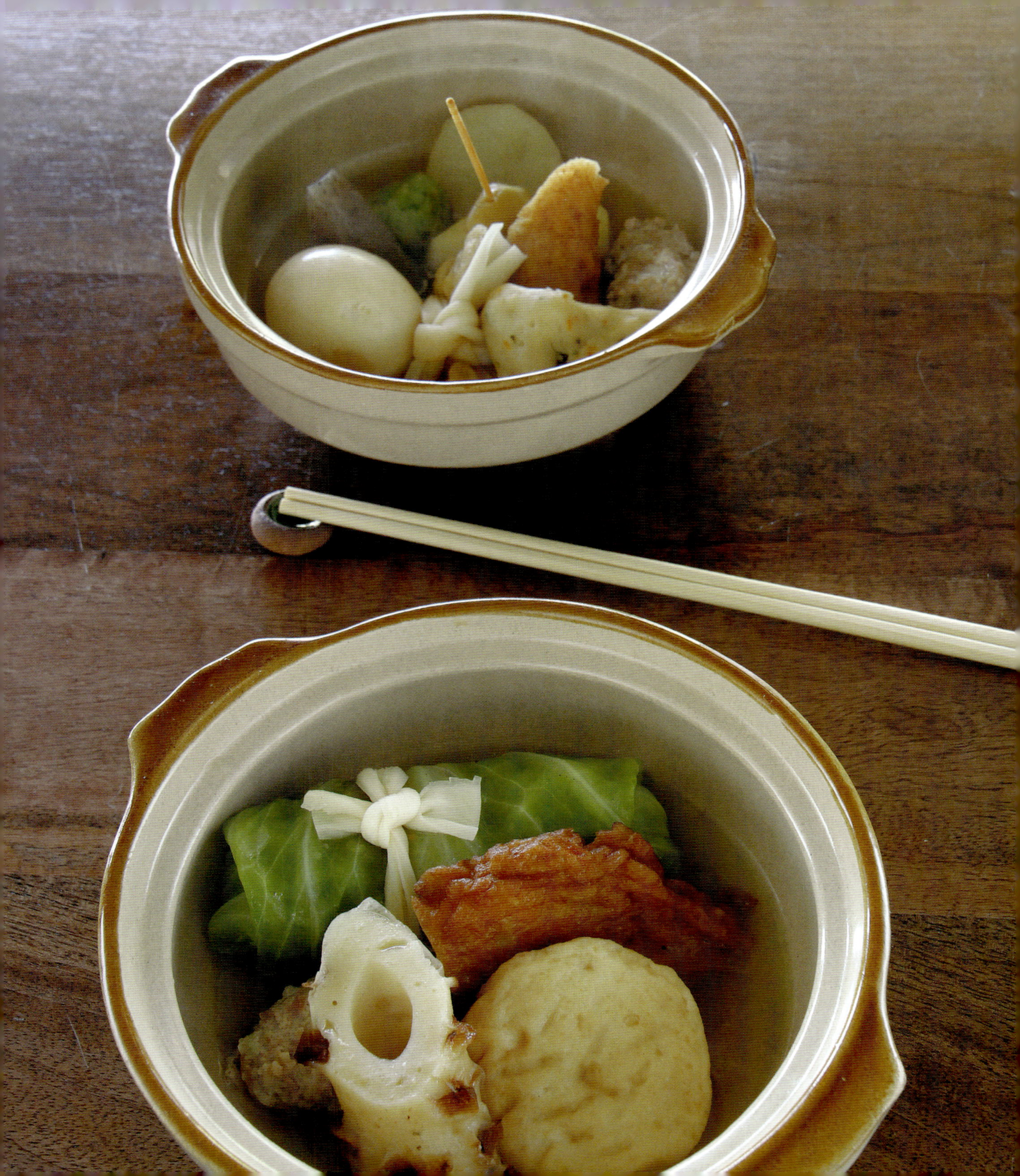

Oden

Oden is a popular stewed dish especially in winter time. The ingredients are quite versatile and in Japan there are shops that specialise in serving Oden dishes with sake, called 'Oden-ya' which are always crowded with people after work, dining or purchasing take-away meals for dinner at home.

The great varieties of fishpaste products used in these dishes are not as easy to find outside of Japan, but you can still enjoy Oden-ya style izakaya at home.

    Oden
    Rolled cabbage
    Chicken ball

Oden

SERVES 4

8cm (3¼ inch) long daikon, peeled, mentori-trimmed* and cut into 2cm (¾ inch) slices

½ (approx. 125g/4½ oz) konnyaku block

4 small waxy type potatoes, such as Charlotte, peeled and soaked in water

4 hard-boiled eggs, peeled

2 atsuage (thick deep-fried tofu), cut in half diagonally

4 rolled cabbage (see opposite)

8 Chicken balls (see opposite)

2 Abura-age (thin deep-fried tofu), pour on boiled water and cut in half lengthways

2 mochi

Fish paste products, such as chikuwa (cylinder-shape fish cake tube) or gobo-ten (deep-fried fish paste with burdock stick)

4 toothpicks

ODEN STOCK

5 cups dashi (see Basics page)

3 tbsp usukuchi shoyu (light colour soy sauce) or 4 tbsp soy sauce

2 tbsp mirin

2 tbsp sake

A pinch of salt

Wagarashi or hot English mustard for serving

一 To prepare daikon, place daikon slices in a pan with water to cover. Bring to the boil and simmer for 15 minutes or until cooked.

二 To prepare konnyaku, cut in half and slice diagonally to make right-angle triangular shapes. Lightly score across one surface diagonally to allow flavour to be absorbed. Lightly boil.

三 To prepare potatoes, place in a pan with water to cover. Bring to the boil and cook for 10 minutes.

四 Prepare rolled cabbages and chicken balls.

五 Open abura-age from cut side, being careful not to tear, and insert mochi into each pocket. Using a toothpick as if sewing to close the pocket.

六 Prepare stock in a large pan. You may add chicken stock for extra flavour if you like.

七 Add daikon, konnyaku, boiled eggs, atsu-age, potatoes and fish products, and simmer for 20 minutes.

八 Add mochi and simmer another 15 minutes.

九 Serving in individual bowls with wagarashi.

Mentori is a presentation method where you trim or curb a piece of vegetable to prevent from losing its shape when cooking.

Rolled cabbage

1 whole cabbage, only used 4 large layers
A pinch of salt
200g (7 oz) minced lean pork
1 stem spring onion, trimmed and chopped
5 dried shiitake mushrooms, soaked in water and sliced
½ tbsp soy sauce
½ tbsp sake
4 sticks

Cut off the stem part of cabbage and gently separate cabbage leaves.

Trim off the hard vein part.

Bring water in a pan to the boil and add a pinch of salt.

Blanch cabbage leaves and drain over a tea towel.

Place minced pork, spring onion and shiitake in a bowl and add soy and sake.

Mix using your hand.

Lay a cabbage leave on a flat board and spoon the pork on the corner of stem.

Wrap pork like a parcel.

Skewer with a stick.

Chicken ball

500g (17½ oz) minced chicken
4 tbsp grated onion
1 egg
½ tbsp sake
A pinch of salt
1 tsp light colour soy sauce

一 Add chicken, onion and egg in a bowl and mix using your hand.

二 Add salt, sake and soy sauce and mix until smooth.

三 Bring water in a pot and with two spoons, shape chicken into balls and transfer to the pot.

四 Chicken will float to the surface when cooked.

五 Transfer into an iced bowl to cool it down.

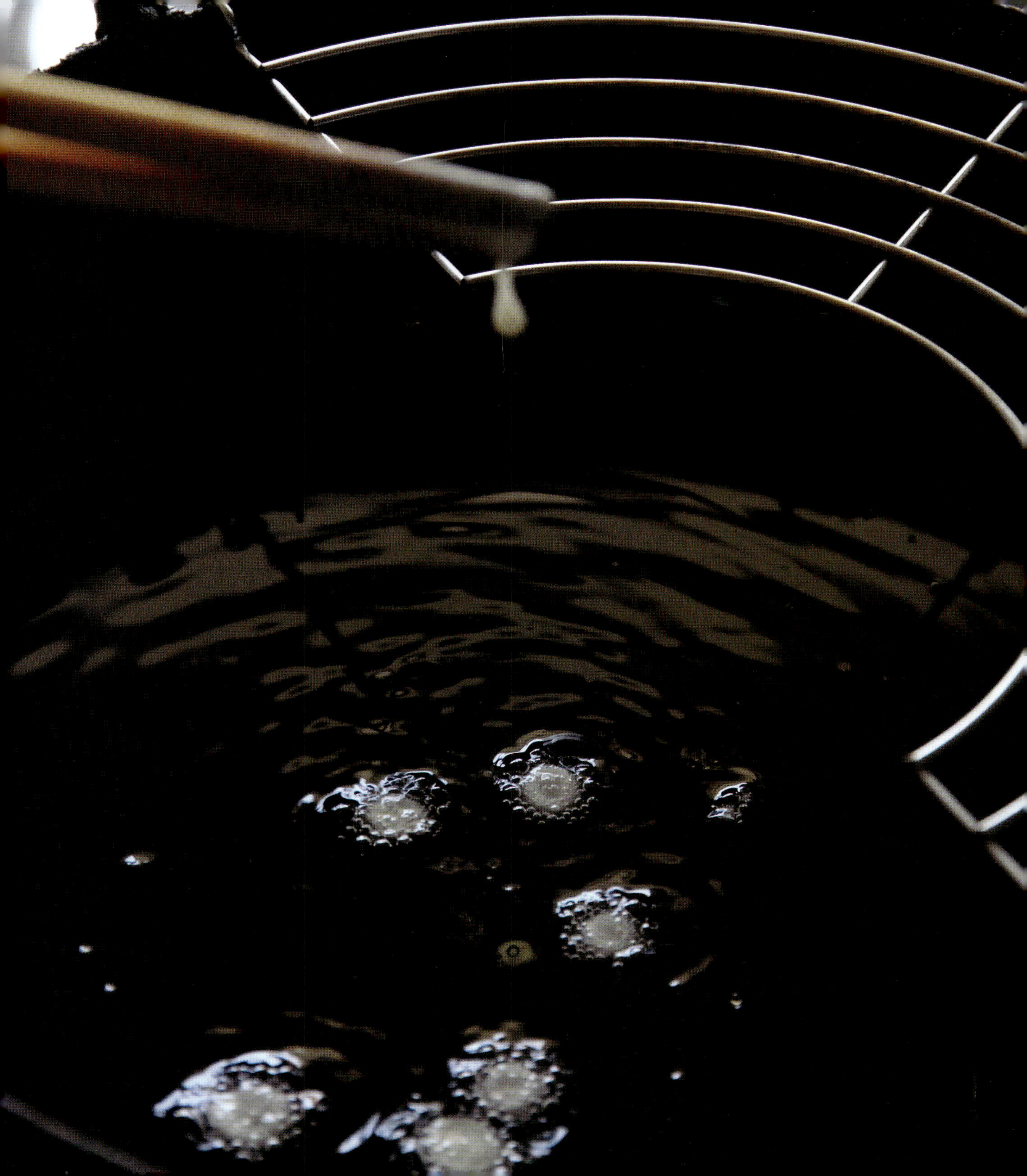

Deep-fried dishes

Beer or chu-hai go particularly well with deep-fried dishes.
Chips: See Tsumami page 29

Tempura

Kaki-age

Dressed up king prawn

Deep-fried zucchini with miso-mayo

Harumaki: Spring roll with king prawn and asparagus

Fishcake with lotus root and carrot garnished with lemon wedge

Deep-fried white fish paste in shiso-leave

Kaki-furai: Deep-fried oyster with breadcrumbs

Japanese croquette in sukiyaki flavour

Potato salad

Renkon senbei karikari chips with sweet soy sauce: Lotus root chips with sweet soy sauce

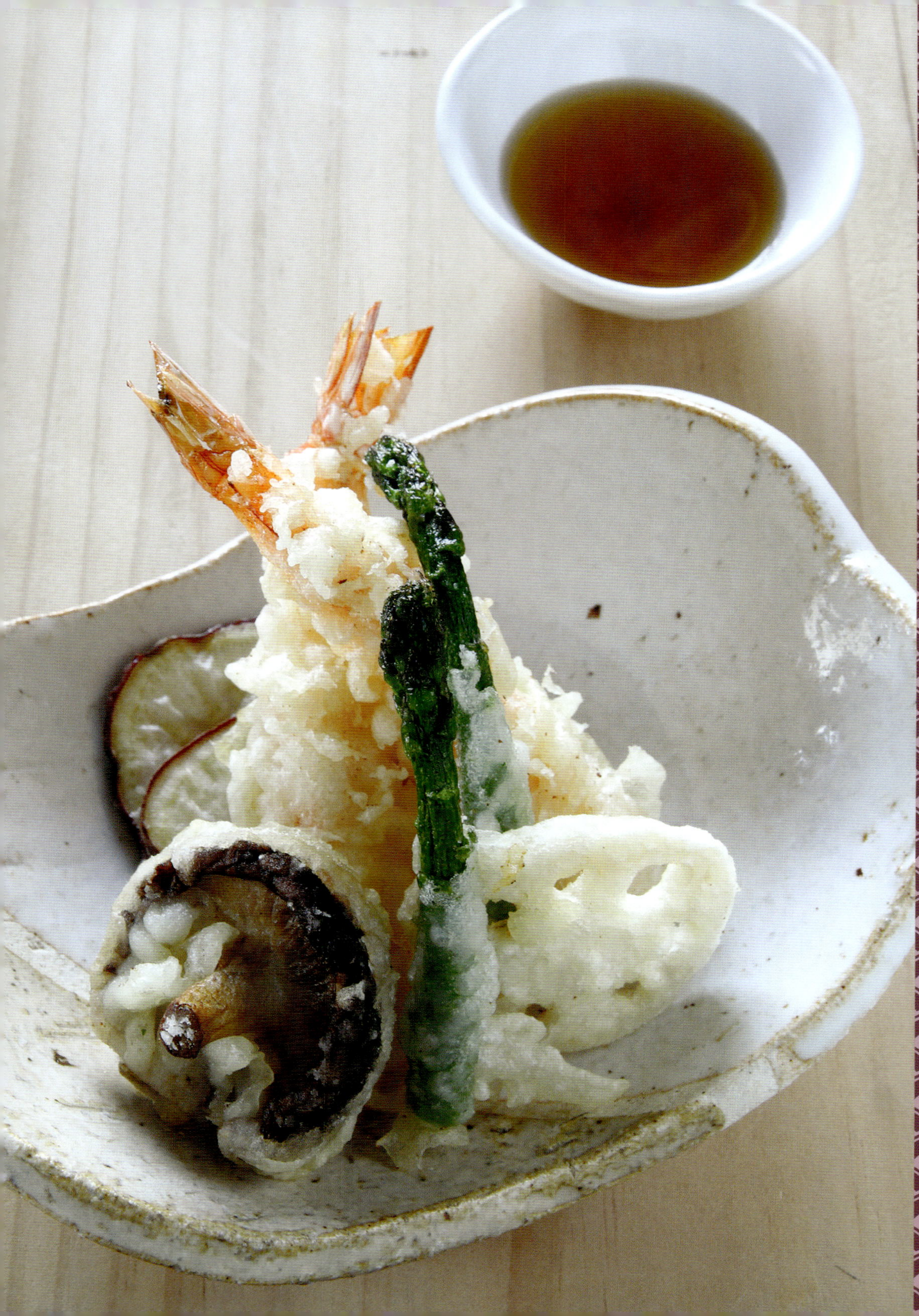

Tempura

SERVES 2

TEMPURA BATTER
150g (5¼ oz) tempura flour or 100g (3½ oz) flour and 50g (1¾ oz) potato starch
150ml (5 fl oz) cold water

2 green king prawns, deveined
2 thinly sliced Japanese sweet potatoes
2 sliced lotus roots
2 asparagus or French beans, trimmed

Potato starch for coating

DIPPING SAUCE
½ cup dashi (see Basics page)
1 tbsp light colour soy sauce
1 tsp mirin

一 To prepare the dipping sauce, add all ingredients in a sauce pan and bring to the boil. Remove from the heat and set aside.

二 To make tempura batter mix, place flour in a bowl. Add refrigerated cold water. Using a pair of chopsticks or fork gently combine.

三 To prepare prawns, remove the head and shell without cutting off the tail. With a small knife, make a slit from the belly side to open like a butterfly.

四 Prepare oil in a deep pan and heat to about 180°C (355°F).

五 Coat the prawns and sweet potato slices with potato starch.

六 To check the temperature, drop a small amount of the tempura batter into the oil, and when it quickly floats up, it is ready. Holding one ingredient with chopsticks or tongs, dip it into the tempura batter and carefully slide it into the oil.

七 Turn over when it becomes lightly golden, and remove when cooked on both sides. Drain on a wire rack or kitchen paper.

八 Repeat with other ingredients.

九 Serve with tempura dipping sauce or just sprinkle salt.

IZAKAYA • DEEP-FRIED DISHES

Kaki-age

150g (5¼ oz) corn kernels, fresh or frozen
5 ham slices, cut into approx. 2 cm (¾ inch) squares
½ cup green soy beans (frozen ones are available from Japanese and Asian grocery stores)
2 tbsp potato starch
½ cup plain flour
¼ cup water
Salt for seasoning

一 If using frozen corn, pat with kitchen paper to dry off moisture.

二 Put corn, ham and soy beans in a bowl.

三 Sprinkle with potato starch and with dry hands combine them.

四 Set aside for 10 minutes.

五 In the meantime, prepare flour and water in a bowl, and mix.

六 Prepare the oil in the deep frying pan and heat to 160°C (320°F).

七 Transfer the vegetables in the mixture and combine.

八 Spoon the vegetable mixture into the oil. Deep-fry over a low heat until crispy.

九 Drain off oil on kitchen paper or a wire rack.

十 Sprinkle salt over while they still hot.

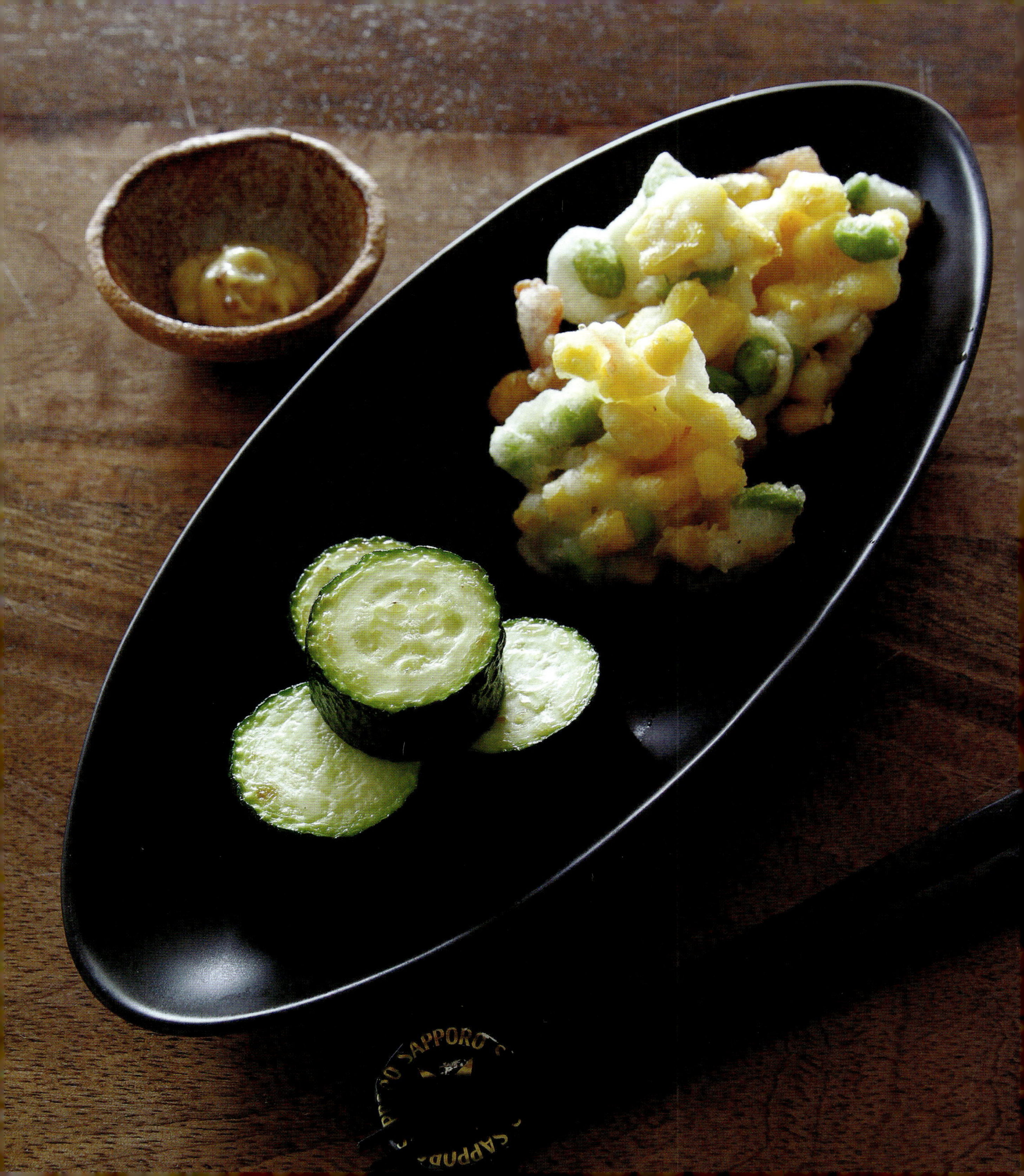
SAPPORO

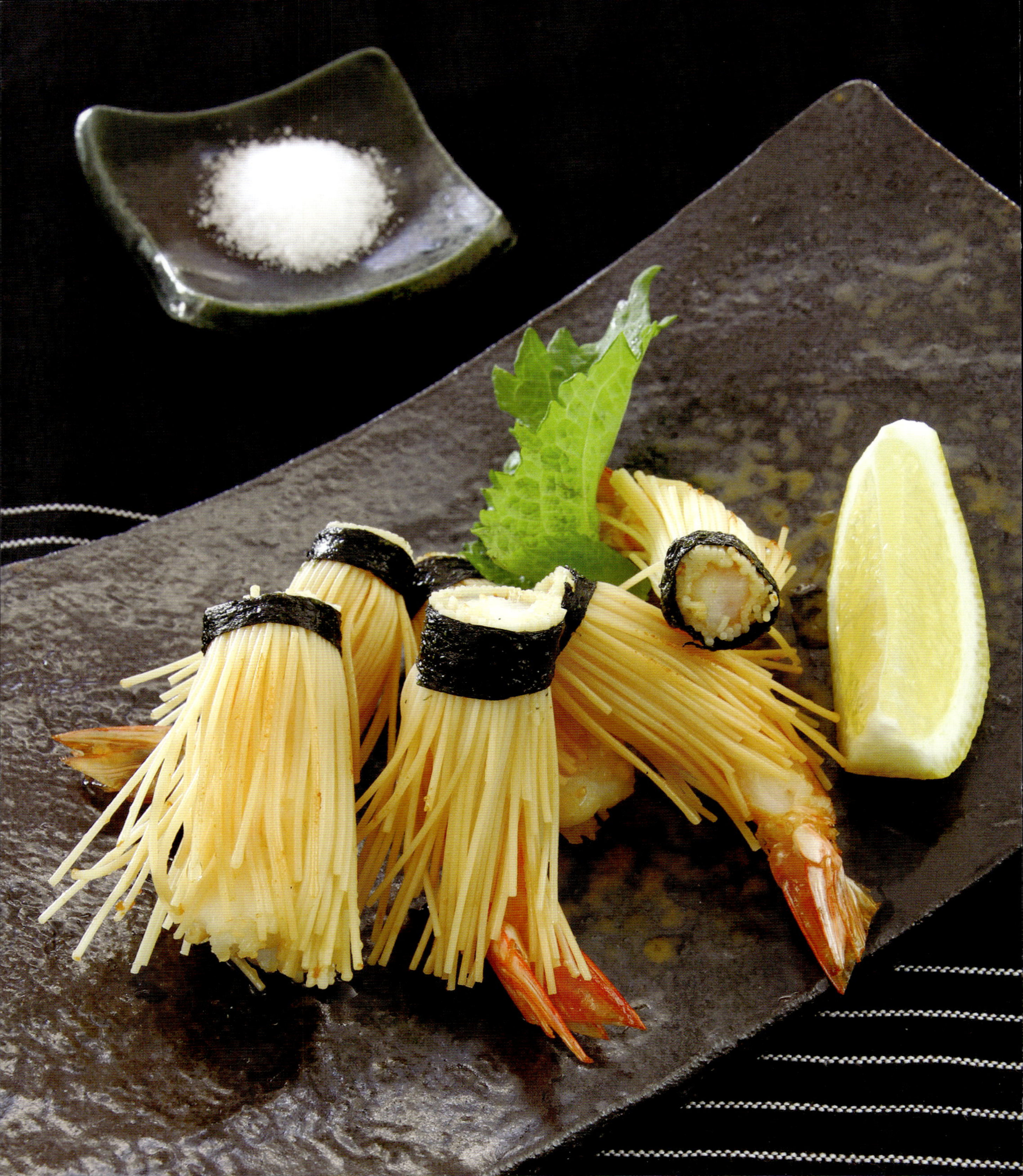

Dressed up king prawn

SERVES FOR 4

8 green king prawns, peeled and deveined
8 Nori strips (1cm x 8cm)
Somen noodles, halved
Shiso (Japanese basil), optional
Salt for sprinkling
4 lemon wedges
Vegetable oil for deep frying

一 Pat prawns dry with kitchen paper.

二 Lay noodles on a plate and coat around prawn.

三 Bind noodles and prawn together with nori strips.

四 Prepare oil in a deep pan, heat to about 180°C (355°F) and deep fry king prawns.

五 Drain off oil over a rack or kitchen paper, and sprinkle with salt.

六 Serve with lemon wedges.

Deep-fried zucchini with miso-mayo

1 zucchini, into 2 cm (¾ inch) slices
3 tbsp mayonnaise
3 tbsp Saikyo miso
1 tbsp mustard seeds
Vegetable oil

一 Heat oil in a deep pan to around 170°C (340°F).

二 Deep fry zucchini for 1 minute or until lightly cooked.

三 Drain oil, arrange zucchini on a tray, and grill for 2–3 minutes.

四 To make miso mayo, mix mayonnaise, Saikyo miso and mustard in a small bowl.

五 Serve zucchini with miso-mayo on the side.

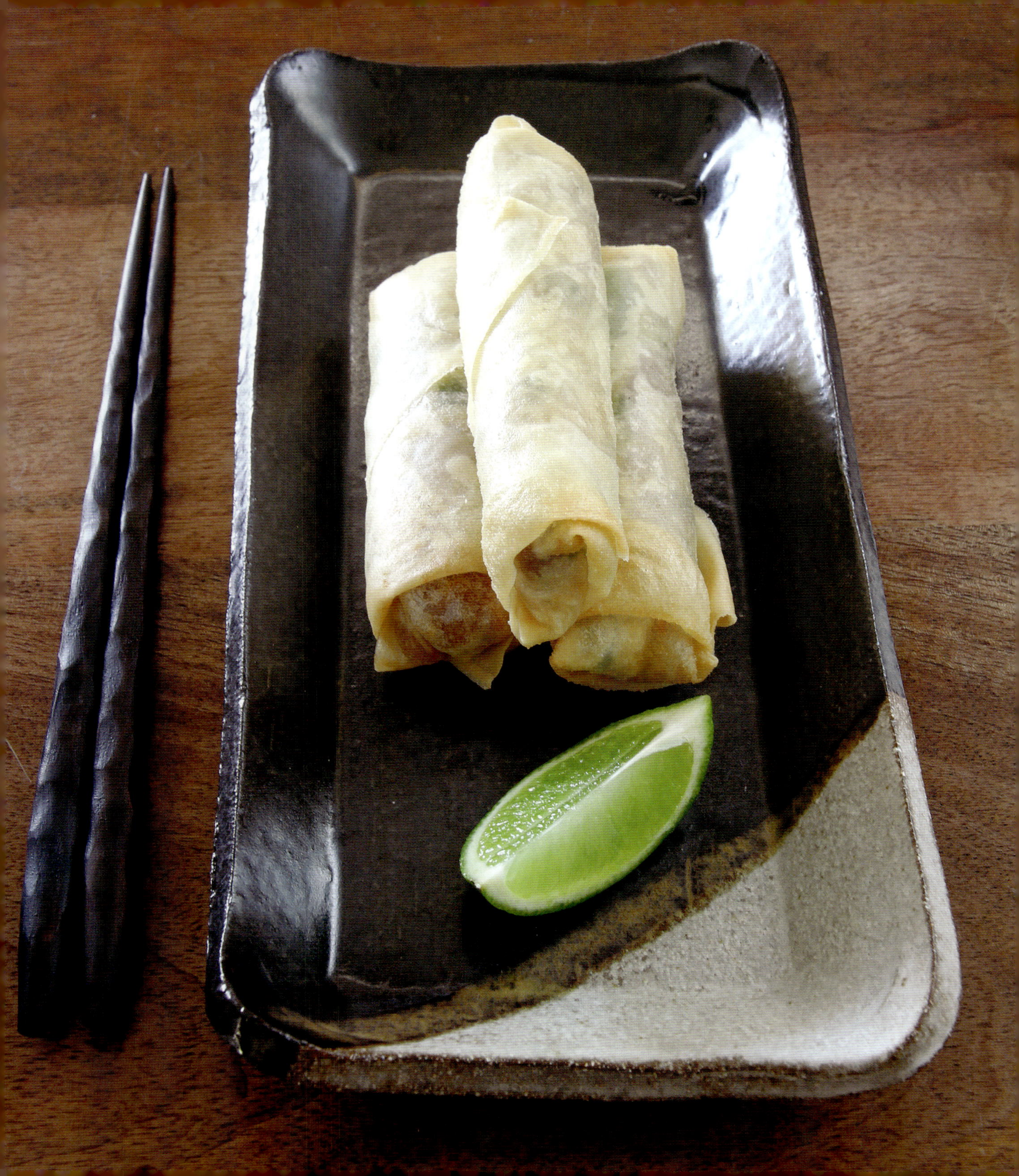

Harumaki: Spring roll with king prawn and asparagus

SERVES 4

4 king prawns

1 tsp sake

200g (7 oz) thinly sliced pork or minced lean pork

2 tsp soy sauce

2 tsp sake

2 tsp potato starch

4 asparagus, trimmed and halved, and precooked

20g (7 oz) rice noodles

2 spring onion, trimmed and chopped

1 tsp chopped ginger

A drop sesame oil

2 tsp soy sauce

2 tsp sake

¼ cup chicken stock

4 spring roll sheets

Vegetable oil for deep fry

1 lime or lemon wedge

一 To prepare king prawns, remove heads, shells and devein. Place king prawns in a pan and sprinkle with sake. Put a lid on and bring it to the boil and cook for 1 minute. Set aside and allow to cool.

二 Place pork in a bowl or zip-lock plastic bag. Add soy sauce, sake and potato starch and marinate.

三 To prepare rice noodles, blanch in boiling water and drain. Refresh under running water and drain, and then cut in 5cm (2 inch) lengths.

四 Drop sesame oil in a frying pan and add spring onion and chopped ginger, then stir for 30 seconds. Add pork and soy sauce, sake and chicken stock, then bring it to the boil. Add cooked rice noodle and stir for 1 minute. Remove from the heat and cool it down.

五 Prepare spring roll sheet on a dry area or plate, place fillings on little bit below the centre of sheet, wrap the filling like parcel, folding the sides as you roll up to the end.

六 Put oil in a deep frying pan and heat it up to 170°C (340°F). Deep fry the spring rolls until lightly brown. Drain off oil on a rack or kitchen paper. Cut in half slightly oblique.

七 Serve with lime or lemon wedge.

Fishcake with lotus root and carrot garnished with lemon wedge

200g (7 oz) white fish
1 tsp caster sugar
A pinch of salt
A small knob of ginger (approx. 10g/⅓ oz), peeled
1 egg
50g (1¾ oz) lotus root, peeled and chopped finely
50g (1¾ oz) carrot, peeled and shredded
Plain flour for dusting
Vegetable oil for deep frying

DIPPING SAUCE
2 tbsp rice vinegar
1 red chilli, deseeded and chopped
1 tbsp caster sugar
2 tbsp soy sauce
Lemon or lime wedges

一 To prepare dipping sauce, mix all the ingredients in a pan and cook until sugar is dissolved.

二 Place fish, caster sugar, salt, ginger and egg in a food processor and beat to a paste texture.

三 Transfer the paste into a bowl and combine with lotus root and carrot.

四 Dust your palm with plain flour. With a tablespoon scoop mixture onto your dusted palm and form mixture into oval or round shapes.

五 Heat up oil in a pan to 180°C (355°F) and deep fry until golden-brown.

六 Serve with lemon or lime wedges.

Deep-fried white fish paste in shiso-leaf

SERVES 4
200g (7 oz) of white fish fillet, such as kingfish, cod
1 pinch of salt
1 tbsp of potato starch
8 shiso (Japanese green basil) leaves
Vegetable oil for deep-frying
4 lemon wedges
soy sauce for serving

一 In a food processor, place the fish, potato starch and salt and whiz until smooth.

二 Spoon the fish paste onto each shiso leaf and fold in half.

三 Heat oil in a pan or wok to 180°C (355°F).

四 Deep fry wrapped fish paste until shiso leaf is crisp and drain well.

五 Serve with lemon wedges and soy sauce.

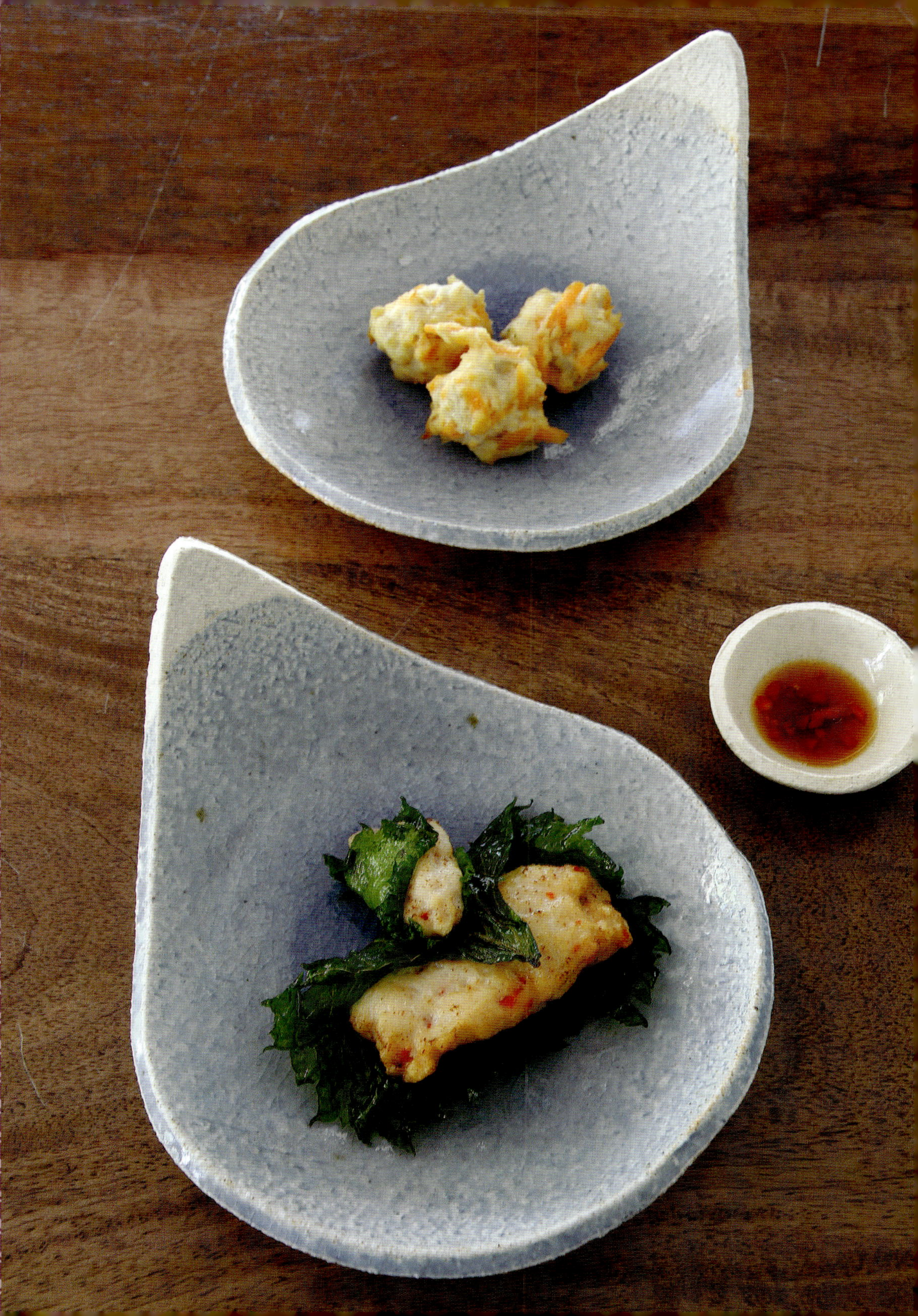

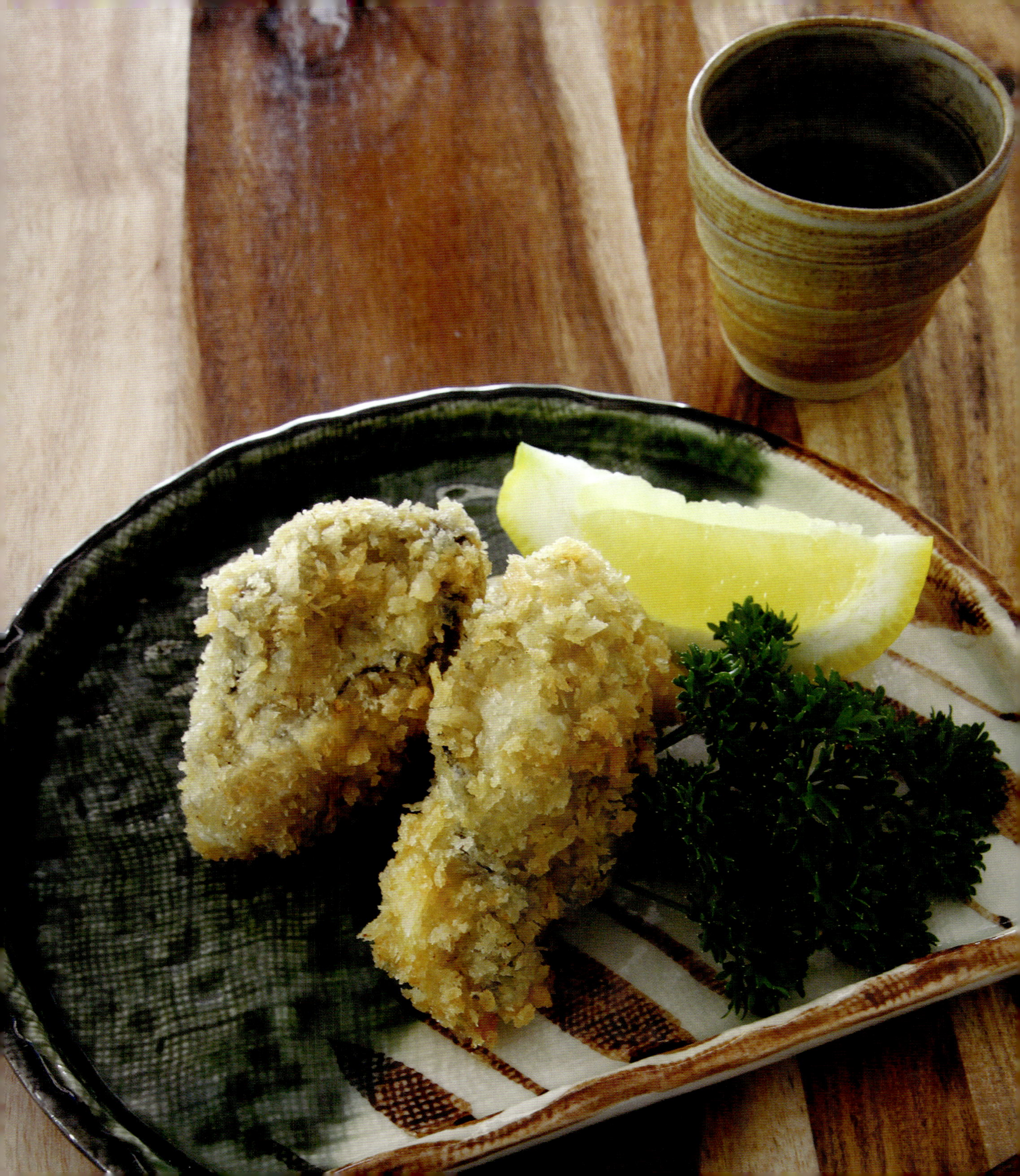

Kaki-furai: Deep-fried oyster with breadcrumbs

3 Pacific oysters
Salt for seasoning
Plain flour for coating
1 egg, beaten
Japanese breadcrumbs for coating
Vegetable oil for deep-frying
Lemon wedges

一 Lightly crack sea salt over the oysters.

二 Prepare flour, beaten egg and breadcrumbs in a line and coat oysters one by one.

三 Prepare oil to 170°C (340°F) in a deep pan and deep-fry until lightly brown.

四 Drain off oil well over a rack or kitchen paper.

五 Serve with lemon wedges.

Japanese croquette in sukiyaki flavour

татин TO MAKE 15~16 PIECES

3 potatoes (approx. 450g/15¾oz), peeled and cut in quarters

1 brown onion, peeled and chopped finely

Small amount of vegetable oil

200g (7 oz) minced beef

2 tbsp soy sauce

1 tbsp caster sugar

1 tbsp mirin

1 cup plain flour

2 cups Japanese breadcrumbs (coarse)

2 eggs, beaten

Cabbage, shredded

2~3 red radish, sliced

1 cucumber, sliced

Vegetable oil for deep frying

一 Cook potatoes until soft and drain, then mash.

二 Meanwhile, fry onion in small amount of oil until golden brown, stirring continuously. Add minced beef, soy sauce, sugar and mirin. Stir until liquid has almost evaporated. Transfer into mashed potato and combine well.

三 Take about 1 tbsp of mixture in the palm of your hand and make a ball. Repeat with the remainder.

四 Line up flour on a plate, beaten egg in a bowl and breadcrumbs on a plate.

五 With hands, pat flour around croquettes.

六 Dip into the egg and coat with flour, dip into egg again and then into breadcrumbs. Repeat with all croquettes.

七 Prepare salad, combine cabbage, radish and cucumber in a bowl. Arrange on a serving plate.

八 Heat up the oil in a heavy pan to about 170–180°C (340–355°F).

九 Deep fry croquettes until a golden colour. Remove from the oil and drain well.

十 Serve with salad.

Tonkatsu sauce (available Japanese or Asian groceries shops) is often used for additional sauce for breadcrumbs.

Potato salad

1 Lebanese cucumber, trimmed and sliced
Salt
4 medium floury potatoes, such as King Edward,
2–3 slices ham, chopped
1 hard-boiled egg, chopped
⅓ cup frozen corn, cooked
¼ cup Japanese mayonnaise
1 tsp roasted white sesame seeds
Freshly grounded salt and black pepper to taste

一 Sprinkle salt over the cucumber and then rub it in. Squeeze to remove excess liquid.

二 To prepare the potatoes, peel and cut coarsely. Put in a pan of lightly salted cold water. Bring to the boil and simmer until cooked, use a skewer to check. Strain and put back in the pan over low heat, shaking the pan and cook until dry or liquid is absorbed. Mash with a masher and cool it down.

三 Add the cucumber into the potato, and add the ham, boiled egg, corn, mayonnaise, sesame seeds and toss well. Season with salt and pepper

Variations : May add hot mustard with mayonnaise.

Renkon senbei karikari chips with sweet soy sauce: Lotus root chips with sweet soy sauce

200g (7 oz) fresh, precooked or frozen lotus root, peel and slice thinly
4 tbsp awase-jyoyu (see Basics page)
2 tbsp caster sugar
Vegetable oil for deep frying

If you are using frozen lotus root, defrost and keep them slightly dry on a tray or kitchen paper before deep-frying. Fresh lotus root is available in the Asian vegetable section at fresh food shops or Asian grocery stores. Frozen and precooked ones are available from Asian or Japanese grocery stores.

一 When using fresh lotus root, peel then using a slicer, slice thinly.

二 Make sweet soy sauce, combine awase-jyoyu and sugar in a small pan and bring it to the boil, simmer to evaporate until slightly thickened.

三 Prepare oil and heat up to 170°C (340°F).

四 Deep fry lotus root until crispy.

五 Drizzle sweet soy over the lotus root immediately before serving at the table.

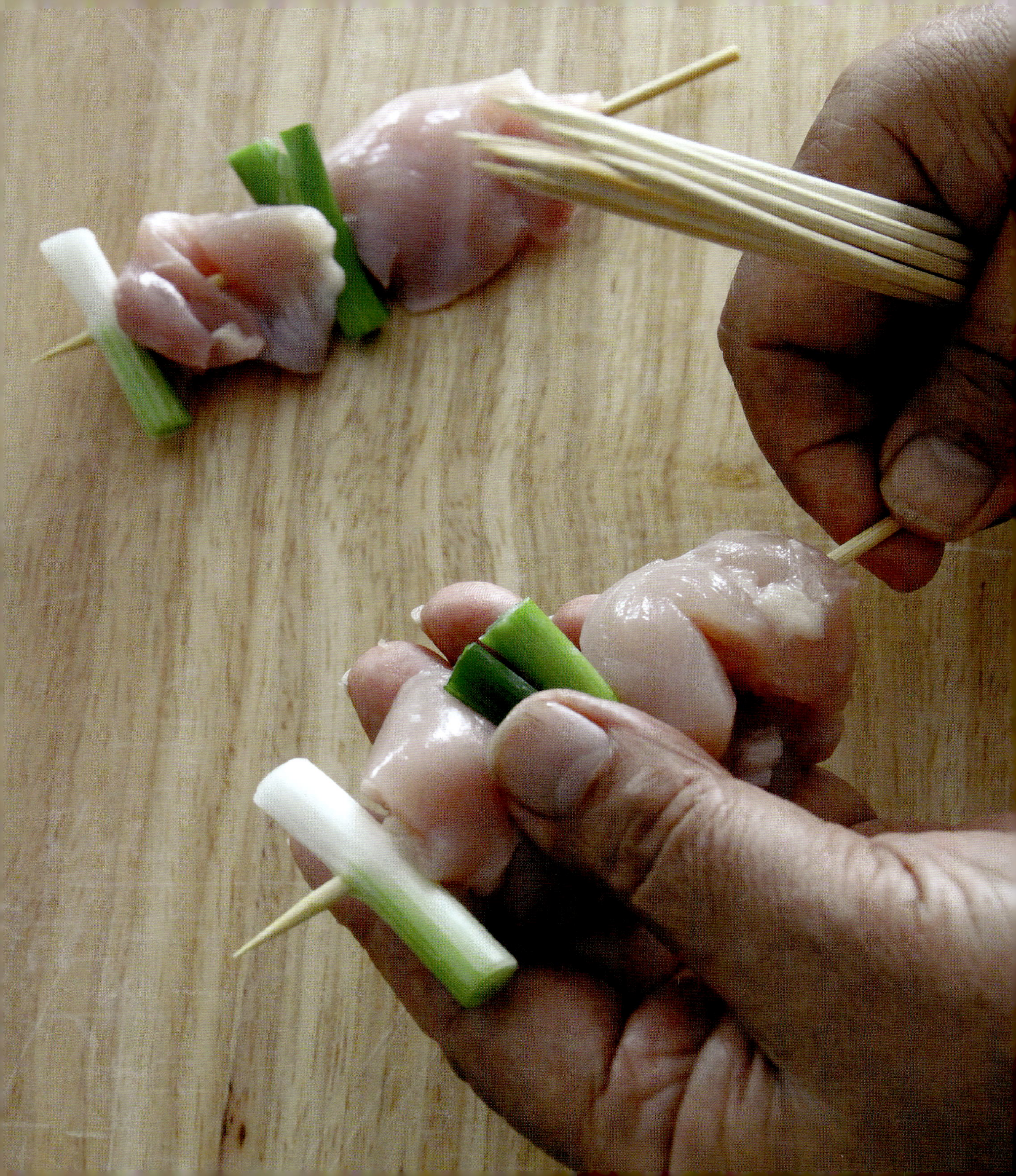

Poultry

Teba to ninniku age: Deep fried chicken wing and garlic
Chicken kara-age
Mizuna salad with onion dressing
Chicken tsukune: Skewered minced chicken
Steamed chicken tenderloin tossed with plum puree
Braised chicken soft bone with garlic, sesame and soy sauce
Chicken giblet with rocket leaves in earthenware pot
Steamed chicken, Yuan style
Dashimaki-tamago: Japanese egg omelette
Japanese egg omelette with scallops

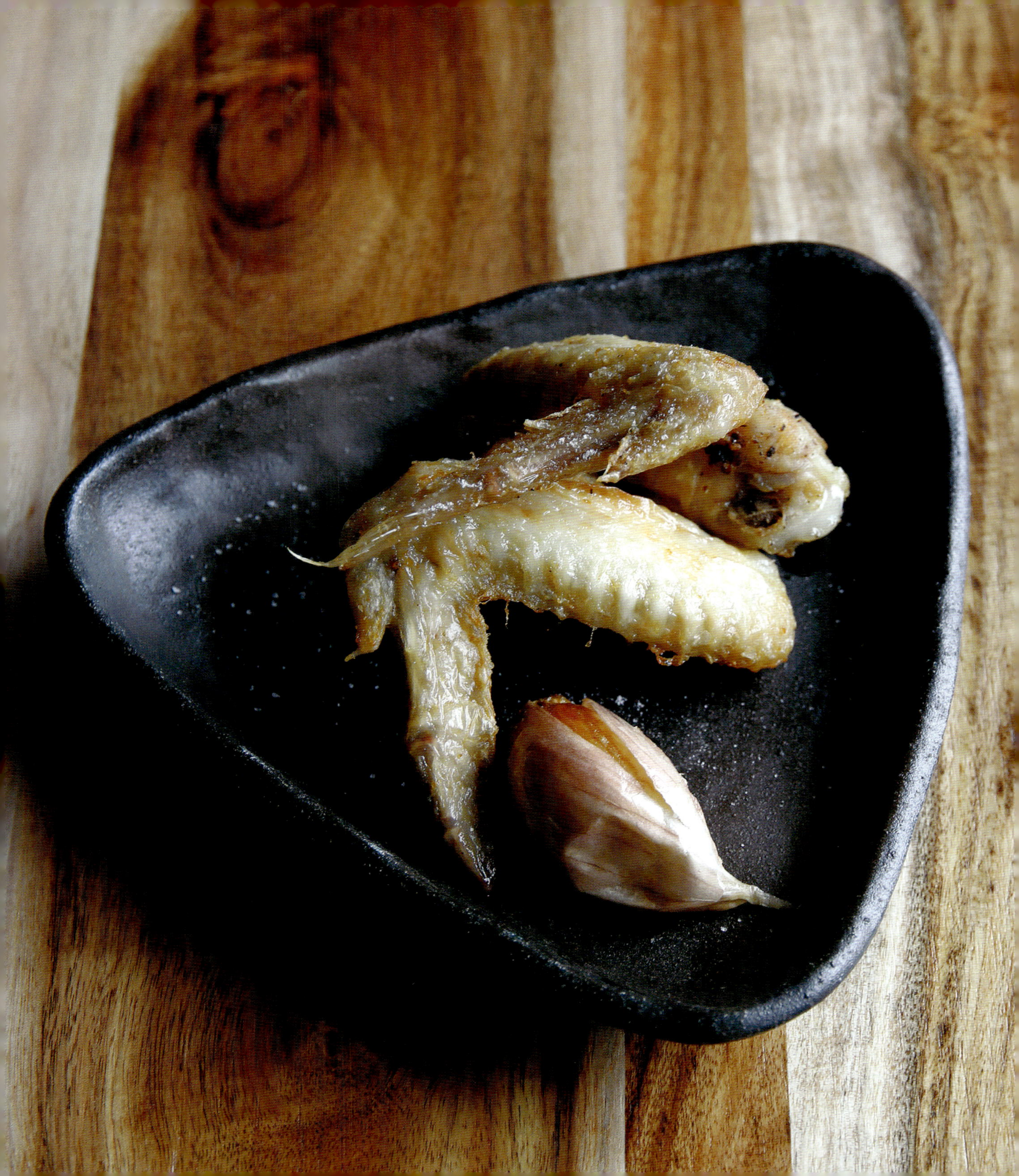

Teba to ninniku age: Deep-fried chicken wing and garlic

SERVES 4

8 Teba (chicken wings)
8 garlic cloves, unpeeled
Vegetable oil for deep frying
Rock salt, cracked

— Wipe off excess moisture from the chicken wings with kitchen paper.

二 Heat oil up to 160°C (320°F) over moderate heat.

三 Deep fry chicken for 4 minutes over low heat and finish with high heat to make it crispy.

四 Drain over a rack or on kitchen paper.

五 Deep fry garlic cloves till they float to the surface. Remove and drain.

六 Sprinkle chicken with salt and eat with garlic.

IZAKAYA • POULTRY

Chicken kara-age

SERVES 2

200g (7 oz) chicken thighs, cut into cubes
2 tbsp soy sauce
1 tbsp honey or caster sugar
1 tsp crushed garlic
1 tsp grated fresh ginger
2 tbsp potato starch, for coating
Vegetable oil for deep frying

一 Marinate chicken cubes in the soy sauce, honey, crushed garlic and ginger and put in refrigerator for at least 30 minutes to rest.

二 Remove chicken from the marinade, drain and pat with kitchen paper.

三 Coat with potato starch.

四 Put oil in a heavy deep frying pan and heat up the oil to about 180°C (355°F).

五 Deep-fry chicken cubes for 1 minute, take out and set aside for 1 minute on a tray. Deep-fry chicken again for two more minutes or until cooked.

六 Drain well on kitchen paper or a wire rack.

Mizuna salad with onion dressing

SERVE 2

200g (7 oz) mizuna salad, rinsed and drained
2 bacon rashers, chopped and deep-fried
Onion dressing (see Basics page)

一 Arrange mizuna topped with chopped bacon and drizzle with onion dressing.

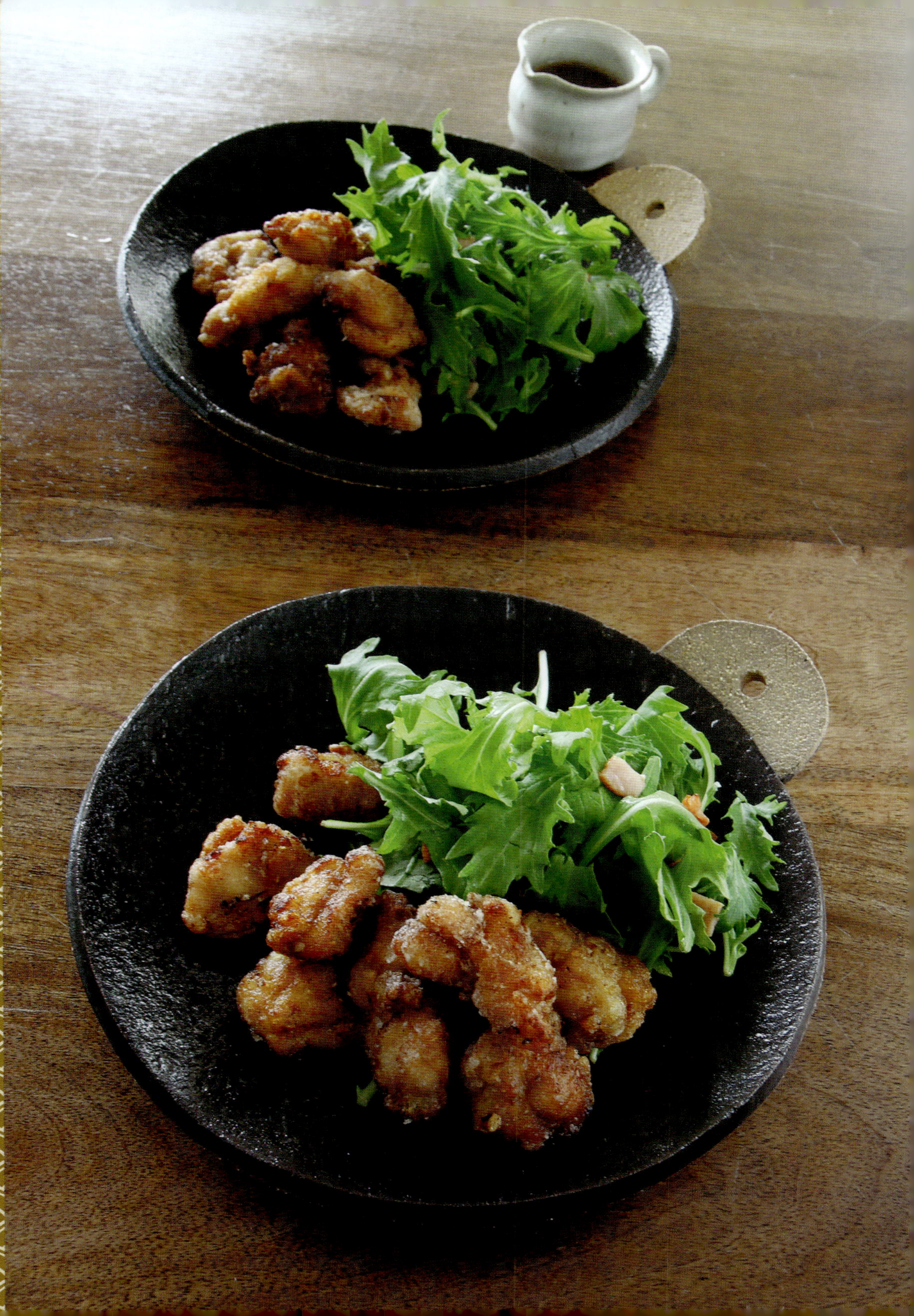

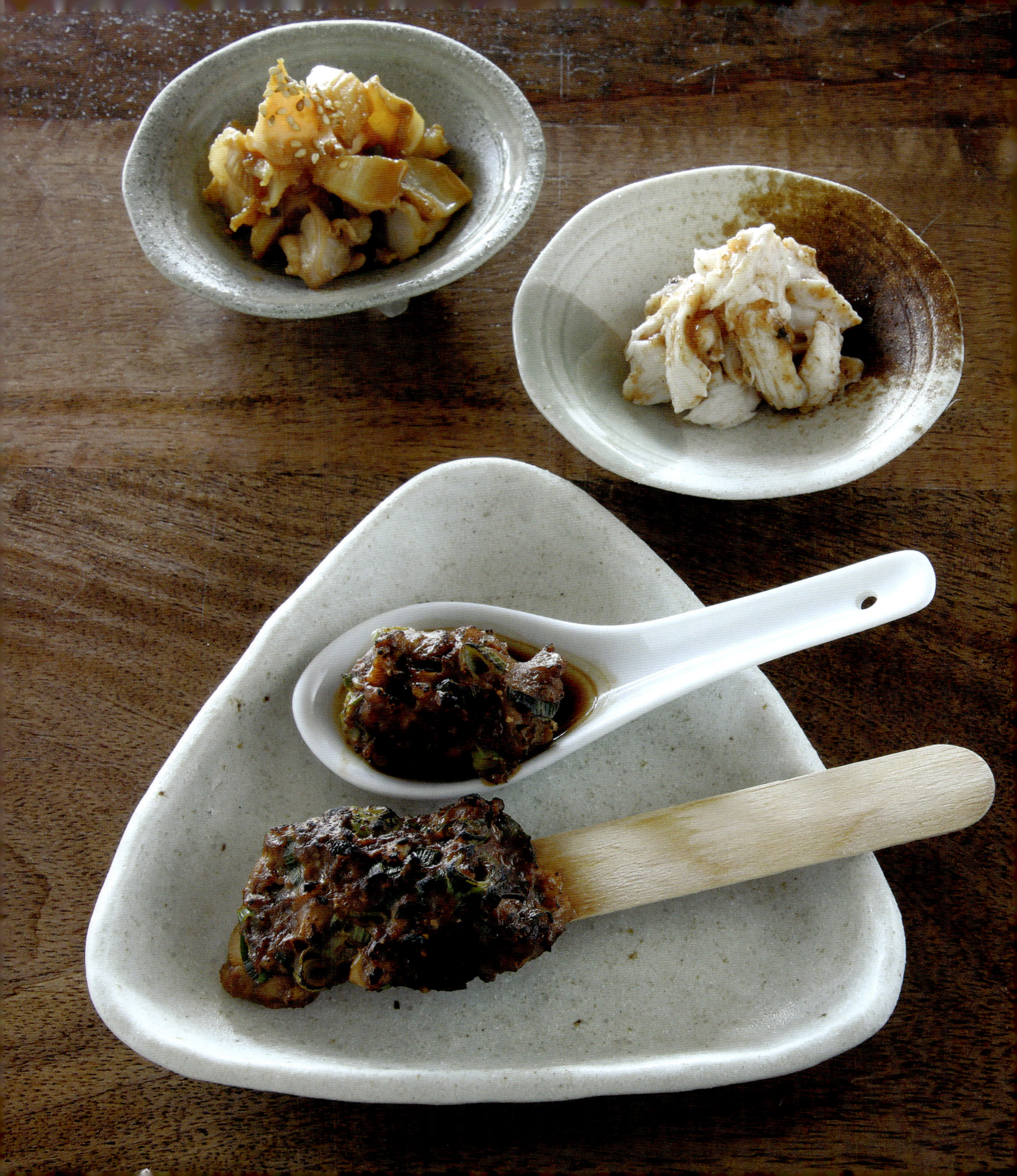

Chicken tsukune: Skewered minced chicken

MAKE 4

50g (1¾ oz) onion, finely chopped
200g (7 oz) minced chicken
1 tbsp hacho-miso
1 tsp grated ginger
1 tsp sake
2 tsp potato starch

DARE (SAUCE)

6 tbsp awase-jyoyu
½ cup dashi
8 bamboo skewers or spoons
Steamer

一 To make sauce, combine awase-jyoyu and dashi stock in a pan and simmer until reduced to half the original quantity.

二 Place all the ingredients in a bowl and combine well using your hand.

三 Divide the chicken mince into 8 and mould each portion around a bamboo skewer in a slightly elongated shape.

四 Prepare steamer and steam chicken until cooked, and then brush with dare sauce and grill.

Steamed chicken tenderloin tossed with plum puree

200g (7 oz) chicken tenderloin
1 tbsp sake
50g (1¾ oz) umeboshi without seeds, chopped
1 tsp mirin
4 tsp caster sugar
2 stems spring onion, trimmed and chopped

一 Sprinkle sake over the chicken.

二 Prepare steamer and bring it to the boil.

三 Arrange baking paper in the steamer and place chicken on the paper.

四 Steam with lid on for 3 minutes or until cooked.

五 Transfer the chicken onto a plate and allow to cool down.

六 Tear chicken into pieces, add umeboshi, mirin and sugar, and toss.

七 Serve in a bowl with spring onion.

Braised chicken soft bone with garlic, sesame and soy sauce

1 tbsp sesame oil
2 garlic cloves, chopped
100g (3½ oz) nankotsu: chicken soft bone/ gristle
1 tsp roasted white sesame seeds
2 tbsp awase-jyoyu (see Basics page)
4 lemon wedges

一 Pour sesame oil in a frying pan, add garlic and leave for 1–2 minutes to infuse on a low heat.

二 Add chicken and stir for 2 minutes.

三 Add sesame seeds and soy sauce, and stir for another 3 minutes.

四 Transfer to a plate and serve with lemon wedges.

*Chicken nankotsu (soft bone) is quite a unique dish and very popular among Izakaya fans. It is not easy to find at shops, so if you cannot buy it one option is to purchase chicken bones and cut off the soft bone from the end of the neck and joints.

Chicken giblet with rocket leaves in earthenware pot

400ml (13½ fl oz) chicken stock
200g (7 oz) giblets such as liver/heart, etc), sliced
1 tbsp soy sauce
A small pinch of salt
1 small brown onion, peeled and sliced
100g (3½ oz) firm tofu, diced
50g (1¾ oz) rocket leaves (optional Shungiku – edible chrysanthemum leaves)
2 tbsp sake

一 Put chicken stock and giblets in a pot and bring to the boil.

二 Add soy sauce and salt and simmer for 3 minutes.

三 Place onion, tofu and rocket leaves in the pot.

四 Drizzle sake and simmer for 3 minutes.

五 Serve in a pot with a lid.

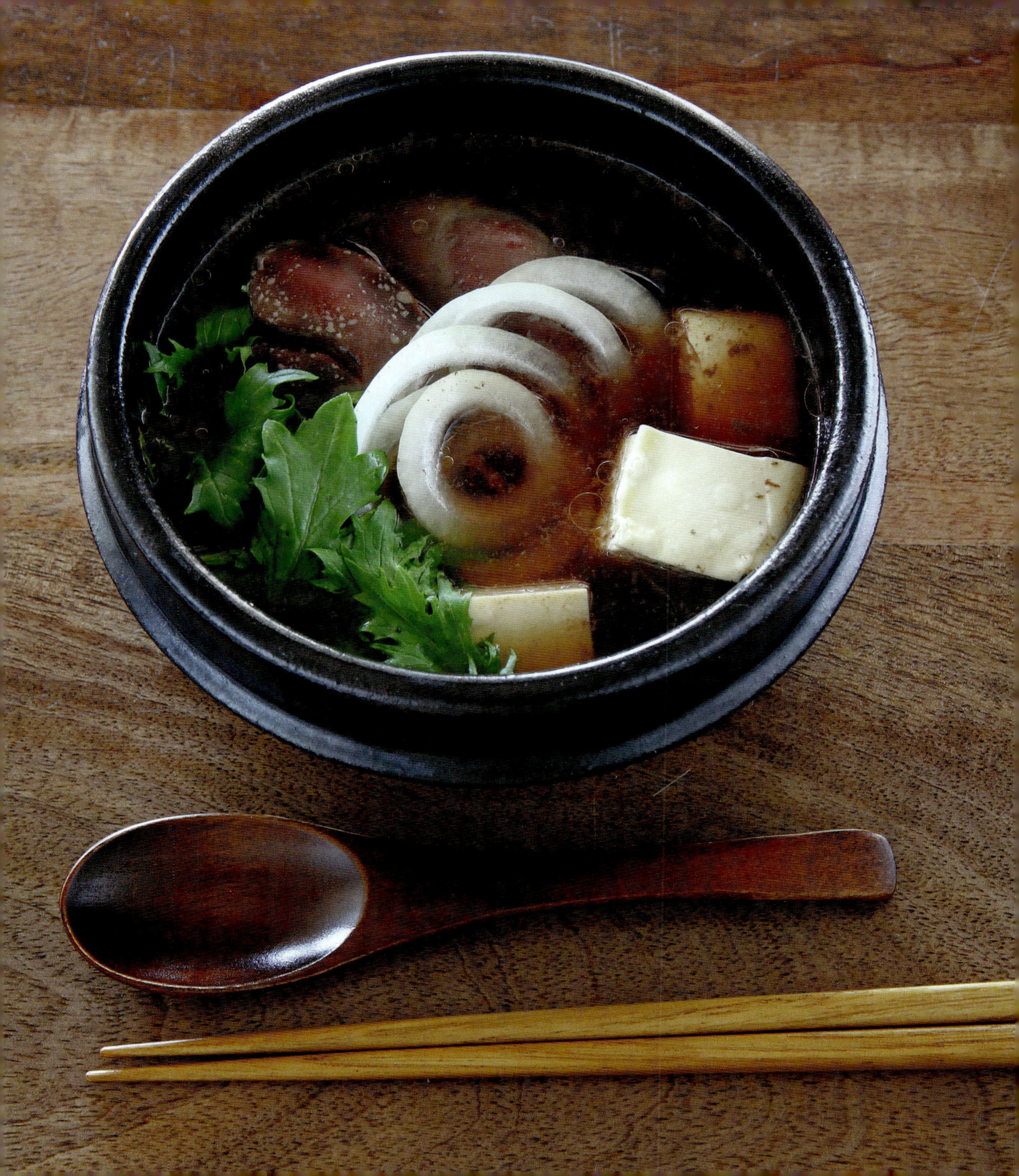

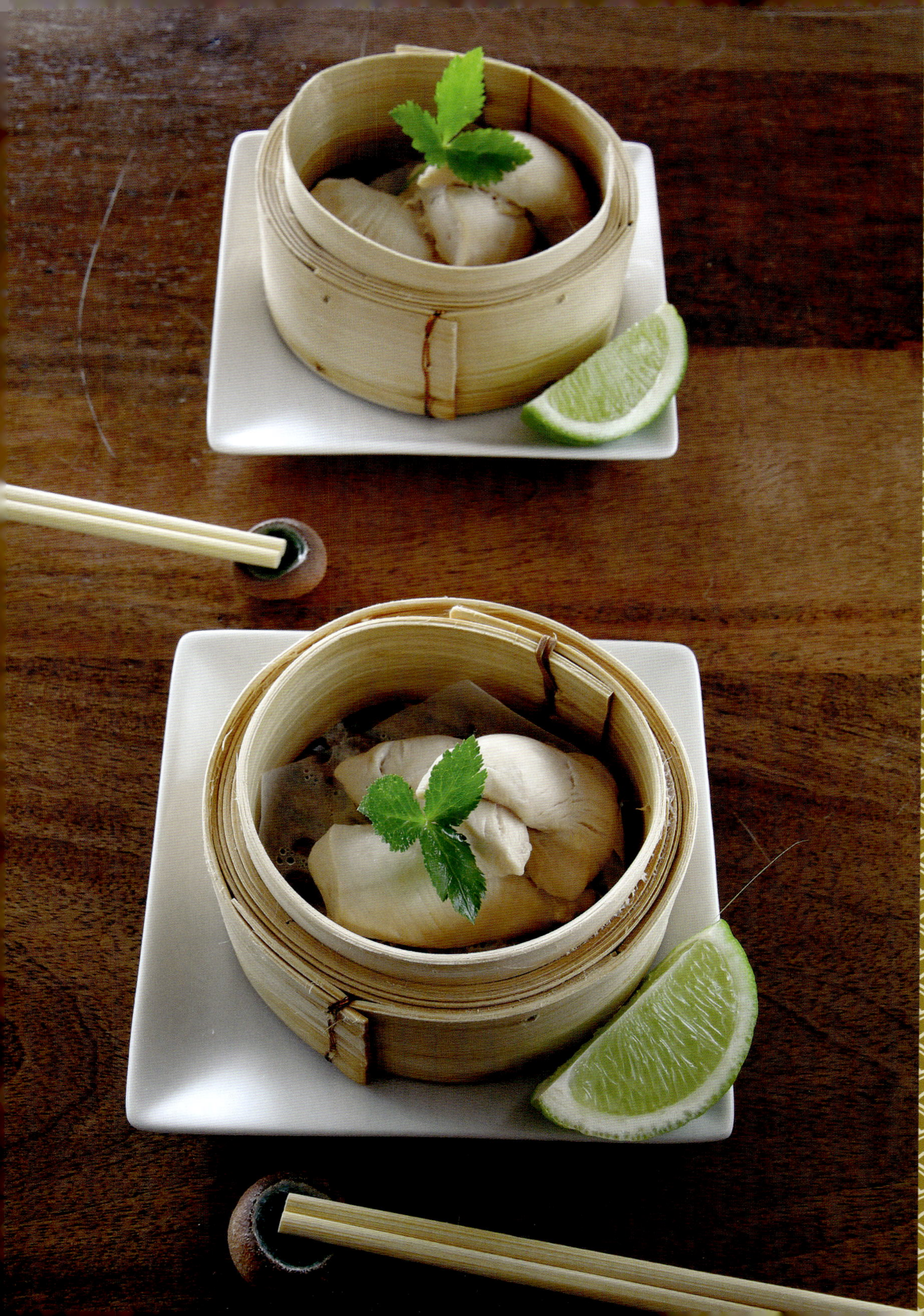

Steamed chicken, Yuan style

SERVES 2

200g (7 oz) chicken breast
½ tbsp soy sauce
1 tbsp sake
1 tbsp mirin
2 lemon or lime slices
2 lemon or lime wedges

一 To prepare marinade, combine soy sauce, sake and mirin in a tray.

二 Add chicken breast and lemon slices, and marinate overnight in the refrigerator.

三 Pat chicken with kitchen paper.

四 Prepare steamer and lay baking paper in the steamer. Transfer chicken into the steamer.

五 Steam until cooked.

Serve on a plate with lemon wedges.

Marinated chicken may be grilled instead of steamed.

Dashimaki-tamago: Japanese egg omelette

SERVES 2

2 eggs
2 tbsp dashi (see Basics page)
1 tbsp caster sugar
1 tbsp mirin
1 tsp light colour soy sauce
1 tbsp vegetable oil
1 tbsp grated daikon radish or red radish

一 Crack eggs into a bowl and add the dashi, sugar, mirin and soy sauce, then whisk lightly.

二 Strain into another bowl.

三 Place a non-stick rectangular shape Japanese omelette pan over a medium heat and heat for 1 minute. Pour in a little oil and swirl evenly over the pan.

四 Pour in one third of the egg mixture and cook until set around the edges.

五 With a spatula fold one third towards the front of the pan, then fold over again in the same direction onto the remaining portion.

六 Add a little more oil to the pan and pour half of the remaining egg mixture onto the empty area of the pan and cook until the edge sets. Again fold one-third towards the folded egg, then fold this over on top of previous roll, making a flat roll on one side of the pan

七 Add oil and pour in the remaining egg mixture, and repeat the folding process. With the spatula, give a little push to mould the shape.

八 When cooked, remove from the heat, and place on a bamboo mat on a dry surface. Wrap the omelette with the bamboo mat and shape.

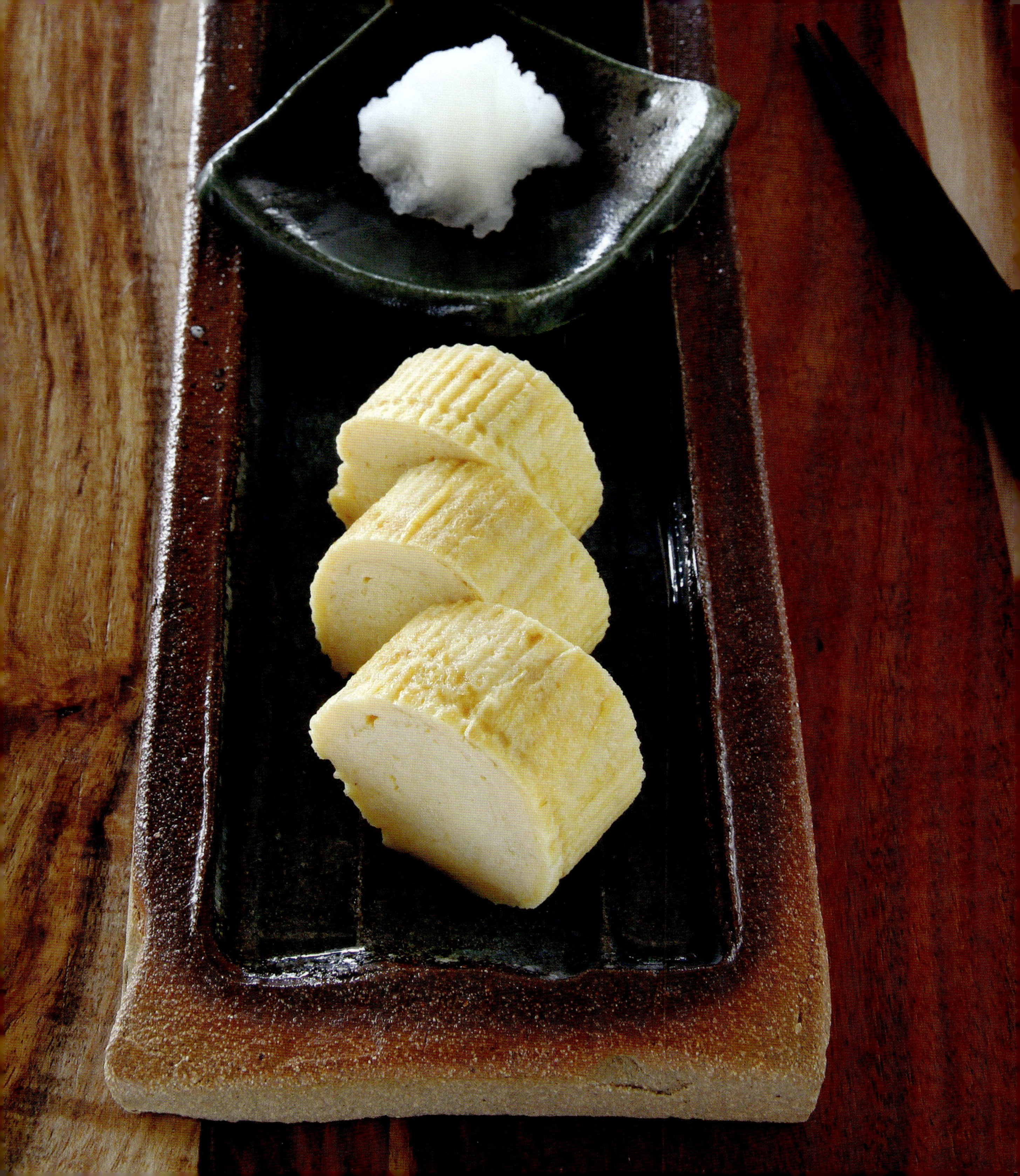

Japanese egg omelette with scallops

MAKES 4 SLICES

3 eggs

3 scallops fresh or frozen

½ spring onion, trimmed and chopped

½ tbsp bonito dashi (see Basics page)

½ tsp usukuchi shyoyu, light colour soy sauce

½ tbsp sake

½ tbsp mirin

½ tsp caster sugar

A few drops of vegetable oil

Extra 1 tbsp oil, soaked onto a piece of kitchen paper

Japanese square omelette pan is required, but if not available, use small non-stick frying pan

一 Break eggs into a bowl and beat.

二 Chop scallops and add to eggs.

三 Add dashi, soy sauce, sake and mirin and mix well.

四 Drop oil onto the pan and spread oil while moving the pan over moderate heat.

五 When the pan is heated gently pour in a third of the egg mixture to cover base of omelette pan.

六 With a cooking chopstick, slightly stir.

七 When the corners are cooked, run a spatula around it to loosen.

八 With spatula or chopsticks, fold one third of omelette from far side toward centre, then fold this over onto the remaining portion closest to you.

九 With the oiled kitchen paper wipe over the empty section of the pan. Slide first omelette portion to the other end of the pan and pour in another third of mixture, lifting cooked omelette up to let it flow underneath. Stir lightly uncooked egg. When it is almost cooked, fold the thicker portion over toward you as before, making a thick flat roll.

十 Continue adding remaining mixture, and repeat to make a triple-layered omelette.

Remove from the heat. Transfer omelette onto a chopping board and slice into quarters.

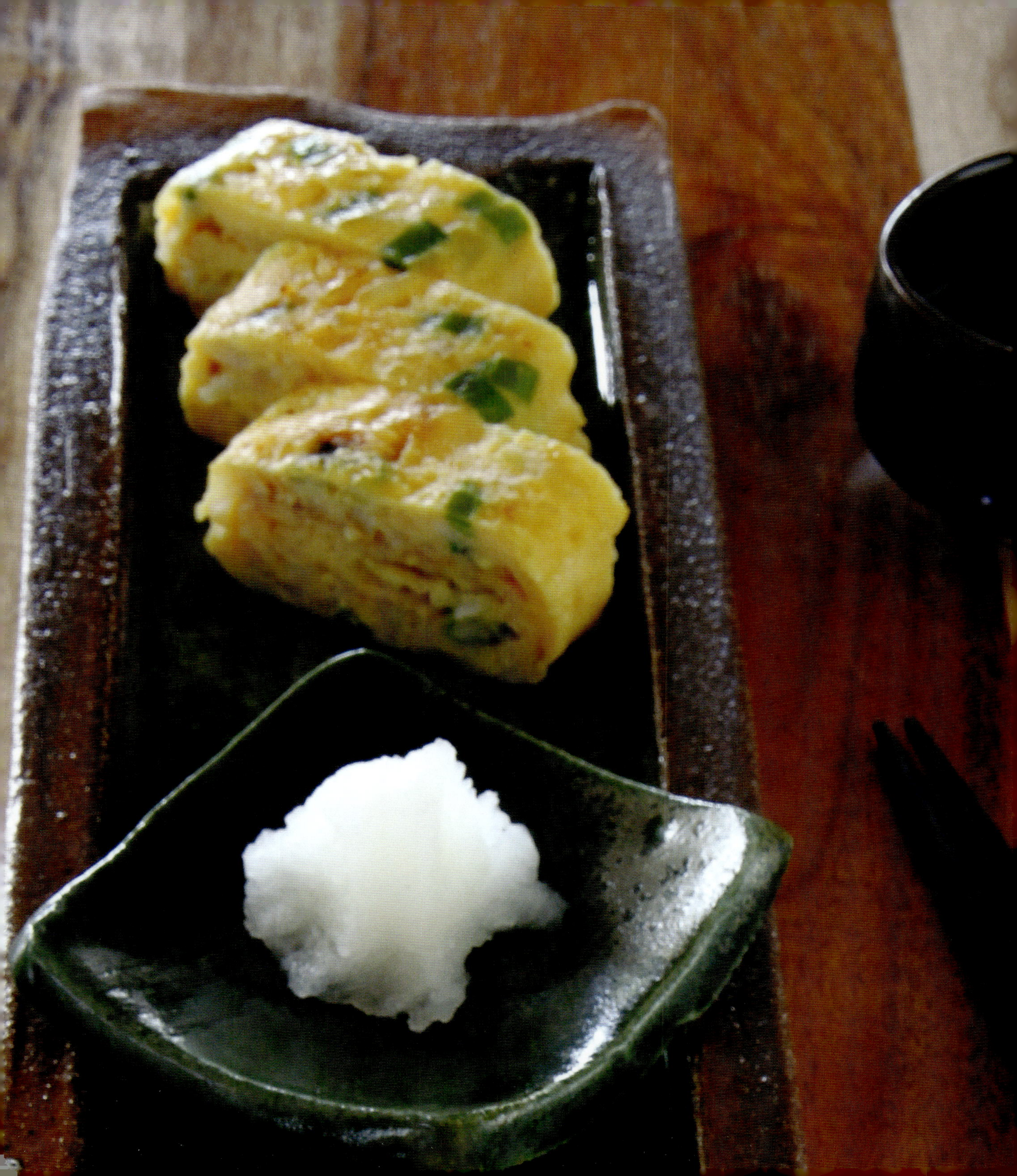

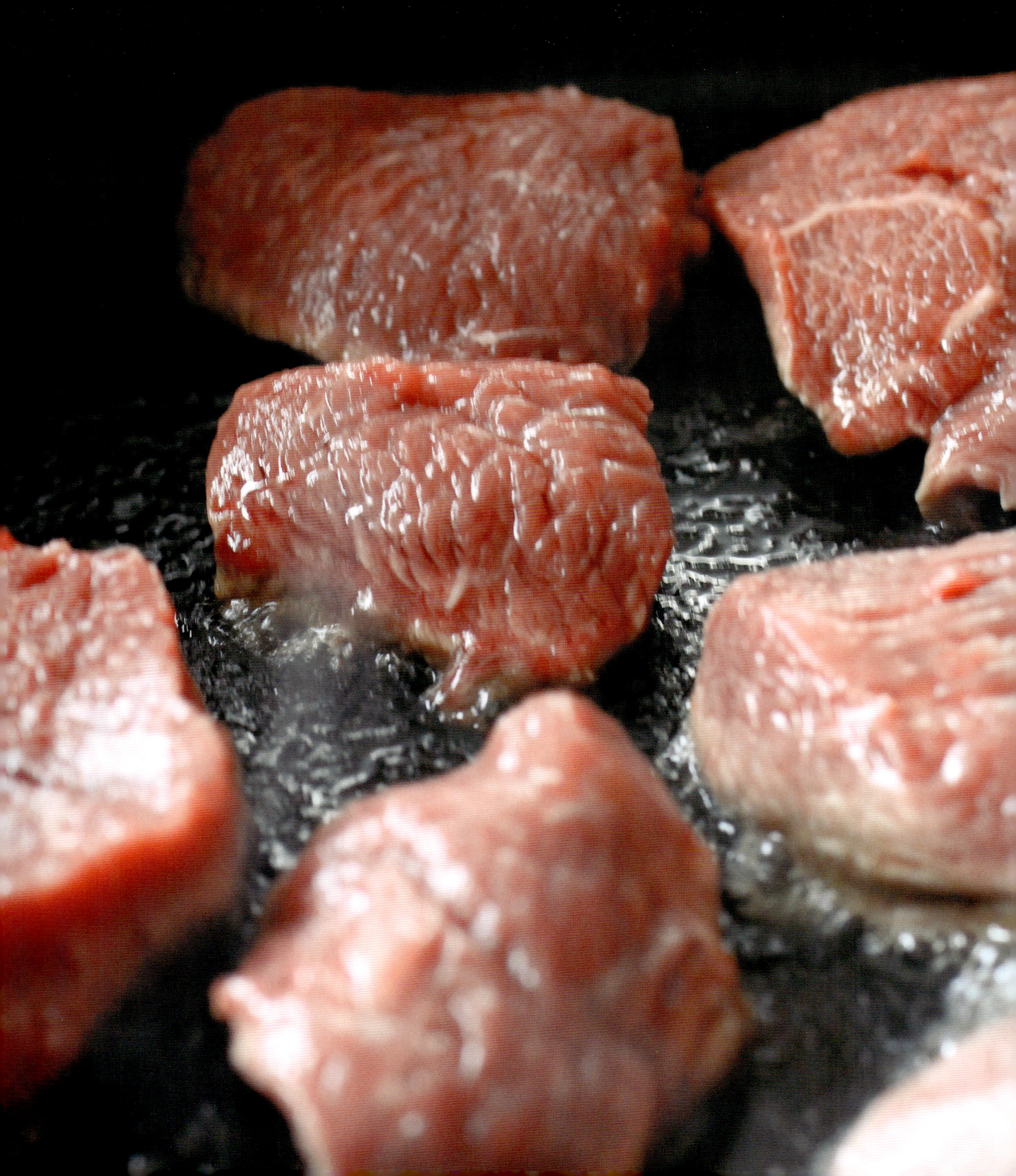

Beef & Pork

Motsu-nabe: soy sauce flavoured slow-cooked beef with fresh spring onion

Motsu-ni: Miso flavoured slow-cooked brisket with daikon

Motsu-ni with chicken offal

Pork Shabu-Shabu salad

Lightly braised thinly sliced beef tongue

Sweet and hot Julianne beef skirt

Topside cubed steak

Blanched beef in rice vinaigrette

Stir-fried lamb liver

Nikujyaga: Beef and vegetable sweet soy sauce stew

Wafu carpaccio

Minudaru: Steamed pork in black sesame

Lamb chop or pork soft rib in chilli miso

Aburi-style marinated pork with miso

Deep-fried diced pork with umeboshi

Gyoza dumpling with stamina sauce

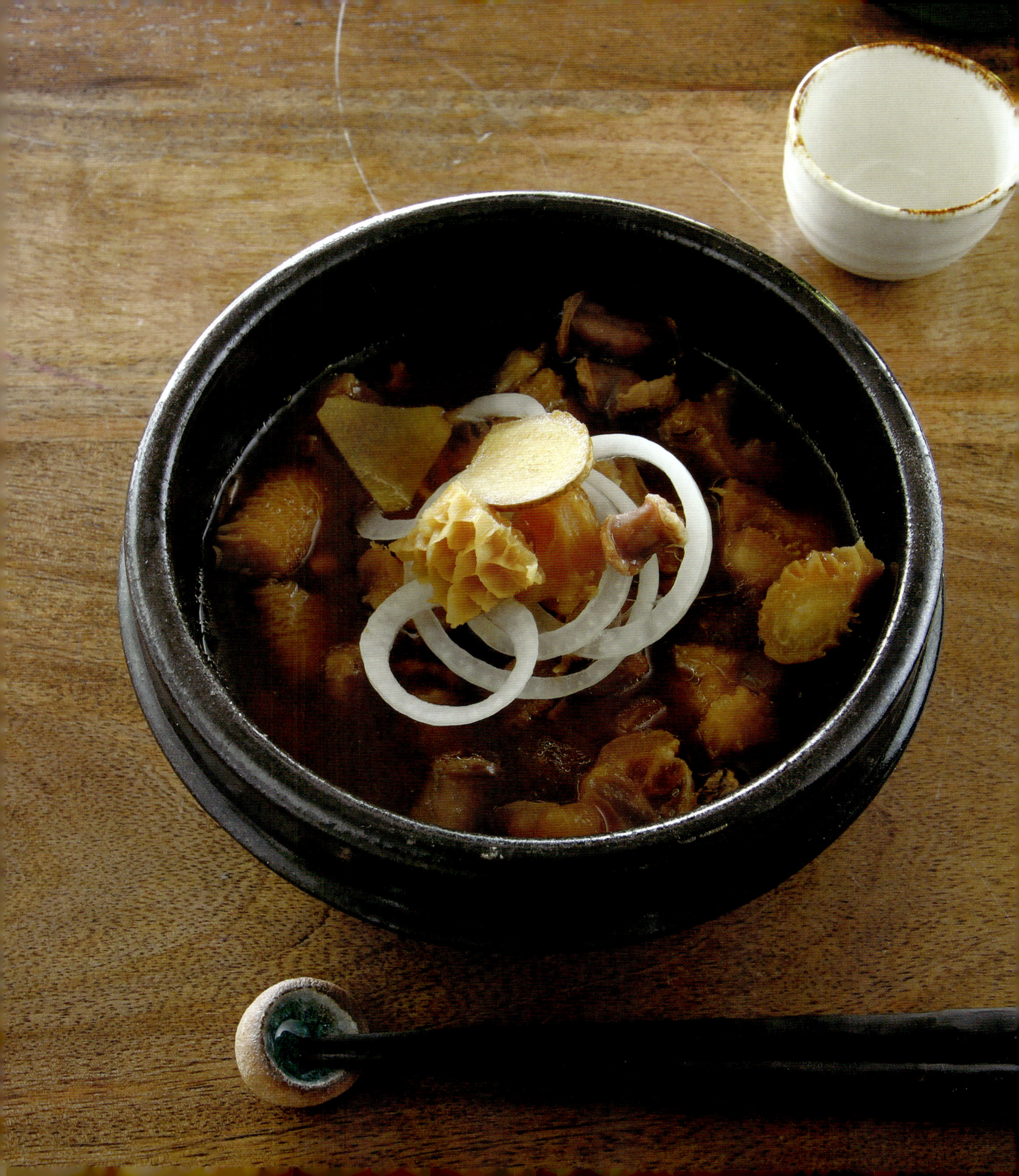

Motsu-nabe: Soy sauce flavoured slow-cooked beef with fresh spring onion

*'Motsu-ni' or 'Motsu-nabe' is a slow cooked dish with beef, pork or chicken offal or secondary cuts in a hot pot. Miso and soy sauce flavours are popular.

SERVES 2

500g (17½ oz) beef shin or cheek
600ml (20¼ fl oz) water
5g (⅐ oz) ginger, sliced
1 clove garlic, sliced
20ml (¾ fl oz) sake
20ml (¾ fl oz) mirin
½ cup awase-jyoyu (see Basics page)
1 tbsp raw sugar
A pinch of salt
1 brown onion, thinly sliced and soaked in water

一 In a pan, place beef, water, ginger and garlic and bring it to boil.

二 Cook for 15 minutes over moderate heat occasionally removing scum from the surface.

三 Add sake and mirin, and simmer for 30 minutes.

四 Add awase-jyoyu, raw sugar and salt and simmer for another 10 minutes with a lid on.

五 Arrange sliced onion on top.

Motsu-ni: Miso flavoured slow-cooked brisket with daikon

SERVES 2

½ daikon (about 500g/17½ oz)
1 tsp rice
½ cup water
200g (7 oz) beef shank or shin, cut into 5cm (2 inch) chunks
2 tbsp miso
1 tbsp mirin
2 tbsp caster sugar
2 tbsp sake

1 tbsp wagarashi or English mustard
Use a pressure cooker to save time.

— To prepare daikon, peel and cut into 4cm (1½ inch) thick pieces, and round off the edges and make a criss-cross scoring over the surface to allow the flavour to penetrate.

二 Place daikon, rice and water in the pan and simmer until soft or about 30 minutes over low heat.

三 In a pan add beef and water just covering the beef. Bring it to the boil and cook for 3 minutes while skimming scum off the surface. Strain.

四 Add miso, mirin, sugar, sake and ½ cup water in a pressure cooker or a pan, and combine well.

五 Place beef and daikon in the pan and cook until the beef is tender, 30–40 minutes, or 10 minutes for a pressure cooker. Once cooked leave for more than an hour to set the flavour.

六 When serving, reheat again and serve with wagarashi (English mustard).

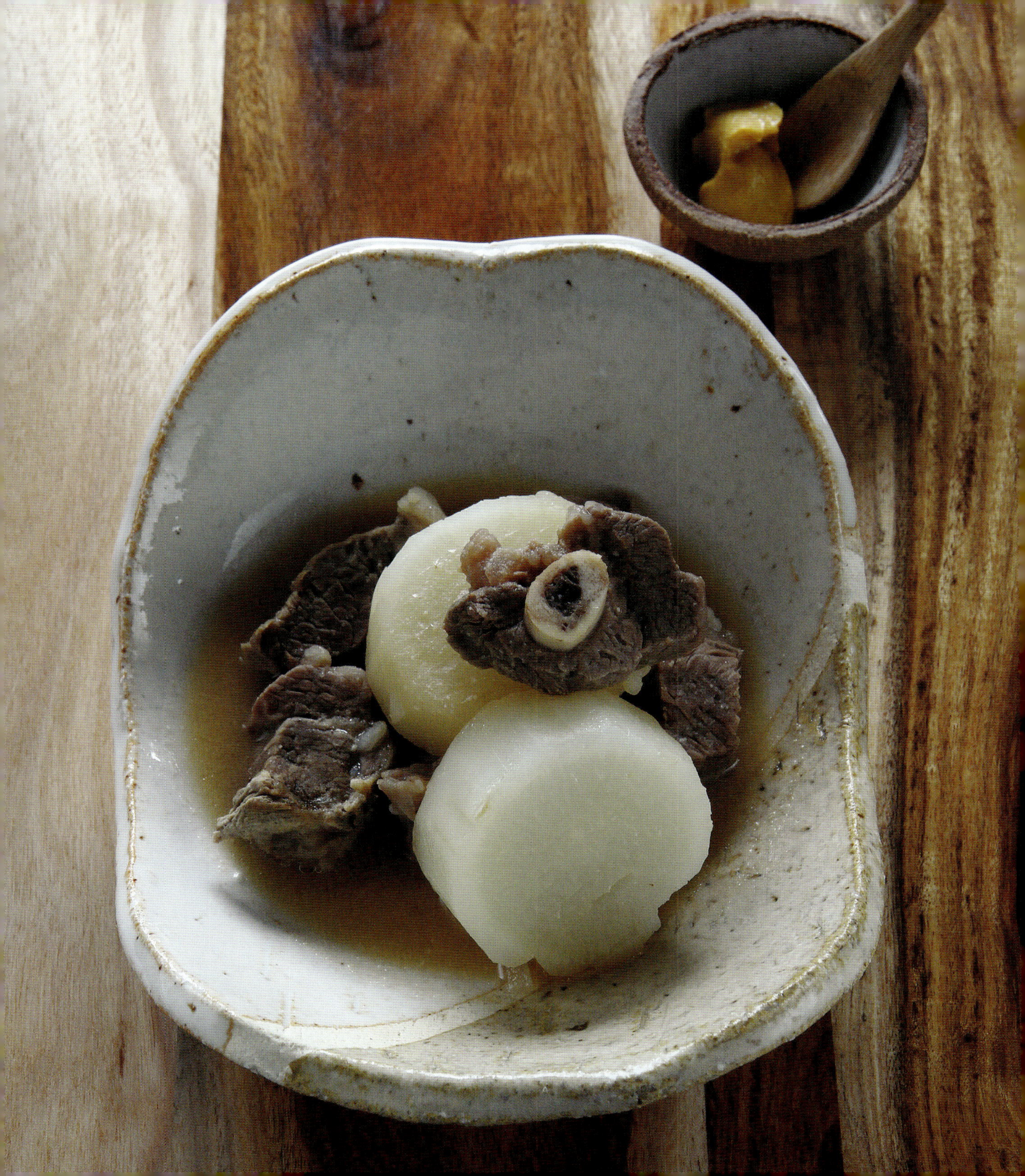

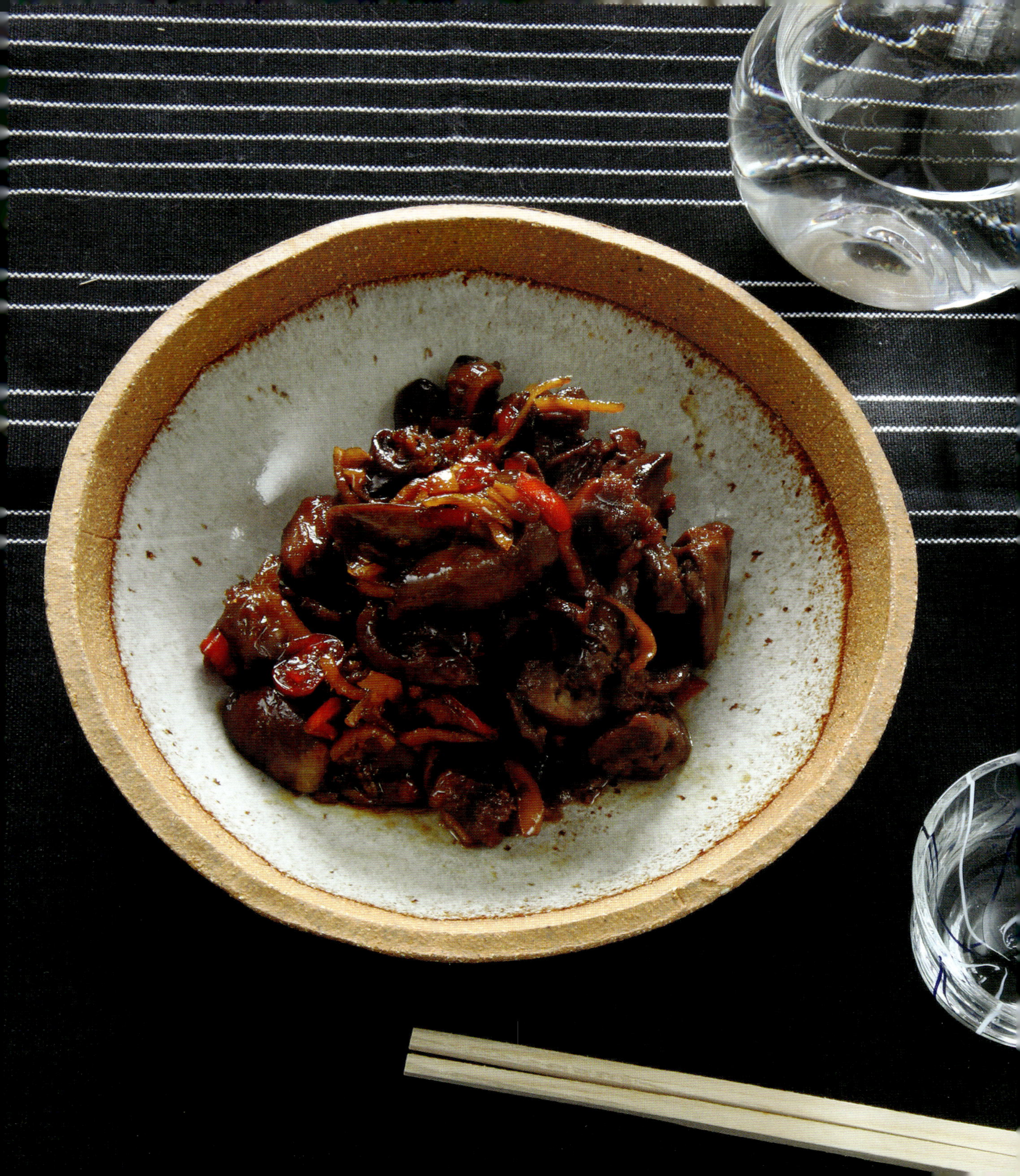

Motsu-ni with chicken offal

SERVES 2

100g (3½ oz) chicken gizzard, cut into bite sizes

100g (3½ oz) chicken liver, cut into bite sizes

100g (3½ oz) chicken heart, cut in half and remove blood

1 cup of milk

2 tbsp vegetable oil

2 fresh or dried chilli, halve and de-seed

2 tbsp soy sauce

1 tbsp caster sugar

3 tbsp sake

½ cup dashi (see Basics page)

1 tbsp ginger, julienne

You may also use only one of the chicken offal from the list.

一 In a pot, place gizzard, liver and heart and add milk. Leave for 10 minutes.

二 Bring it to the boil and simmer for 3 minutes. Discard milk over the strainer and rinse chicken with lukewarm water, and drain.

三 In a frying pan, add oil and chilli, and stir for 1 minute for deep-fried chilli.

四 Add chicken in the pan and stir for 2 minutes. Add soy sauce, sugar, sake and dashi and ginger, and simmer until most of the liquid evaporates.

五 Serve in a bowl.

Pork Shabu-Shabu salad

SERVES 2

1 litre (4 cups) water
1 tbsp of sake
200g (7 oz) thinly sliced pork (available frozen from Asian butchers or Japanese grocery stores)
½ Spanish onion, thinly sliced and soaked in water
½ brown onion, thinly sliced and soaked in water
1 tbsp awase-jyoyu
1 tbsp rice vinegar* Yuzu-zu (Yuzu citrus vinegar is used as a substitute)
1 tsp lemon/lime juice
1 tsp caster sugar
2 stems spring onion, trimmed and chopped
A pinch of bonito flakes as your preference

一 Bring water to the boil in a pan and add sake.

二 Prepare a bowl of water to the side.

三 With chopsticks or tongs, blanch pork until it just changes colour and transfer into the water. Repeat with all slices.

四 Drain water and pat pork with kitchen paper, and transfer onto a plate.

五 Strain onions and drain well. Arrange onions on top of pork and sprinkle with spring onion.

六 Combine awase-jyoyu, rice vinegar and citrus juice and serve with pork salad.

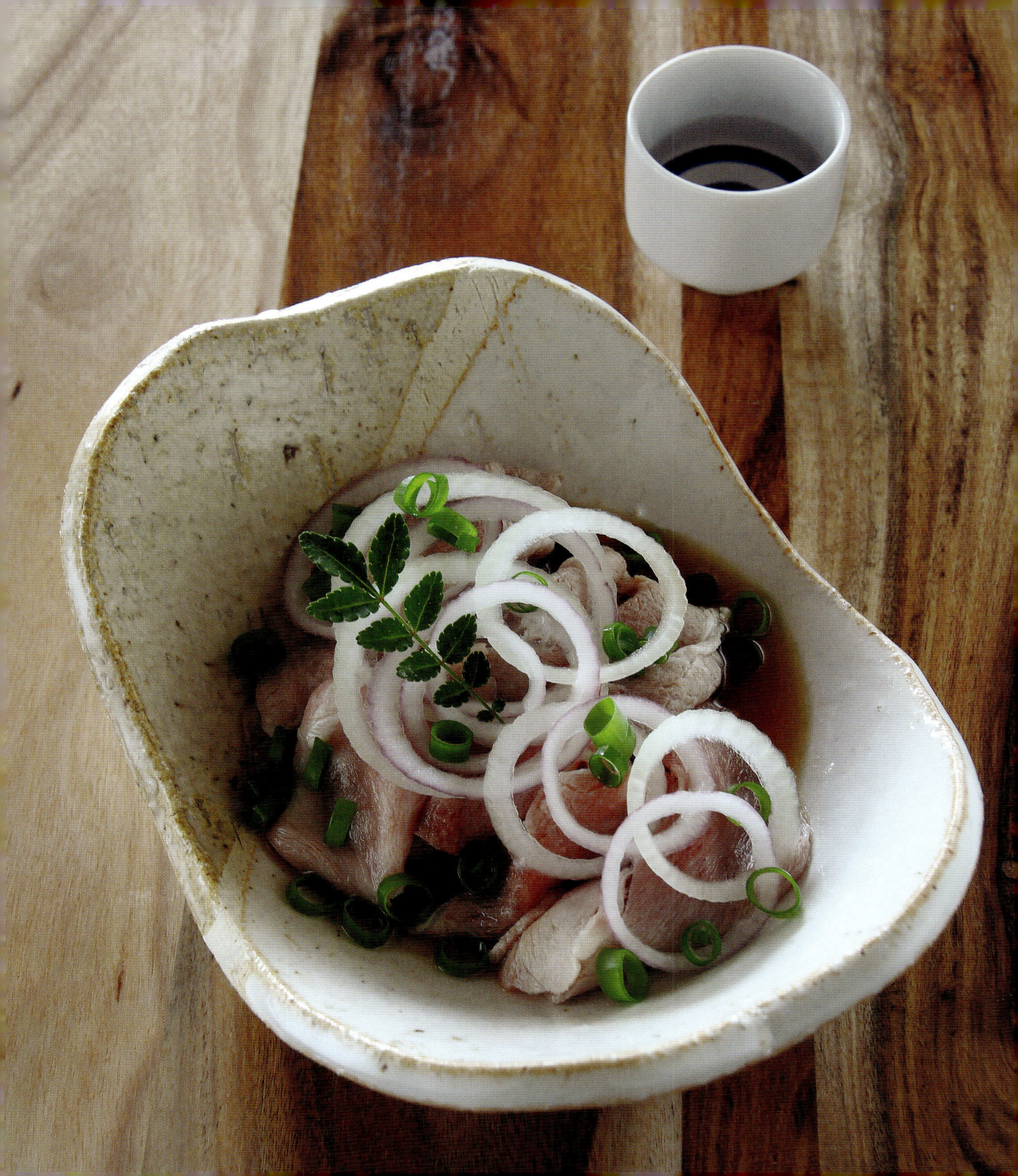

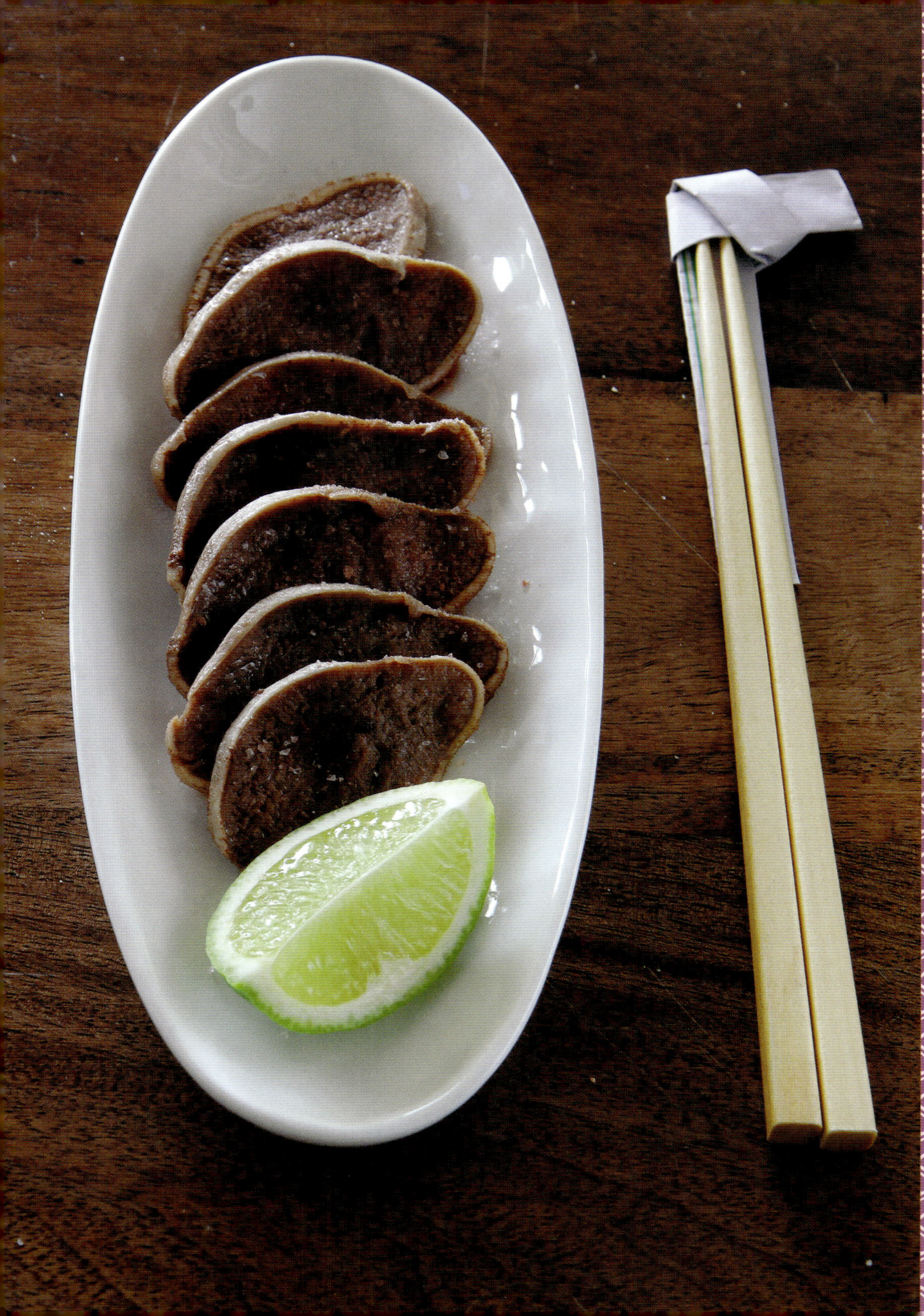

Lightly braised thinly sliced beef tongue

200g (7 oz) beef tongue, thinly sliced
2 tbsp sake
A drop olive oil
A pinch of sea salt
1 lemon or lime wedge

一 Sprinkle sake over the thinly sliced beef tongue.

二 Drop olive oil into the frying pan and braise beef tongue while stirring until lightly cooked or 2 minutes over moderate heat.

三 Sprinkle salt.

四 Transfer the beef tongue onto a plate with lemon wedge.

Sweet and hot Julianne beef skirt

SERVES 2

200g (7 oz) beef skirt, julienne

1 tbsp vegetable oil

1 tsp chopped red chilli or shichimi

5 tbsp awase-jyoyu (see Basics page)

1 tbsp caster sugar

1 tbsp potato starch, dissolved with 1 tbsp of water

20g (¾ oz) rice noodle, deep-fried in vegetable oil

一 Heat oil in a frying pan.

二 Add beef and chilli, and braise for 1 minute.

三 Add awase-jyoyu and sugar and stir for 2 minutes.

四 Add potato starch to make it thicken.

五 Serve onto a plate or a bowl.

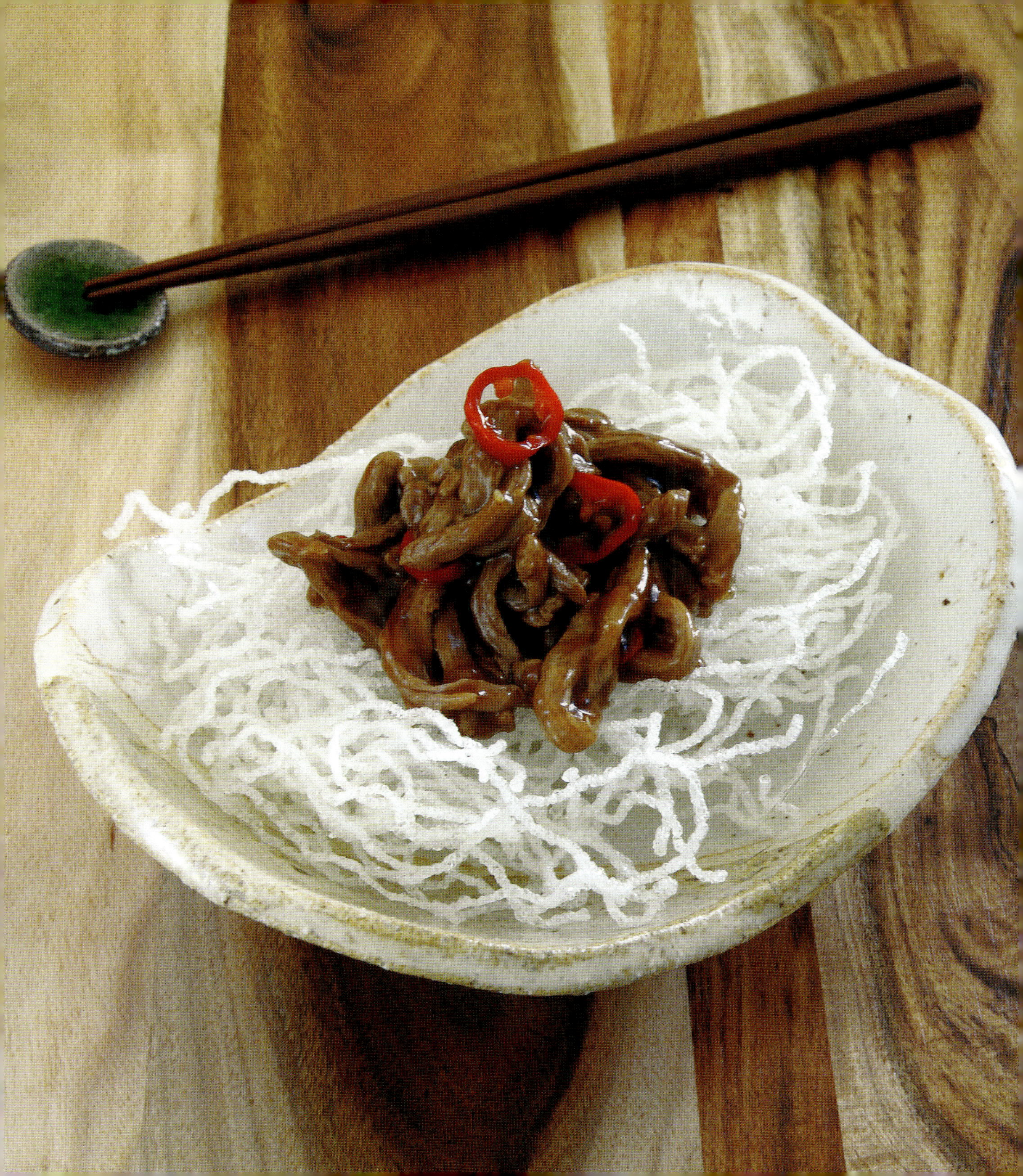

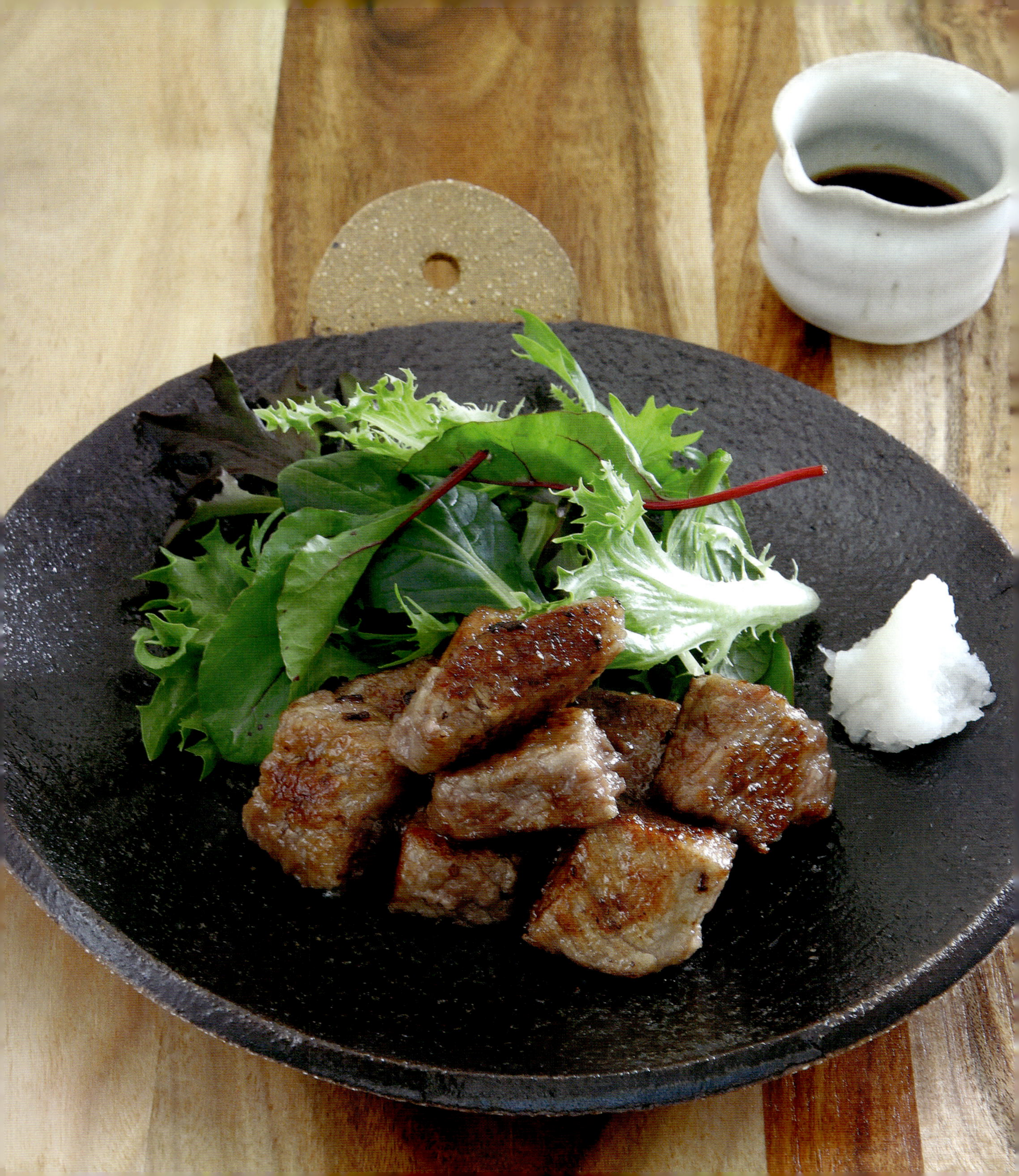

Topside cubed steak

SERVES 2

200g (7 oz) rump steak, cut into 2cm (¾ inch) cubes
Vegetable oil for deep fry
1 tbsp potato starch
4 tbsp grated daikon, lightly squeezed
Soy sauce or awase-jyoyu to serve
Green salad leaves on side

一 Coat steak with potato starch.

二 Heat oil in a deep pan to 170°C (340°F).

三 Deep fry beef to your preference and drain well over a rack or kitchen paper.

四 Serve onto the plate aside with grated daikon and green salad leaves.

五 Serve with soy sauce or awase-jyoyu.

Blanched beef in rice vinaigrette

200g (7 oz) beef rump
1 brown onion, peeled, sliced and soaked in water
¼ cup rice vinegar
4 tbsp caster sugar
20g (¾ oz) ginger, julienne
1 clove garlic, peeled and chopped
¼ cup water
2 stems of spring onion, trimmed and chopped

一 To make the marinade mixture, add onion, rice vinegar, sugar, ginger, garlic and water in a container and mix well.

二 Bring water in a pan to the boil and blanch beef for 30 seconds.

三 Transfer into iced water for 3 seconds. Drain and pat dry with kitchen paper.

四 Place beef in the vinegar mixture and refrigerate for 20-30 minutes.

五 Transfer beef to a chopping board and slice thinly with a sharp knife.

六 Arrange slices of beef on a plate and add marinade mixture.

七 Sprinkle over spring onion.

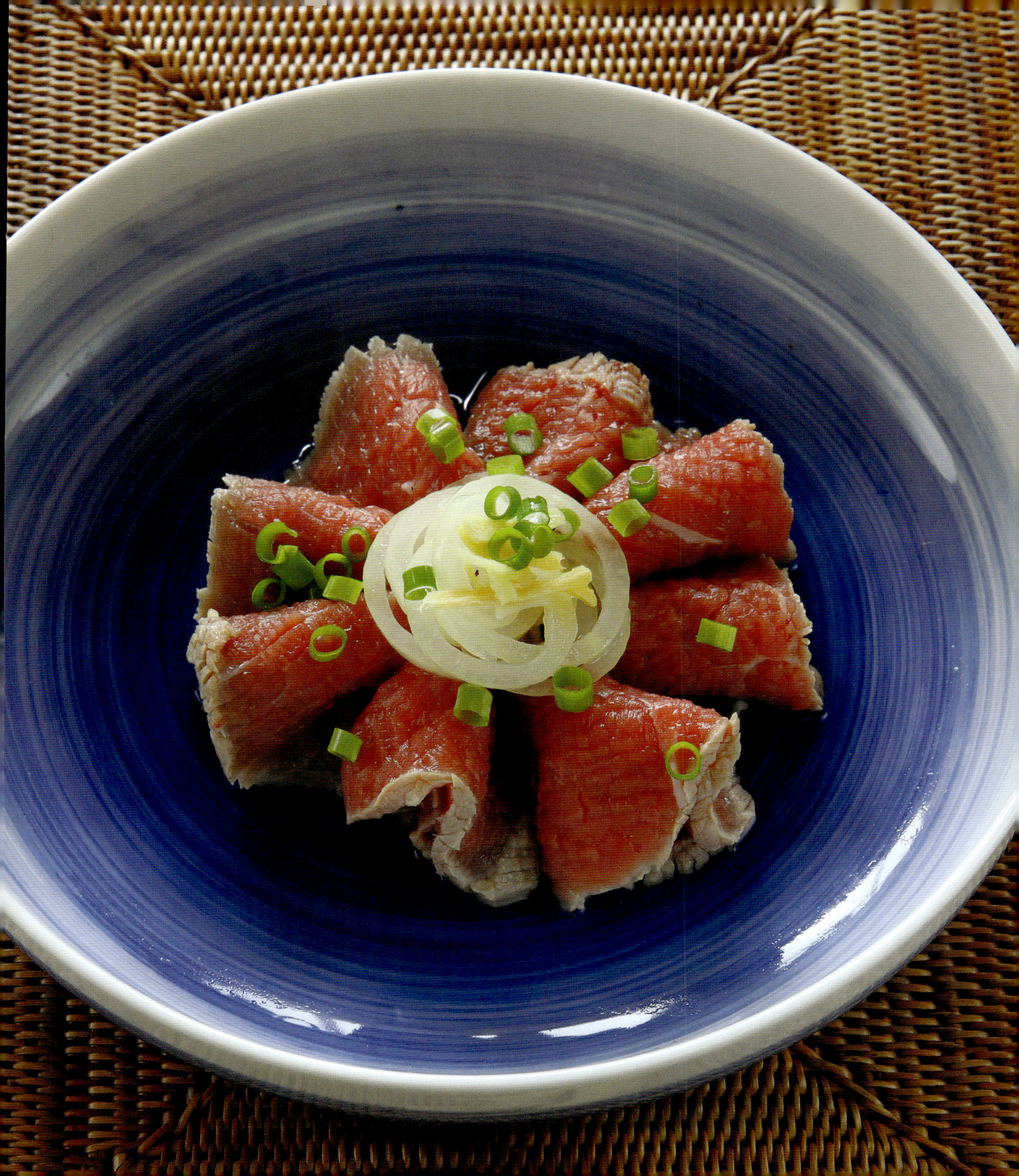

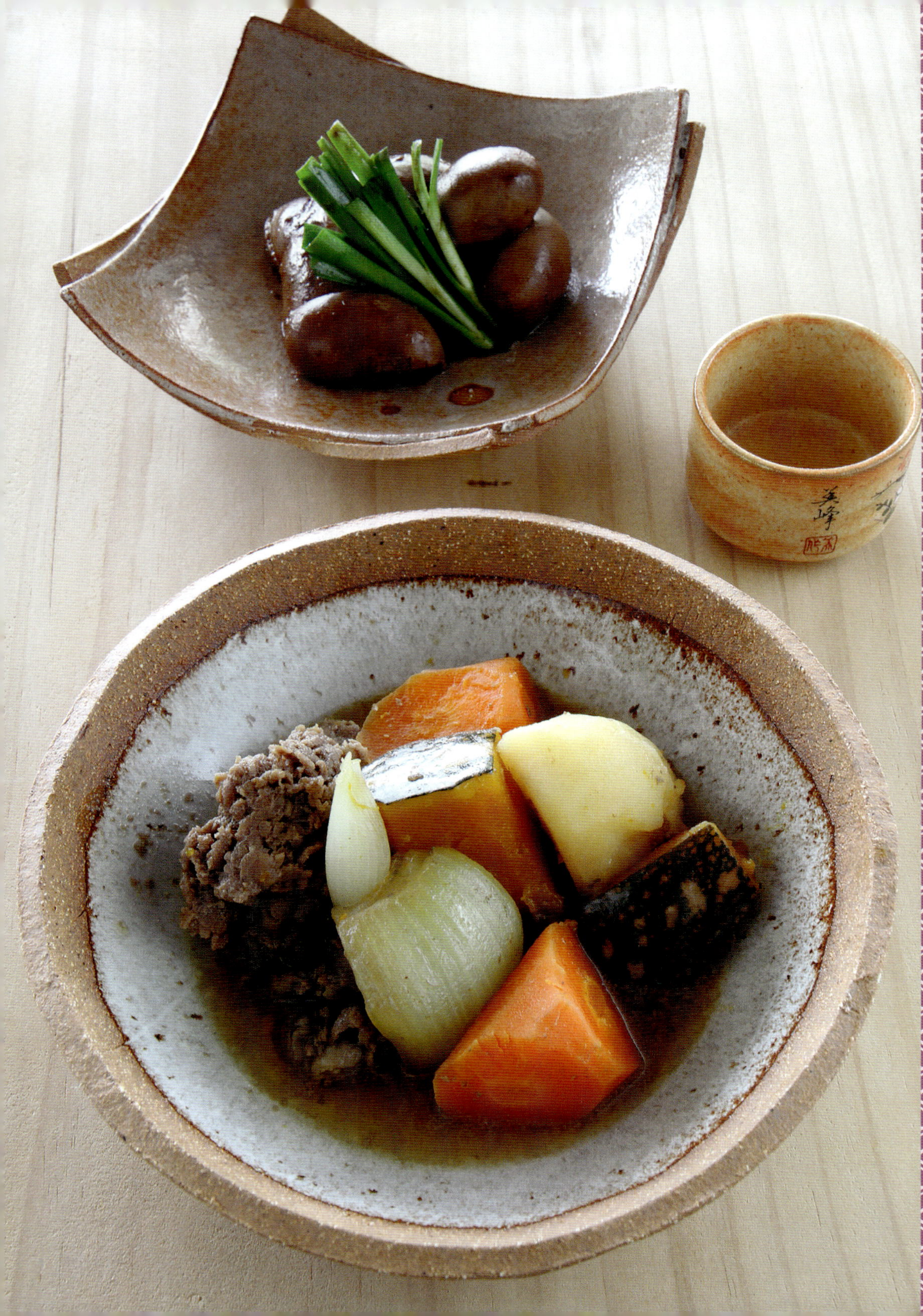

Stir-fried lamb liver

200g (7 oz) lamb or beef liver, chopped into bite sizes
A pinch salt
A drop vegetable oil
1 tbsp awase-jyoyu (see Basics page)
1 tbsp sake
¼ bunch garlic chives, cleaned and cut into 4cm (1½ inch) strips

一 Sprinkle salt over liver.
二 Heat oil and stir liver in pan for 1 minute.
三 Add awase-jyoyu and sake and stir until cooked.
四 Finish with garlic chives and stir, then serve on a plate.

Nikujyaga: Beef and vegetable sweet soy sauce stew

SERVES 2
Vegetable oil
200g (7 oz) of thinly sliced brisket beef or oyster blade (they are available from Asian butchers or Japanese grocery stores)
1 brown onion, peel and sliced
1 carrot, peeled and cut into pieces
2 new potatoes, cut into about 4 cm (1½ inch) chunks
200g (7 oz) Japanese Pumpkin, cut into about 4cm (1½ inch) chunks
2 tbsp caster or raw sugar
1 tbsp sake
3 tbsp soy sauce
½ cup water
4 snow peas or spring onion (sliced diagonally)

一 Drop oil in a pan and swirl over the base. Add beef, onion, carrot, potatoes and pumpkin and stir for a minute.
二 Add sugar, sake, soy sauce and water and bring it to the boil.
三 Simmer for 10 minutes with a lid on occasionally stirring. Turn off the heat and steam for 20 minutes.
四 When serving add snow peas or spring onion in the pan and reheat.
五 Serve in a bowl.

IZAKAYA • BEEF & PORK

Wafu carpaccio

SERVES 2

200g (7 oz) beef tender loin or sirloin, thinly sliced

½ small brown onion, peeled and chopped

2 tbsp olive oil

A drop of soy sauce or awase-jyoyu (see Basics page)

2 tbsp lemon juice

1 tbsp chopped parsley

Salt and pepper to taste

一 Arrange beef slices on a plate.

二 Place olive oil, soy sauce and then lemon juice in a bowl.

三 Add parsley and onion.

四 Crack salt and pepper over the beef.

五 Place the mixture on top of beef.

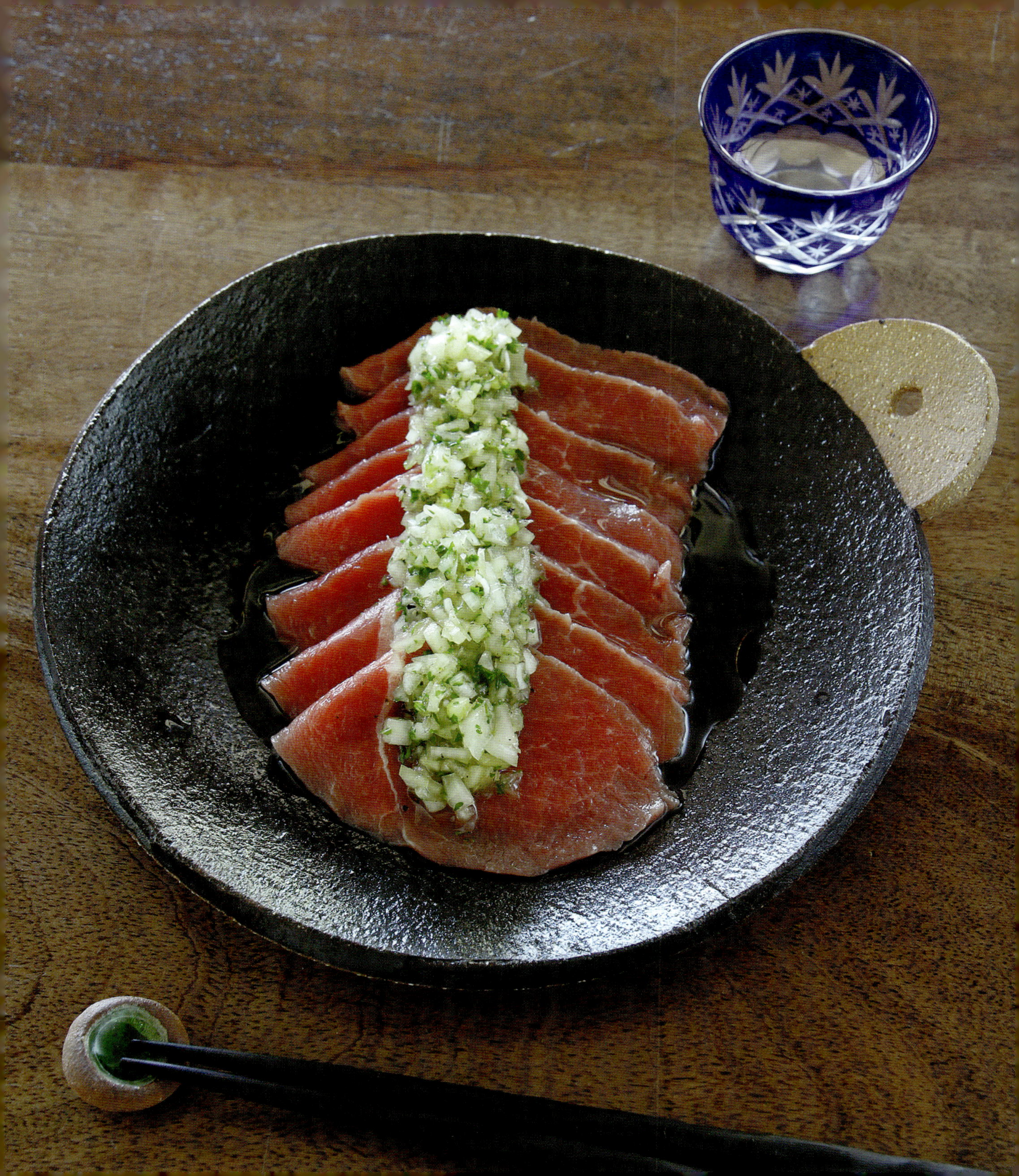

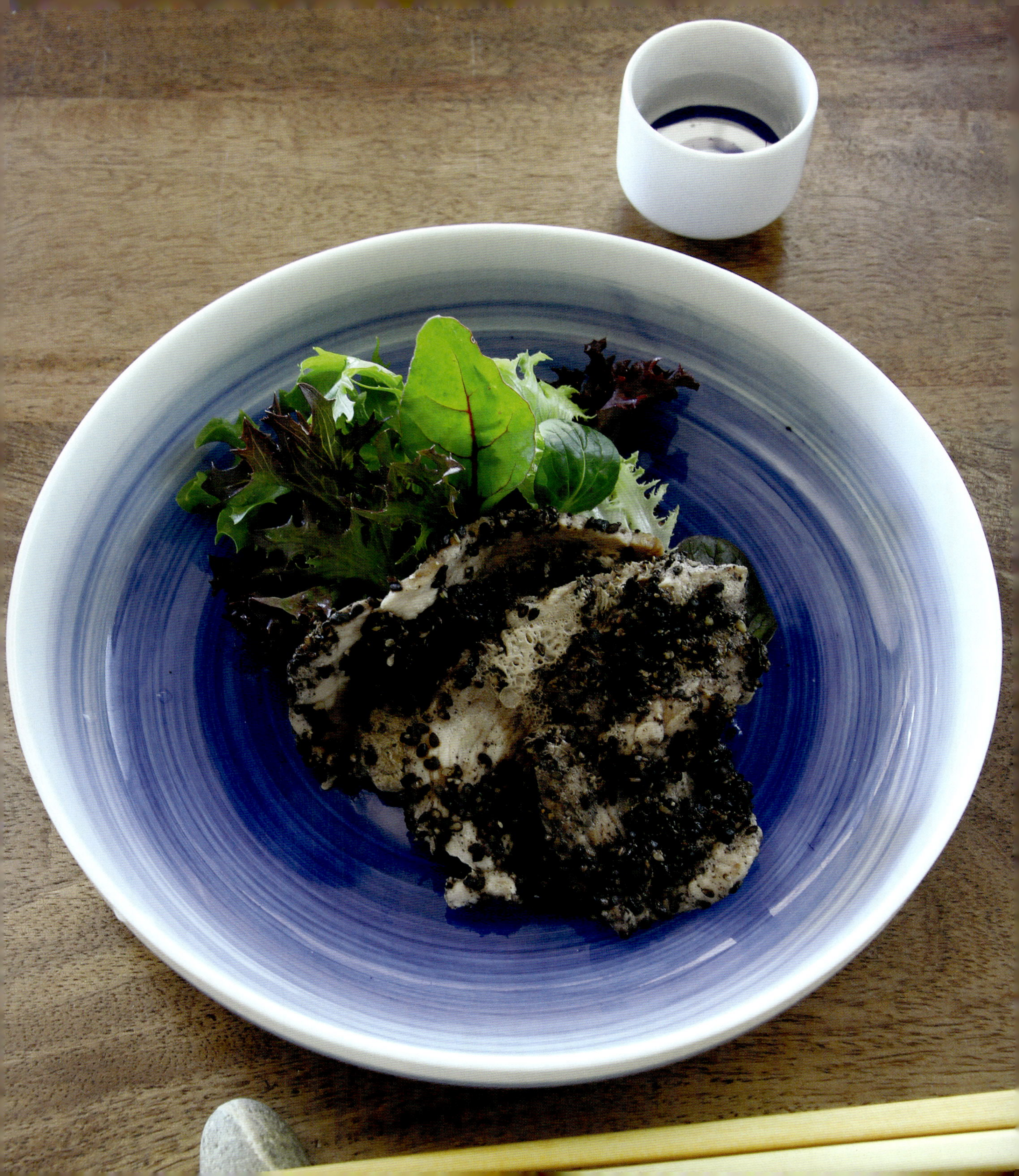

Minudaru: Steamed pork in black sesame

This is one of the regional cuisines from Okinawa.

BLACK SESAME PASTE
50g (1¾ oz) of roasted black sesame
2 tbsp caster sugar
2 tbsp soy sauce
1 tbsp mirin

300g (10½ oz) pork loin 0.5cm (¼ inch) thickness
Green salad

一 To make a black sesame paste, grind sesame in a grinder or use suribachi (a ribbed mortar) and surikogi (pestle) until powdery.

二 Add the caster sugar, mirin and soy sauce and combine well.

三 Paste the sauce over the pork and set aside for 1 hour.

四 Prepare steamer and steam for 20 minutes.

五 Cool it down and slice.

六 Serve on a plate with green salad.

Lamb chop or pork soft rib in chilli miso

4 lamb chops or 8 pieces of pork rib
Salt and pepper for seasoning
1 fresh chilli, deseed and slice
4 tbsp saikyo-miso, dissolved with 4 tbsp water
1 tbsp mirin
1 tbsp brown sugar

一 Season the lamb with salt and pepper.

二 Add the chilli, miso mixture, mirin and brown sugar in a container and marinate the lamb for 1–2 hours.

三 Preheat the oven 200°C (390°F). Transfer lamb in the oven tray and bake for 20 minutes or until cooked.

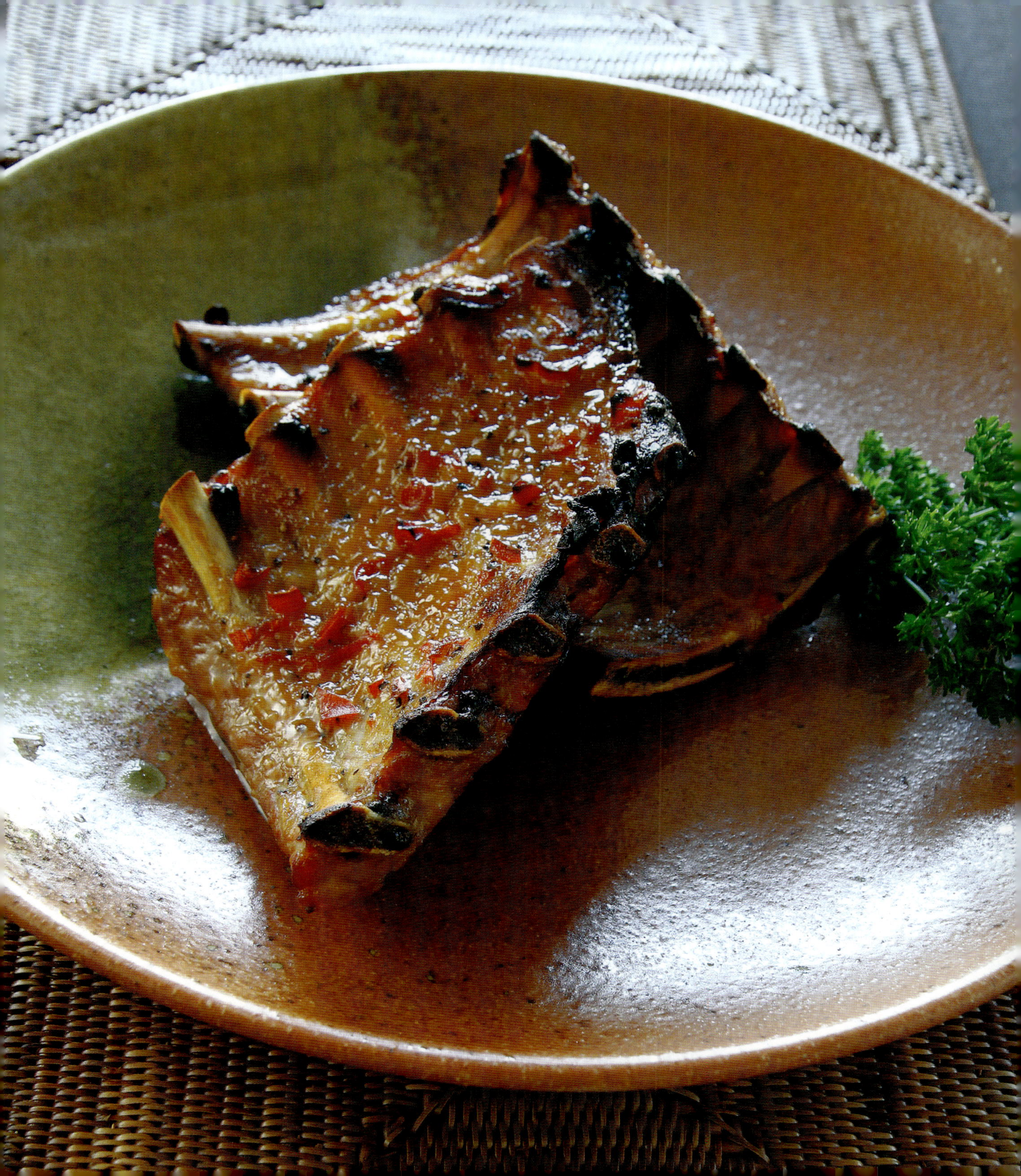

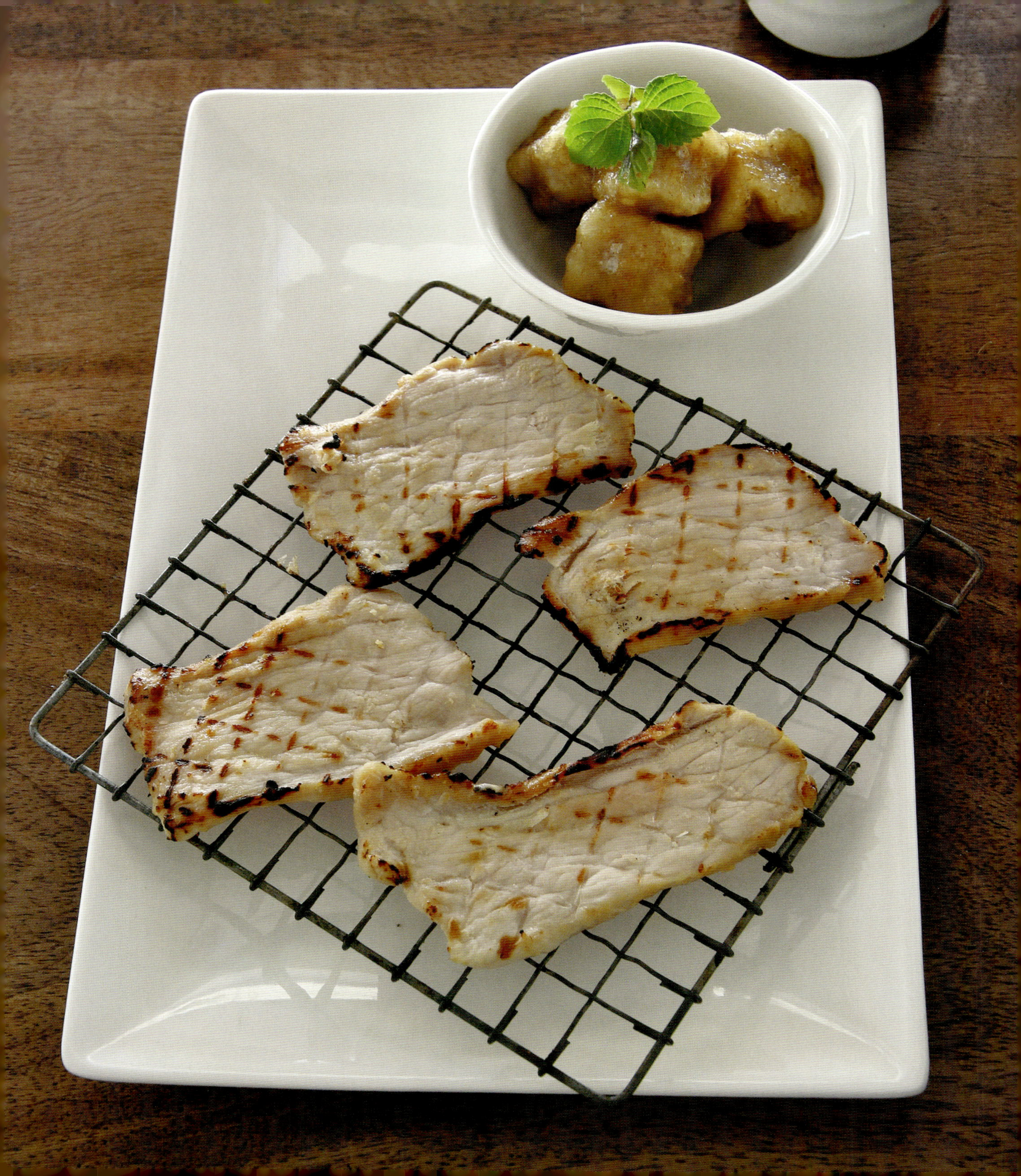

Aburi-style marinated pork with miso

400g (14 oz) lean pork
3 tbsp miso or sakiyo miso
60ml (2 fl oz) sake
60ml (2 fl oz) mirin
1 tbsp brown sugar
A pinch of salt

一 Mix the miso, sake, mirin, brown sugar and salt in a container.

二 Place the pork and coat with mixture, and marinate overnight in the refrigerator.

三 Transfer pork to the chopping board and slice.

四 Lay slices on the baking tray and scorch with a blow torch or grill over the hibachi.

Deep-fried diced pork with umeboshi (pickled plum)

200g (7 oz) of pork rump, cut into bite-size cubes
3 tbsp of potato starch
½ cup of bonito dashi
1 tbsp mirin
1 tbsp sake
4 tbsp soy sauce
1 tbsp honey
4 umeboshi, deseed
2 shiso leaves, sliced
Vegetable oil for deep fry

一 Coat pork with potato starch.

二 Heat oil in a deep pan to 180°C (355°F).

三 Deep-fry pork for 1 minute and drain oil.

四 Place dashi in a pan and bring it to the boil.

五 Add mirin, sake, soy sauce, honey and umeboshi and cook until well mixed.

六 Place pork in the dashi and simmer for 10 minutes over low heat.

七 Serve in a plate topped with shiso leaves.

Gyoza dumpling with stamina sauce

MAKES 12

100g (3½ oz) cabbage or Chinese cabbage, trimmed and chopped finely

100g (3½ oz) lean minced pork

A little pinch of salt

50g or ½ bunch of garlic chives, chopped finely

½ tsp ginger juice

1 tsp sake

1 tsp caster sugar

1 tsp sesame oil

1 tsp soy sauce

½ tbsp potato starch

12 gyoza or gow gee wrappers

Extra potato starch or a sheet of kitchen paper for resting gyoza

1 tbsp sesame oil

½ cup chicken stock or water

STAMINA DIPPING SAUCE

1 clove garlic, grated

1 tsp chopped garlic chives

1 tbsp soy sauce

1 tbsp rice vinegar

1 tbsp chilli oil or fresh small chili, chopped

2 tbsp grated daikon for condiment

COMMON DIPPING SAUCE

1 tbsp soy sauce

1 tbsp rice vinegar

1 tsp sesame oil or chilli oil

一 In a bowl place the cabbage and salt. Give a little massage and leave for 5 minutes. With both hands squeeze out excess liquid.

二 Add garlic chives, ginger juice, sake, caster sugar, sesame oil, and soy sauce and with combine well with hands.

三 Prepare a small bowl of water.

四 Place a wrapper in your left palm or on a plate, spoon filling in the centre of the wrapper.

五 Fold the wrapper over the filling, seal the edges together by pressing and making small pleats. Rest on a potato starch dusted plate or tray. Repeat with remaining wrappers.

六 To cook, drop sesame oil over the non-stick frying pan, swirling around the pan.

七 Lay gyoza side by side in one or two rows in the pan (depending on size of pan), and cook on one side until golden brown over moderate heat. Then add chicken stock or water and put a lid on to steam. Steam for 2–3 minutes or until most of the liquid has evaporated over high heat.

八 To make the dipping sauce add all the ingredients except daikon and combine.

九 Serve hot with dipping sauce with daikon on the side.

For the novices, there is a useful tool to fold gyoza, which is available from Japanese or Asian shops.

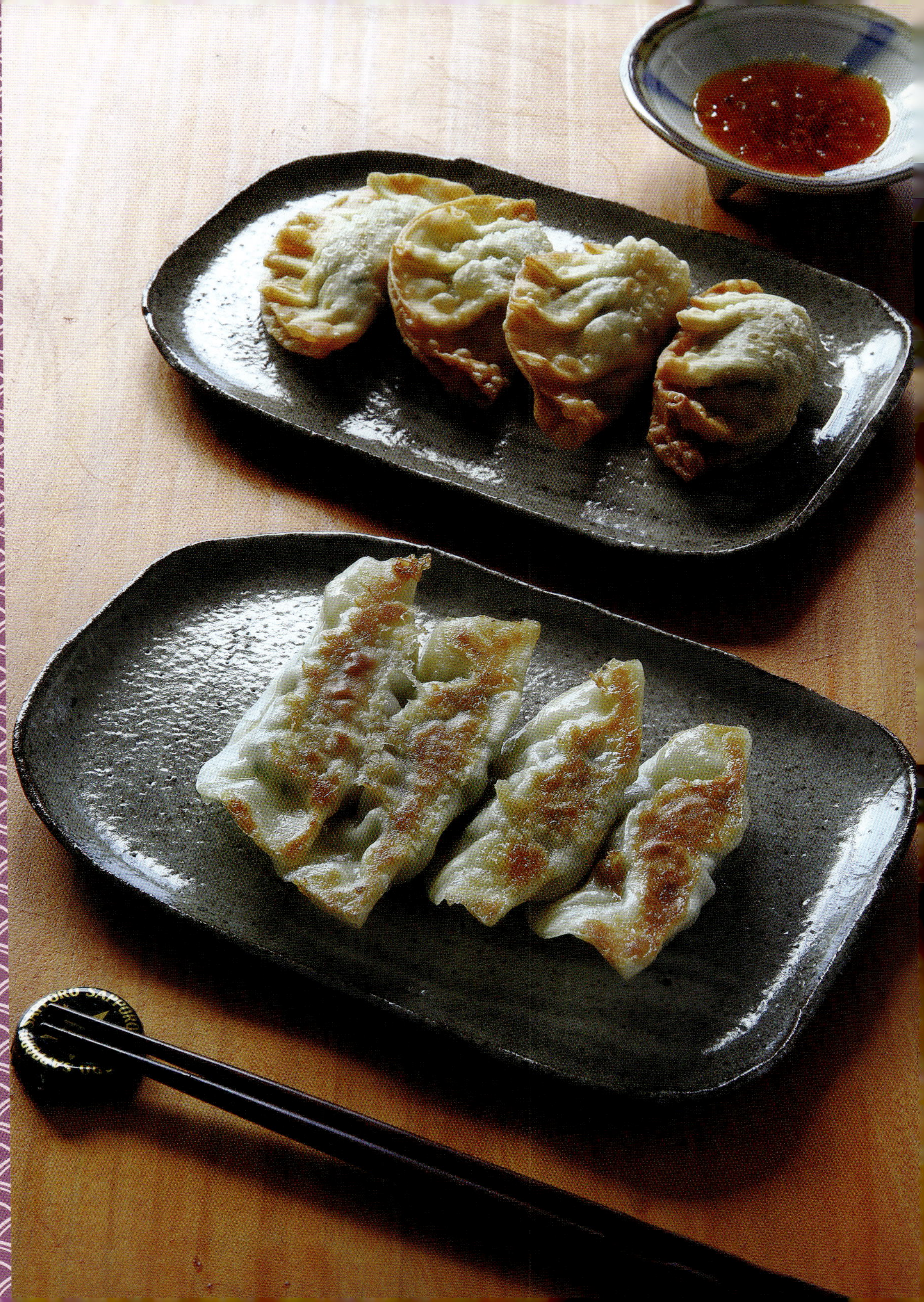

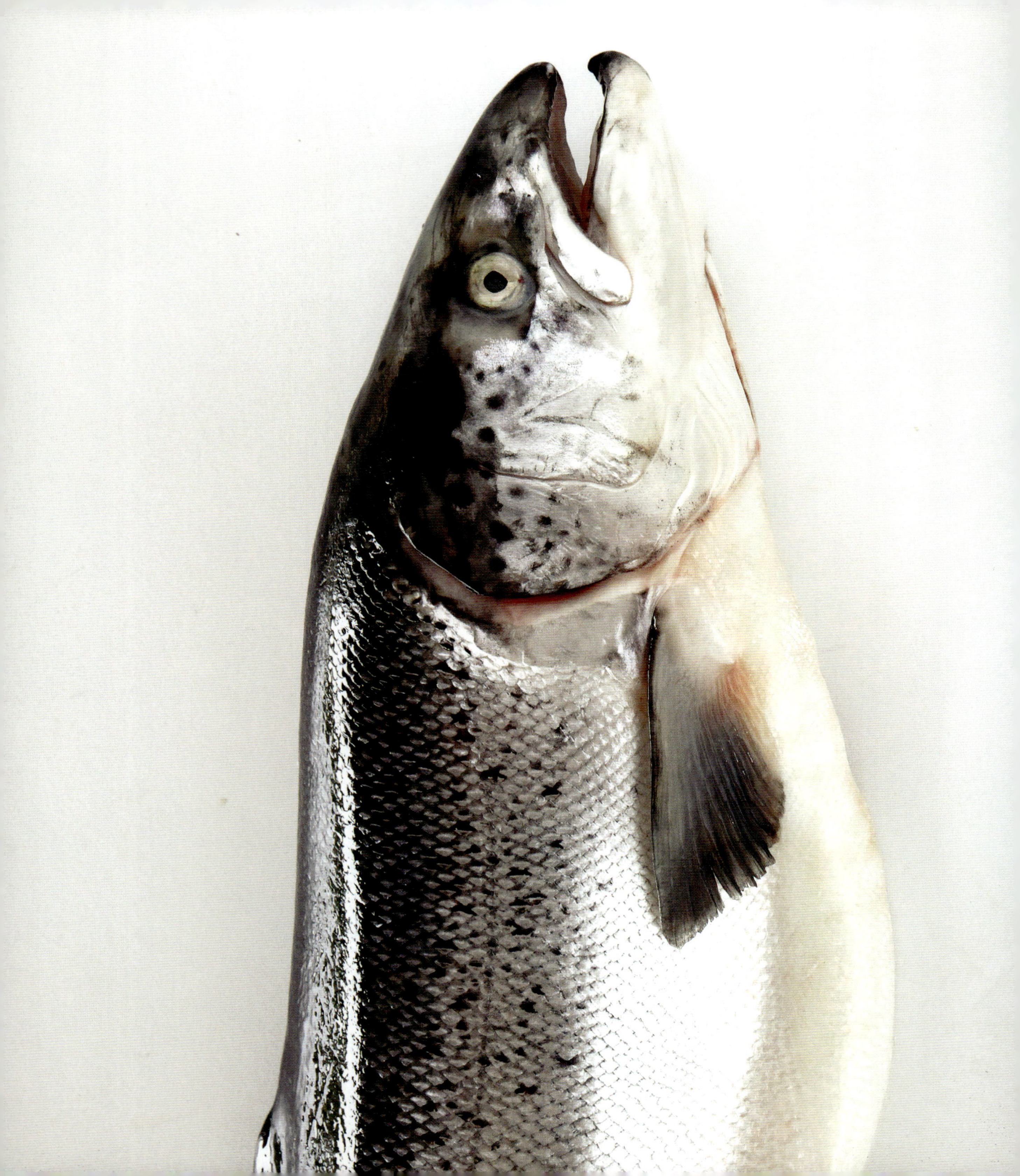

Seafood

Basics
    Filleting (shima-aji in sanmai oroshi, three pieces filleting)
    Sashimi slicing techniques
    Preparing daikon-tsuma

Sashimi

Tuna sashimi combined with natto

Tuna sashimi with avocado

Snapper carpaccio

Ika-somen

Cuttle fish with mentaiko and green salad leaves

Fresh pacific oyster combined with plum and soy sauce

Octopus in vinaigrette

Octopus with daikon and bainiku sauce

Kara-age: Deep fried flounder with shiitake glazing sauce

Grilled squid tube with shichimi

Grilled tiger prawn stuffed with mango and chilli

Grilled sundried whiting with mirin

Grilled clam stuffed with sea urchin

Baby octopus crackers

Steamed baby abalone

Grilled skewered whiting

Sardine tatsuta-age

Mackerel cooked in miso

saikyo-style grilled cod

Teriyaki kingfish

Hotate with soy sauce butter

Saikyo-style grilled scallops

IZAKAYA • SEAFOOD

Filleting

SHIMA-AJI IN SANMAI OROSHI, THREE PIECES FILLETING

1 sashimi quality Shima-aji (trevally)

— Make a slit from the tail to the head along the belly with a sharp knife and open. Pull out and discard the insides and rinse the cavity under running water.

二 Scale the fish using an uroko-tori (Japanese fish scaler) if possible, as it causes less damage to the fish.

三 Wipe the fish dry so that it is easier to work with. Position the fish flat on a board with the tail on the right hand side if you are right-handed, and hold the fish with your left hand. Reverse if you are left-handed. Insert the knife at the top of the fish head, just behind the head bone, with the blade angled slightly toward the fish head. Following the natural curve of the cheek, continue slicing in one smooth stroke behind the gills to the depth of the backbone, until you reach the underside of the fish. Holding the knife flat and the blade facing away from the fish head, insert the knife into the very top ridge of the fish head just behind the head bone. In one swift movement, slice the knife diagonally through the fish with the knife kept flat along the back bone, allowing the knife to cut through the flesh of the belly edge too.

四 Continue in a drawing motion until you reach the tail and the fillet is free.

五 Set the fillet aside and turn the fish over, again placing the tail on the right hand side of the board. Repeat all steps as above, but when making the second cut (along the backbone), insert the knife point sideways at the underside edge rather than the top of the fish.

六 Place the fillets cut side up on the board. Holding the knife on a fairly flat angle, cut from the centre of the fillet to belly edge, removing lower belly parts with bones.

七 Place the fillet on the board, skin side down. Run your finger along the fillet to check for bones. Remove any bones with a pair of tweezers.

八 Wipe the knife clean. Hold onto the tail end of a fillet with one hand (your left if you're right handed), skin side down. Insert the knife at a slight angle just above the skin at the tail end, and move the knife along the skin about 5cm (2 inches) into the fillet. Holding the fish firmly, remove the knife. Gently pull the free flesh back just enough to hold the knife vertically above the skin you've just cut free from the fish. Make a 2cm (¾ inch) incision into the skin, cutting lengthwise about 2cm (¾ inch) from the tail edge. This will create a buttonhole that runs parallel to the length of the fish. Insert your left thumb into the buttonhole in order to prevent the slippery skin from moving. Hold the knife flat side facing up and begin cutting from the tail end near the buttonhole, just above the skin. Keeping the knife held flat just above the skin, carefully slice towards the head end in one continuous movement to free the flesh from the skin. Repeat with the other fillet.

Sashimi slicing techniques

Sashimi slicing techniques vary according to the type of fish. Here are the two main techniques:

HIKI-ZUKURI

Need a long fillet of fish that is 6cm (2⅓ inches) wide and a clean, wet cloth.

This is a basic sashimi technique to slice fish into pieces.

— Place the fillet on a chopping board and hold onto the fillet with your left hand (reverse if you are left-handed). With a sashimi (filleting) knife, slice the fish into pieces 2.5cm (1 inch) wide. Arrange the pieces neatly in a layered row. Balance the layered pieces on the flat side of the knife and transfer to serving dishes.

SOGI-ZUKURI

Need a long fillet of fish that is 6cm (2⅓ inches) wide and a clean, wet cloth.

A technique for sashimi and sushi tops. This slice is thinner than Hiki-zukuri so it creates a different sensation in the mouth.

— Hold onto the thicker end of the fillet with your left hand (reverse if you are left-handed) Insert the sashimi knife at a 45-degree angle into the fish and slide the knife towards the left to make a thin slice about 1cm (⅓ inch) thick. Slice the remaining fillet into 1cm (⅓ inch) thick pieces.

SEAFOOD • IZAKAYA

Preparing daikon-tsuma*

About 10cm (4 inch) long daikon, peeled

一 Using a vegetable-carving knife or paring knife, peel a section of daikon. Alternatively, use a peeler.

二 Place knife at a right angle to work surface, cut daikon into very thin slices.

三 Separate slices and place in bowl of water, or refrigerate in water for 15 minutes. Drain well before using.

*This method is also used to prepare cucumber-tsuma

四 Using a vegetable peeler, cut daikon 20cm (7¾ inches) long and slice off thin daikon strips. Then roll up and cut into thin julienne.

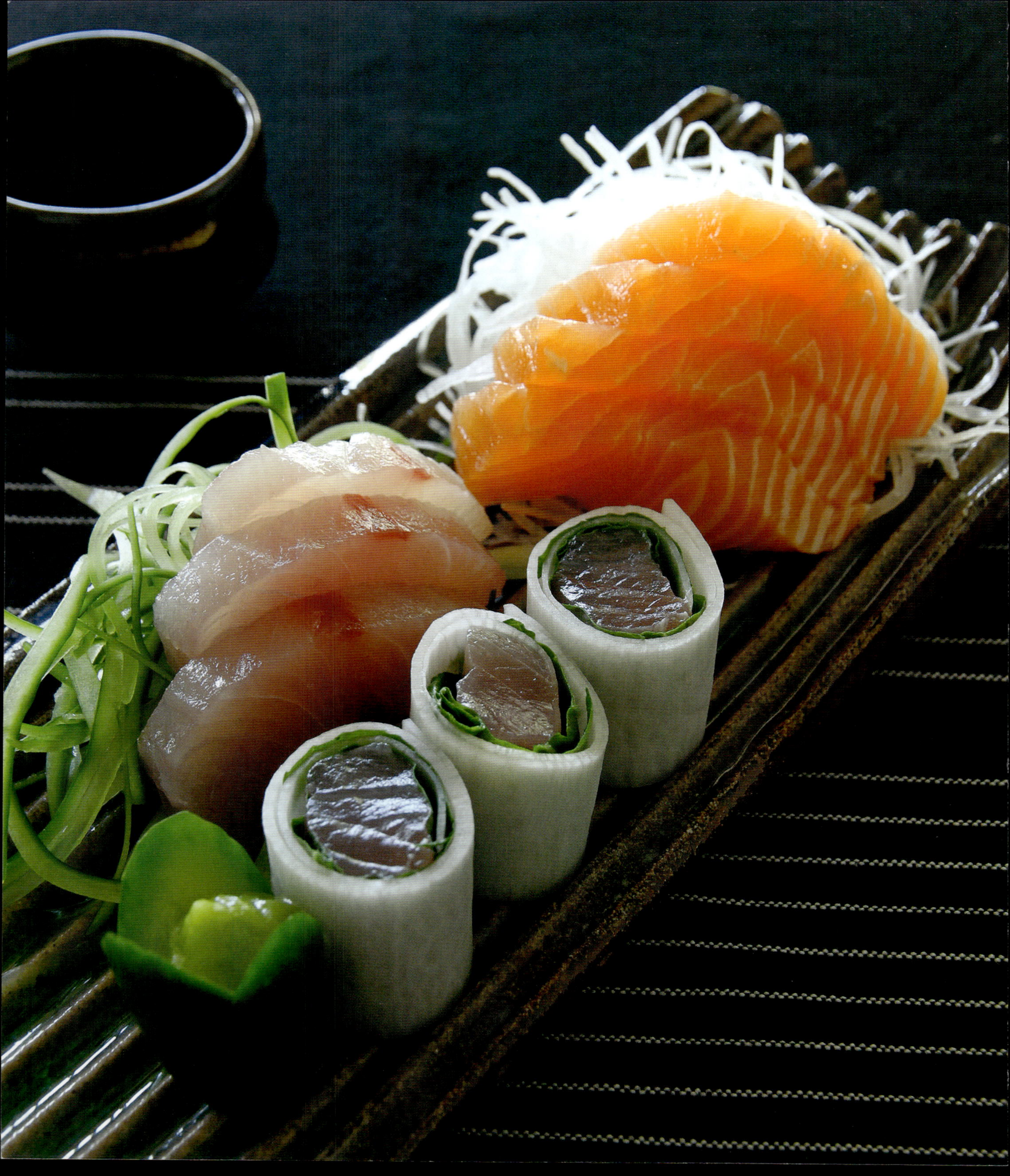

Sashimi

SERVES 2

100g (3½ oz) sashimi quality salmon slices

100g (3½ oz) sashimi quality kingfish slices

1 tuna block 2 x 2 x 10cm (¾ x ¾ x 4 inches) long

2 green shiso (Japanese basil) leaves

1 daikon strip (10cm/4 inches long)

1 cucumber garnish

100g (3½ oz) cucumber tsuma for garnish (see page 159)

100g (3½ oz) daikon tsuma for garnish (see page 159)*

Soy sauce for serve

Wasabi for serve

Tsuma, or edible garnishes are an essential component of sashimi.

一 To prepare a cucumber flower cup, cut 5cm (2 inches) of cucumber and cut off one side straight. With a small knife, insert the tip of the knife and make three cuts, making sure that the cuts meet near the bottom as rounding the cucumber. Holding the bottom of the cucumber, gently top off with your other hand. Put a little knob of wasabi in the centre.

二 Prepare salmon and kingfish slices according to the Sogi-zukuri (see page 158).

三 Lay the sheet of daikon, arrange the shiso leaves on the corner and top with the tuna block. Roll up tightly and slice into 3 pieces.

四 Arrange daikon and cucumber tsuma and place kingfish and salmon sashimi on them. Transfer tuna rolls beside with cucumber.

五 Serve with soy sauce.

Tuna sashimi combined with natto

SERVES 2

200g (7 oz) sashimi quality tuna block
1 packet natto* along with a sachet of sauce and karashi (hot mustard)
1 stem spring onion, chopped
Soy sauce for serving

一 In a small bowl with chopsticks or fork mix natto with its sauce and karashi until creamy.

二 With a knife, cut tuna into 1cm (¾ inch) cubes.

三 Serve tuna cubes in a bowl and place natto on top.

四 Sprinkle spring onions.

五 Serve with soy sauce

*Natto is fermented soy beans with quite a unique smell. Instead of natto, okura or avocado could be used.

Tuna sashimi with avocado

SERVES 2

200g (7 oz) sashimi quality tuna, block
½ avocado, peeled and pit removed
Lemon juice
A pinch of nori strips
Soy sauce for serving
Wasabi for serving

一 With a knife, cut tuna into 1-cm (¾-inch) cubes.

二 Cut avocado into 1-cm (¾-inch) cubes and drizzle lemon juice.

三 Place tuna and avocado in a bowl and lightly toss.

四 Arrange tuna and avocado in a serving bowl and top with nori strips.

五 Serve with wasabi and soy sauce.

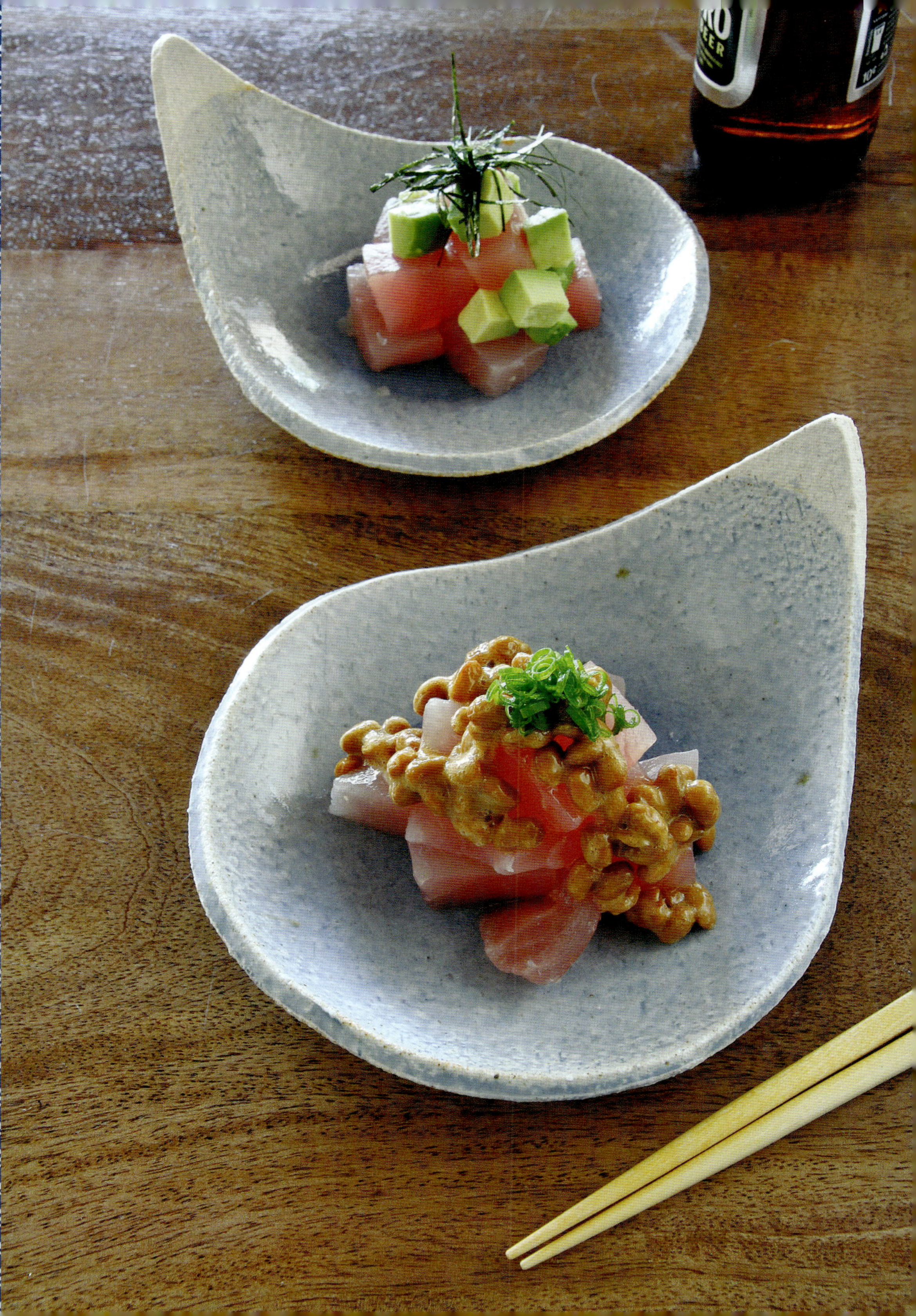

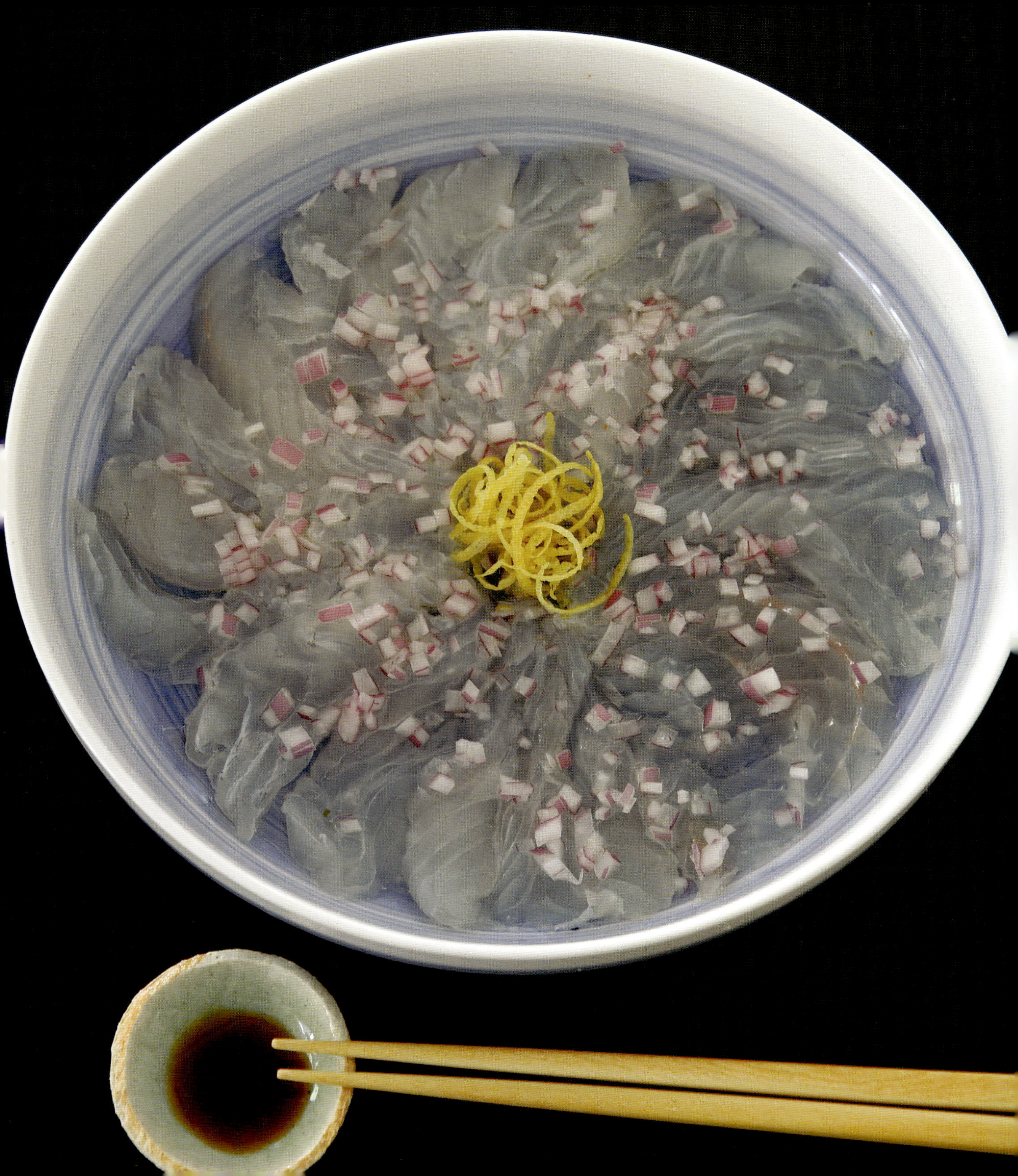

Snapper carpaccio

SERVES 2

200g (7 oz) sashimi quality snapper fillet without skin
½ small red onion (about 20g/¾ oz), peeled and chopped
½ tsp olive oil
1 tsp rice vinegar
1 tsp caster sugar
Juice of ½ lemon
A pinch salt
A pinch of lemon zest
Soy sauce for serving

— Thinly slice the snapper fillet in Sogizukuri style (see page 158).

二 To make vinaigrette, add the olive oil, rice vinegar, caster sugar, lemon juice and salt in a bowl and mix well.

三 Arrange snapper slices in a circle on a shallow plate and drizzle over vinaigrette sauce. Sprinkle the chopped red onion and top with the lemon zest.

IZAKAYA • SEAFOOD

Ika-somen

4 Sashimi quality cuttlefish, 80g (2¾ oz) each
4 shisho, Japanese basil leaves, sliced
Wasabi for serving
Soy sauce for serving

一 Hold the calamari in one hand and with the other hand pull out the tentacles and entrails, being careful not to break the ink sac.

二 Rinse under running water. The tentacles can also be used for sashimi or other dishes. To use, cut them off below the eyes and remove beak. Cut tentacles into bit-sized pieces.

三 Slit the edge only half way on the inside of the mantle. With a firm hold, pull the silky skin from the edge of the fillet. Using a cloth makes skinning easier.

四 Place fillet on board and use tip of knife to slice in julienne strips.

五 Toss cuttlefish with shiso strips.

六 Serve with soy sauce and wasabi.

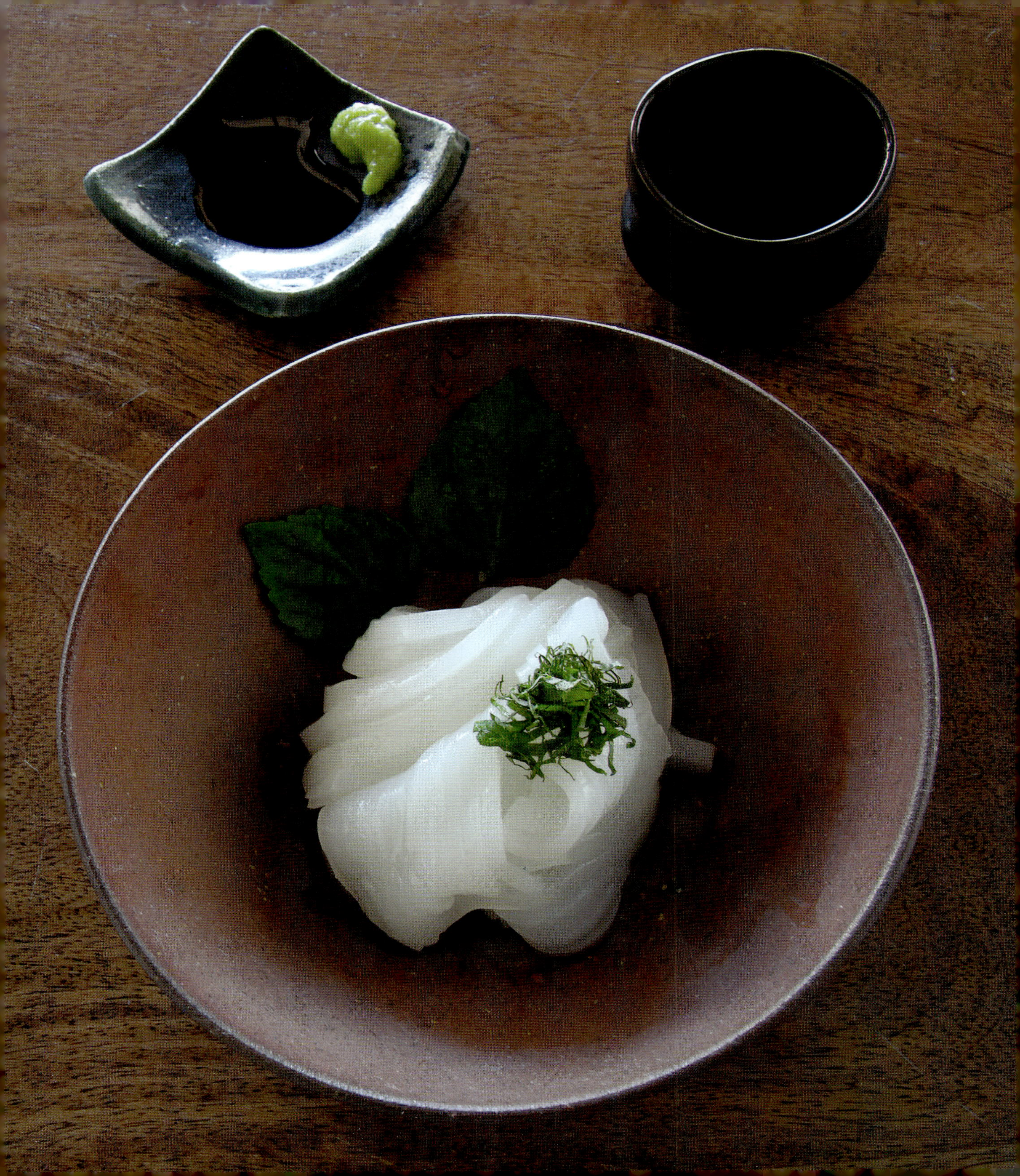

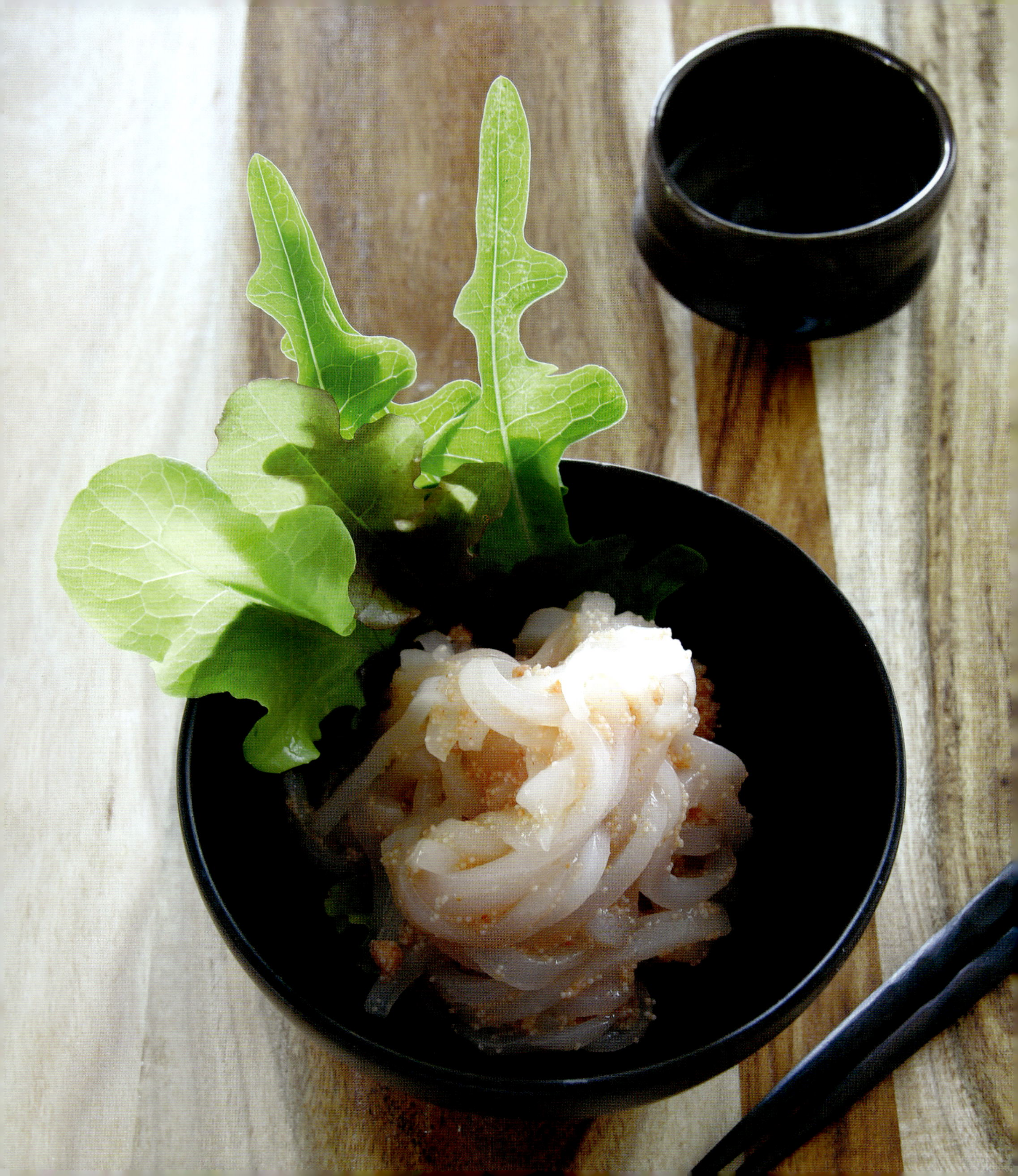

Cuttle fish with mentaiko and green salad leaves

4 Sashimi quality cuttlefish, prepare like Ika-somen (see page 166)
15g (½ oz) mentaiko, salted Alaska Pollack roe in chilli pepper
Green salad leaves

一 Grill mentaiko for about 6 minutes or until cooked.
二 Cool it down and with fingers make into flakes.
三 Combine mentaiko and cuttlefish together.
四 Serve with green salad leaves.

*Mentaiko is edible both raw and cooked, in this dish we use it cooked as it is easier to flake.
Tobikko (preserved flying fish roe) is another option instead of Mentaiko.
Mentaiko is available from Japanese or Korean grocery shops.

IZAKAYA • SEAFOOD

Fresh pacific oyster combined with plum and soy sauce

3 fresh pacific oysters in half shell
1 litre (4 cups) water (5% salted)
2 tbsp bainiku: plum puree
1 tsp soy sauce
1 tsp mirin

— Lightly rinse the oysters in salted water and tip out the excess water.

二 Serve onto a plate.

三 Combine plum puree, soy sauce and mirin in a small bowl and serve with oysters.

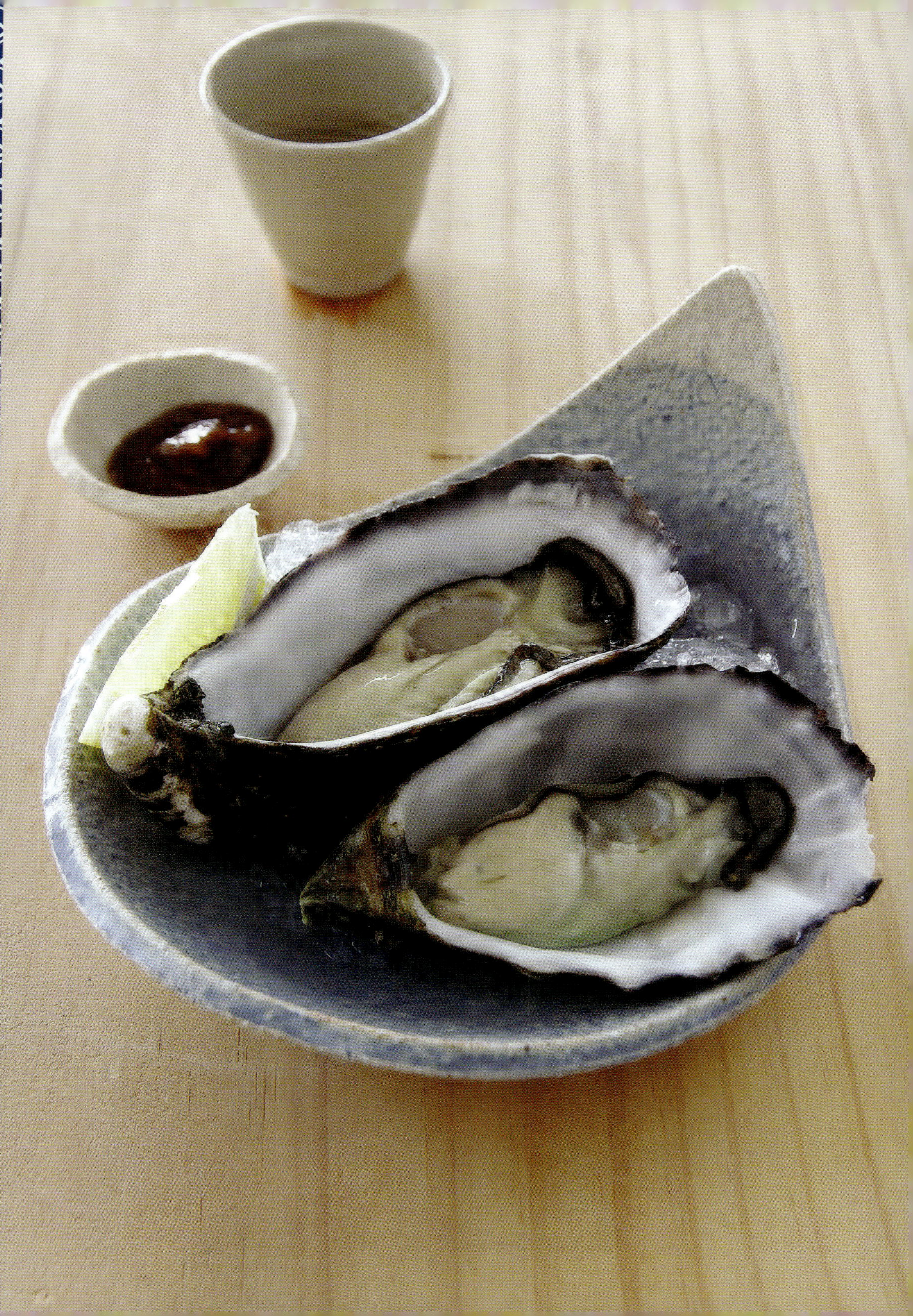

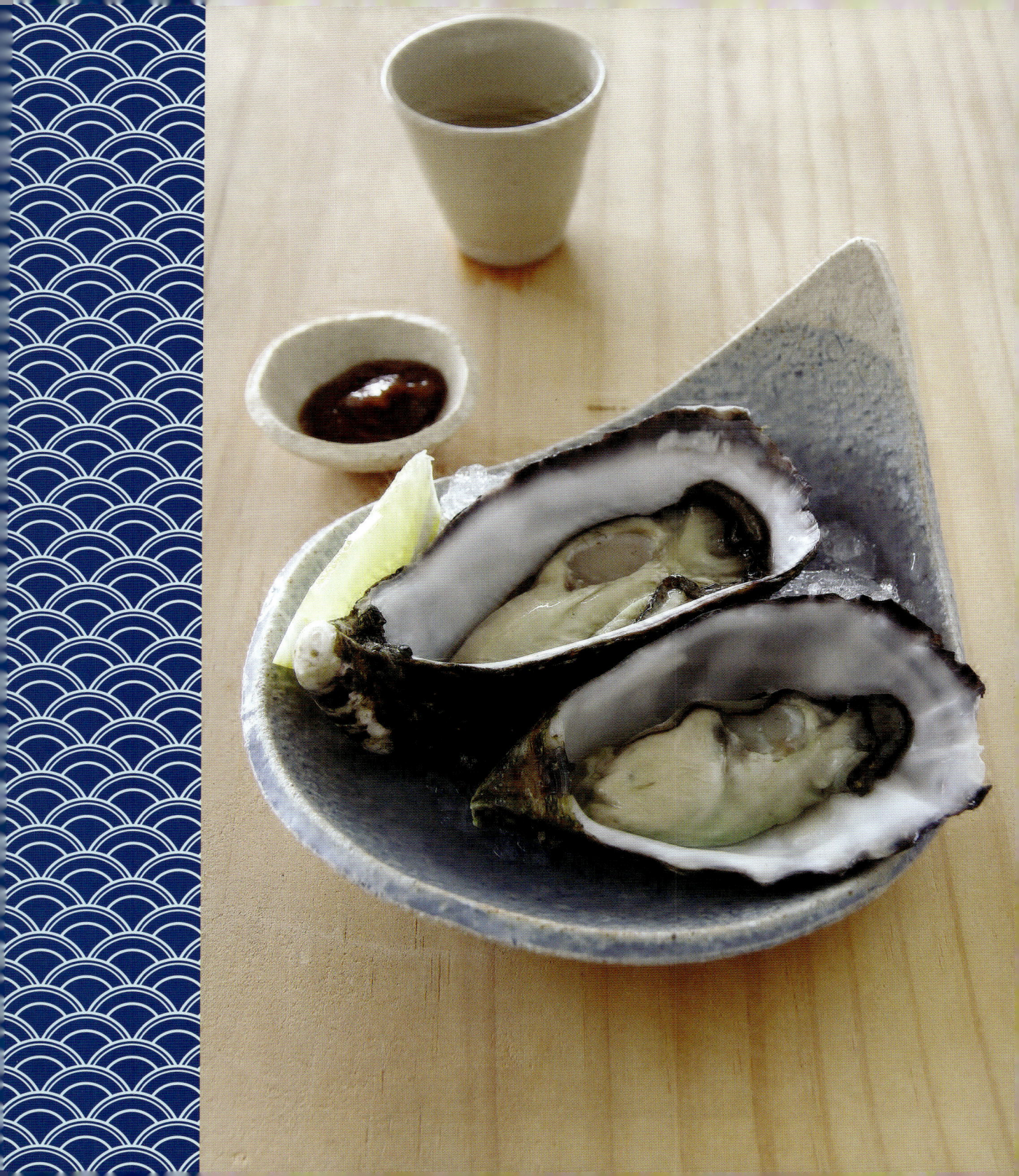

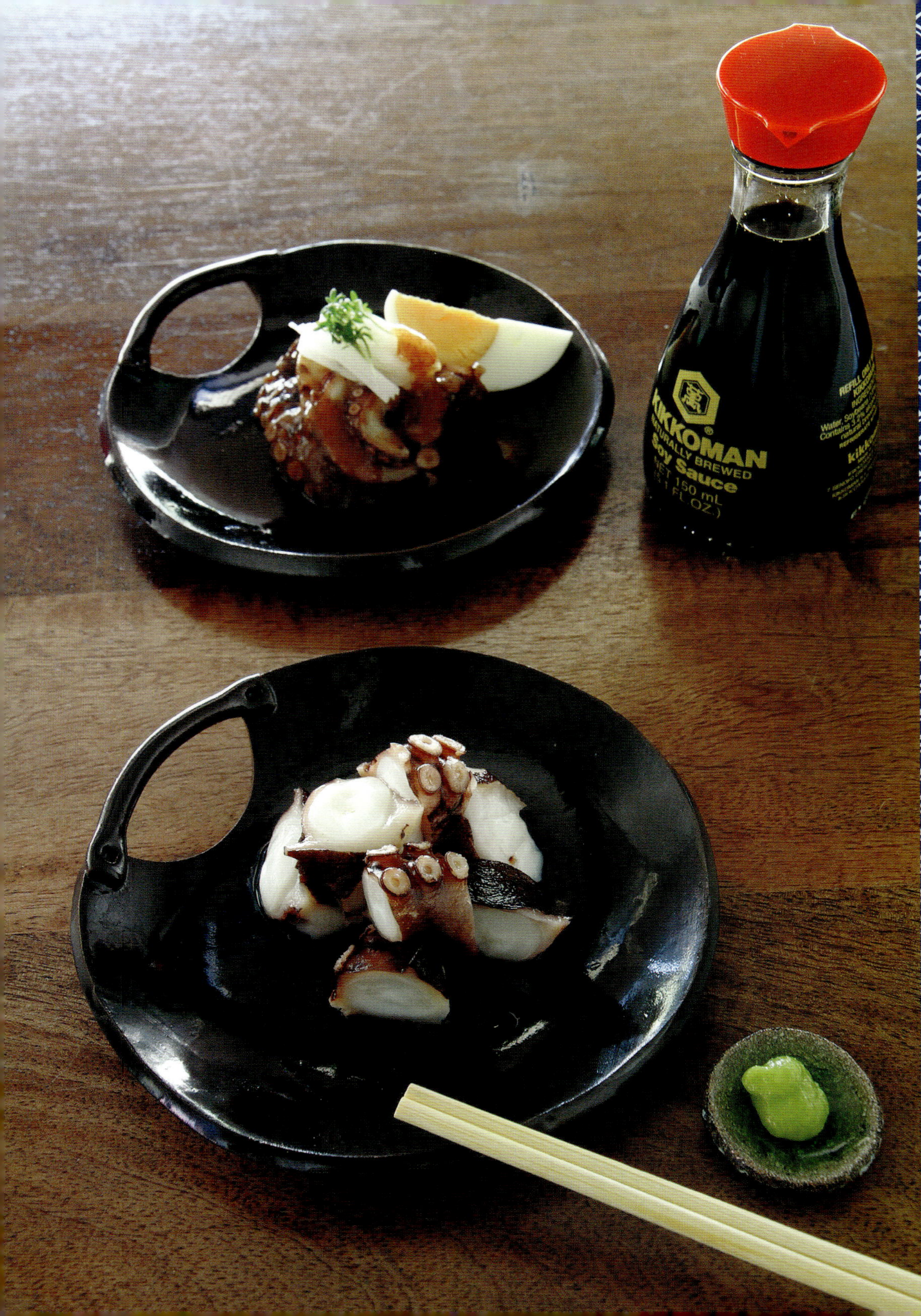
KIKKOMAN
NATURALLY BREWED
Soy Sauce
NET 150 mL

Octopus in vinaigrette

SERVES 4

About 500g (17½ oz) fresh octopus
2 tbsp salt
1 tbsp rice vinegar
1 tbsp red wine, (optional, used to add colour and enhance taste)
½ cup rice vinegar
¼ cup caster sugar
1 tbsp mirin
Soy sauce for serving
Wasabi for serving
Yuzu (optional)

一 Rub the octopus with salt.

二 Bring water to boil in a pan and add the vinegar and red wine.

三 Holding the head with your hand, slide the octopus into the boiling water tentacles first. Blanch octopus until slightly red.

四 Take out and rest in water to cool it down.

五 In the meantime, make the marinade sauce. Add the rice vinegar, sugar and mirin. Transfer the octopus to the sauce and marinate for 2 hours in the refrigerator.

六 Transfer the octopus onto the chopping board. Cut the head, then each tentacle and separate. Slice each tentacle slightly diagonally. Slice the head.

七 Serve the octopus on a plate with soy sauce and wasabi.

Octopus with daikon and bainiku sauce

SERVES 2

Use the octopus from 'Octopus in vinaigrette' above.
200g (7 oz) octopus, prepared according to 'Octopus in vinaigrette'
1 hard-boiled egg, remove shell and halve lengthways
50g (1¾ oz) of daikon radish, peeled and julienne
A handful of daikon-sprout or other sprout

BAINIKU (PICKLED PLUM PUREE) SAUCE

1 tbsp bainiku
½ tsp caster sugar
½ tbsp usukuchi shoyu: light colour soy sauce
½ tbsp rice vinegar
1½ tbsp vegetable oil

一 Prepare the octopus.

二 Make the bainiku sauce, add all ingredients in a bowl and mix well.

三 Arrange the octopus slices, boiled egg, radish and daikon-sprout on a plate and drizzle over with the sauce.

IZAKAYA • SEAFOOD

Kara-age: deep-fried flounder with shiitake glazing sauce

SERVES 4

4 baby flounder (about 150–200g/ 5¼–7 oz each)

Freshly ground salt for seasoning

1 tsp sake for drizzling

¼ cup of potato starch for coating

Vegetable oil for deep-frying

SHIITAKE-MUSHROOM GLAZING SAUCE

50g (1¾ oz) fresh shiitake mushrooms, discard stem and slice

1 dry or fresh chilli, deseeded and sliced

1 tbsp chopped ginger

½ cup bonito dashi, (see Basics page)

2 tbsp usukuchi-shoyu: light coloured soy sauce

4 tbsp caster sugar

1 tbsp potato starch, dissolved with 2 tbsp water

4 stems spring onion, trimmed and chopped

4 lemon wedges

一 Scale off and gut out to clean the flounders. Rinse under running water. Pat with kitchen paper.

二 Place the flounders on a tray. Sprinkle salt and set aside for a couple of minutes.

三 Sprinkle sake on the flounders and set aside for a couple of minutes.

四 Coat each flounder with potato starch.

五 To make ankake-sauce (glazing sauce), add mushrooms, chilli, ginger and dashi in a pot, then bring it to the boil.

六 Add soy sauce and sugar, and add potato starch to thicken the sauce while stirring.

七 Prepare vegetable oil in a tempura pan or a deep pan, such as a wok and heat it up to 180°C (355°F).

八 Deep-fry each flounder until crispy and drain oil well on a wire rack or kitchen paper.

九 Serve on each individual plate and pour warmed sauce. Sprinkle spring onion and aside with lemon wedge.

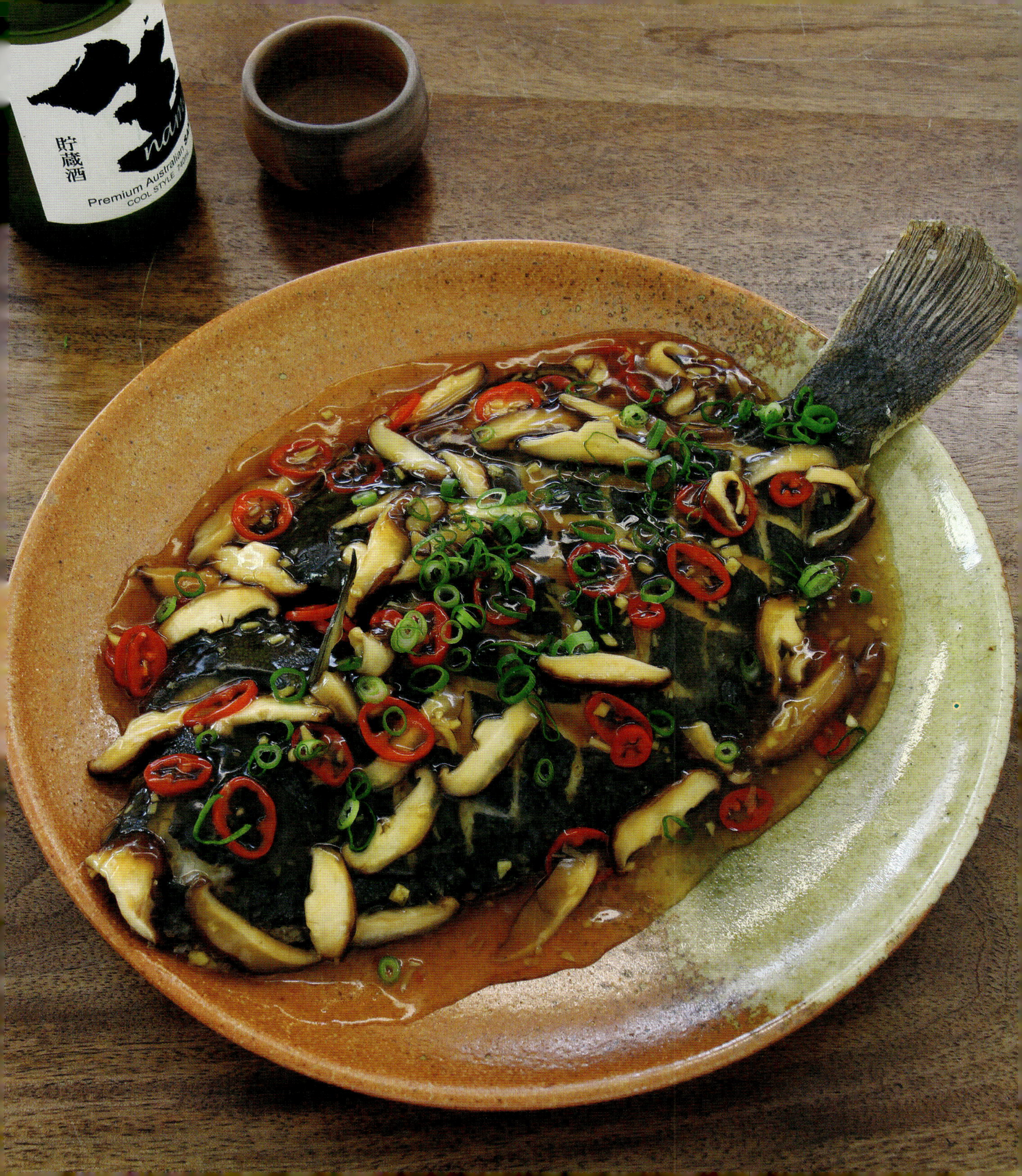
貯蔵酒
Premium Australian
COOL STYLE

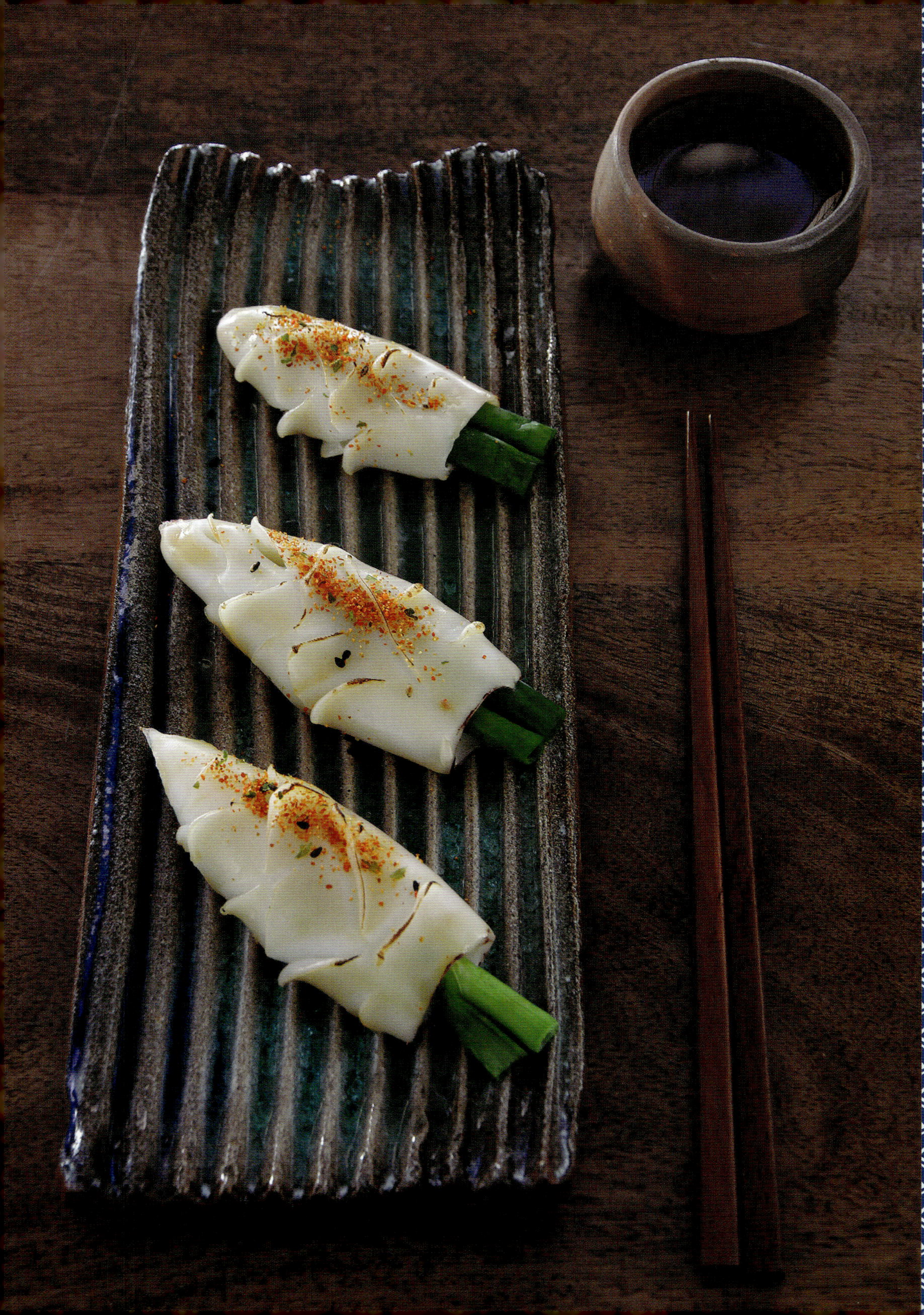

Grilled squid tube with shichimi

6 small squid tubes (approx. 60g/2 oz each)
12 x 10cm (4¾ x 4 inches) long spring onion stems
1 tsp mirin
Sea salt for seasoning
1 tsp shichimi (Japanese seven peppers)

一 With a small knife make criss-cross slits over one side of each squid.

二 Insert two stems of spring onion into each squid tube.

三 Drizzle mirin over squids and crack salt over for seasoning.

四 Place squids on a baking tray with the criss-cross side facing up.

五 Grill under the griller until lightly cooked through or using a blow torch, scorch both sides.

六 Transfer squids to a plate and sprinkle shichimi.

Grilled tiger prawn stuffed with mango and chilli

SERVES 4

8 fresh tiger prawns

A pinch of sea salt

½ cup mango cubes (approx. 0.5cm/ ¼ inch)

1 dry chilli, chopped

1 tbsp mirin

1 tsp potato starch

4 bamboo skewers

一 With a knife make a slit on the shoulder side of the tiger prawn to make a pocket.

二 Sprinkle salt over it.

三 Skewer each king prawn straight with bamboo skewers.

四 Combine mango, chilli and mirin in a bowl.

五 With a tsp, stuff mango chilli into the king prawns' pocket.

六 Grill until cooked.

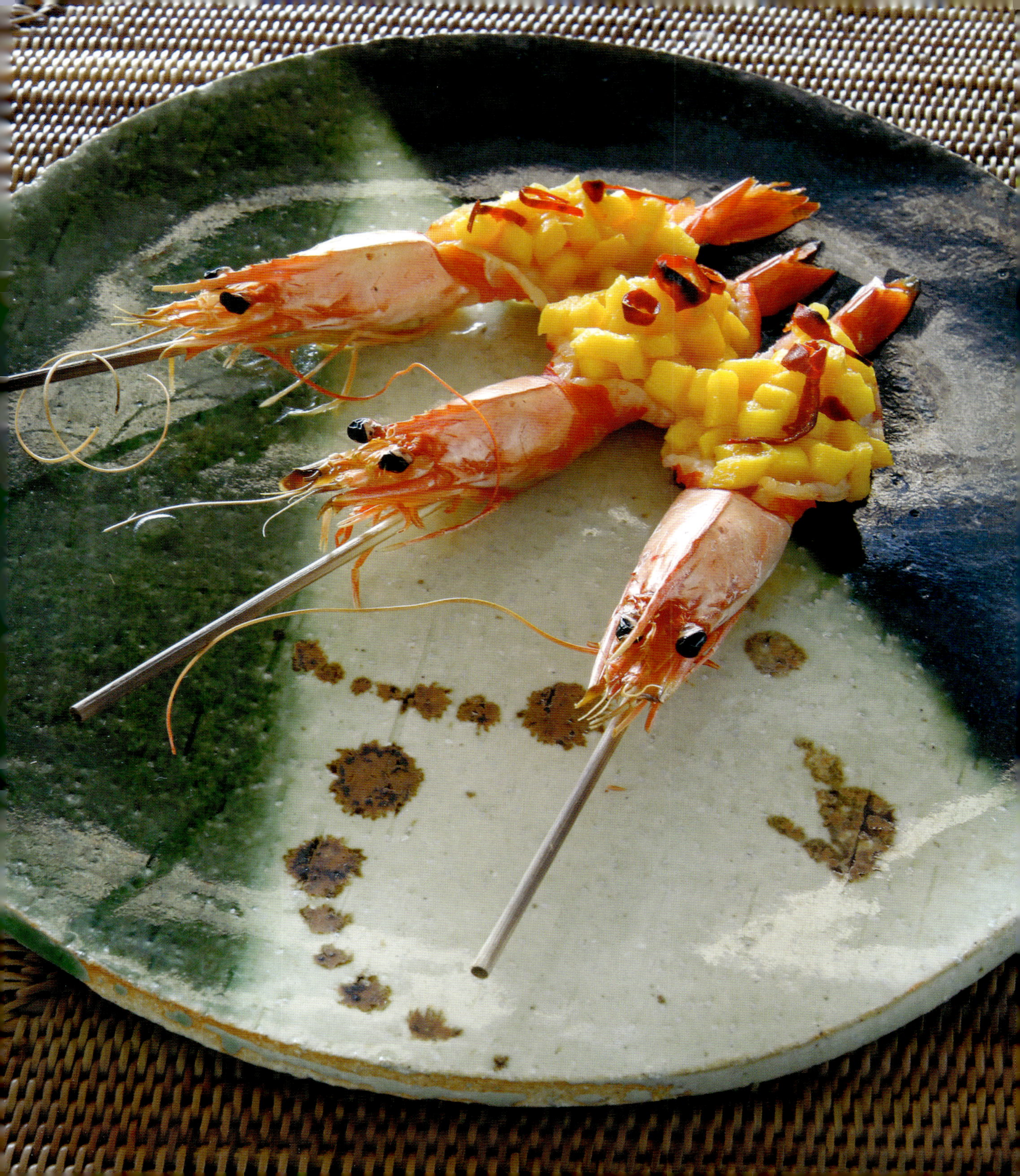

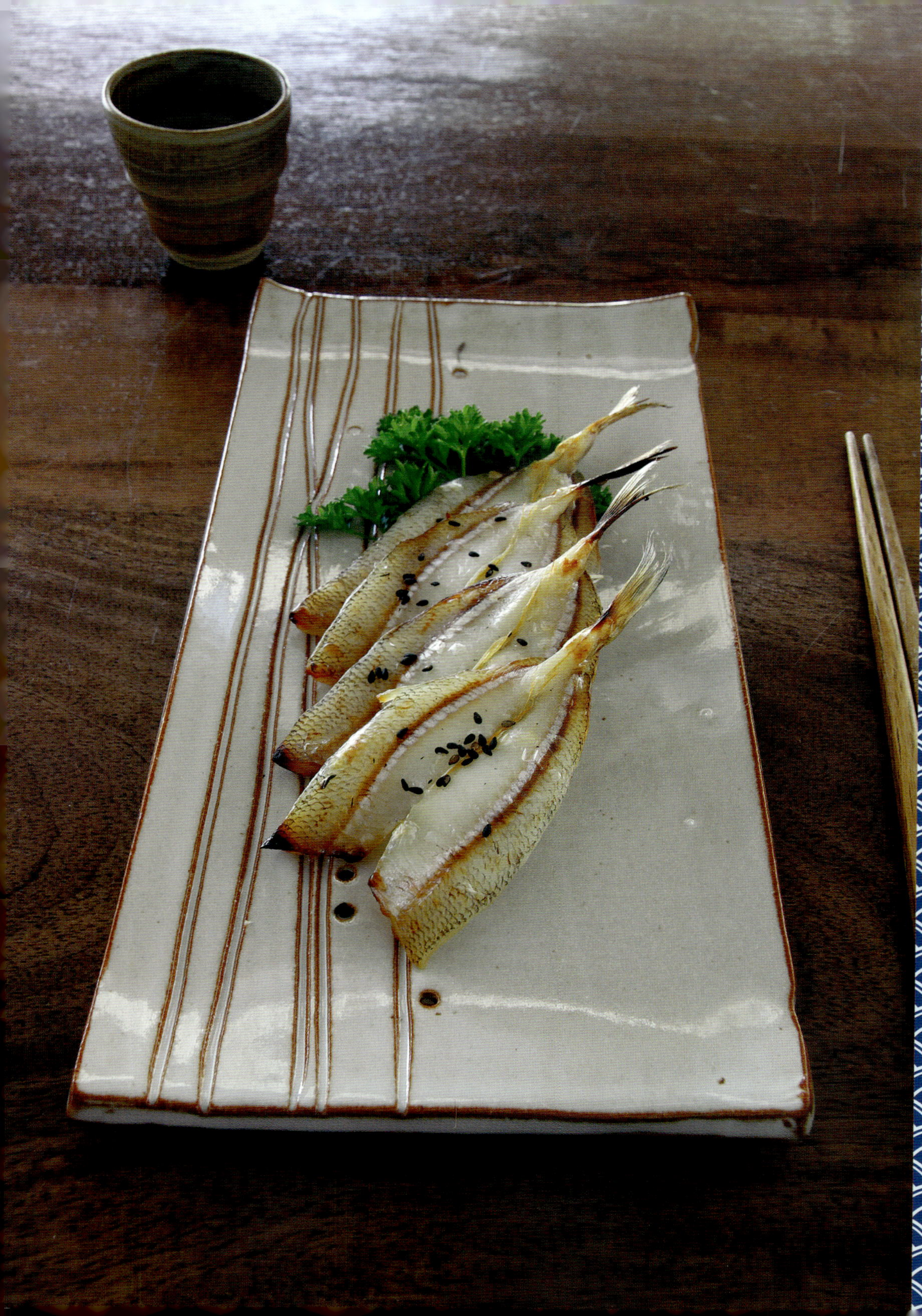

Grilled sundried whiting with mirin

SERVE 4
4 small kisu (whiting)
1 tbsp salt
2 tbsp mirin
1 tbsp black sesame

一 With a sharp knife, cut the head off the fish and trim off the belly side and gut.

二 Rinse under running water.

三 Insert the tip of the knife and start cutting into the fillet from the (missing) head part to the tail, along the backbone of the fish, from the shoulder and slide the knife along the center bone. Turn over the fish and repeat with the other side. Open up the butterfly and cut off the bone to discard.

四 Place fish on a mesh and brush with mirin over the fish.

五 Place fish in a mesh hanging box or a clothing net to sun-dry, and hang in a good breeze for a day.

六 Remove the fish and grill until cooked.

七 Sprinkle with black sesame over whiting.

Grilled clam stuffed with sea urchin

12 clams
100g (3½ oz) sea urchin
1 tbsp mirin
1 tbsp salt
Nori sheet, tear into pieces

一 With a table knife, open clams up and remove one side of the shell.

二 Sprinkle with salt and mirin.

三 Arrange sea urchin on top of clams.

四 Lightly grill.

五 Serve with nori.

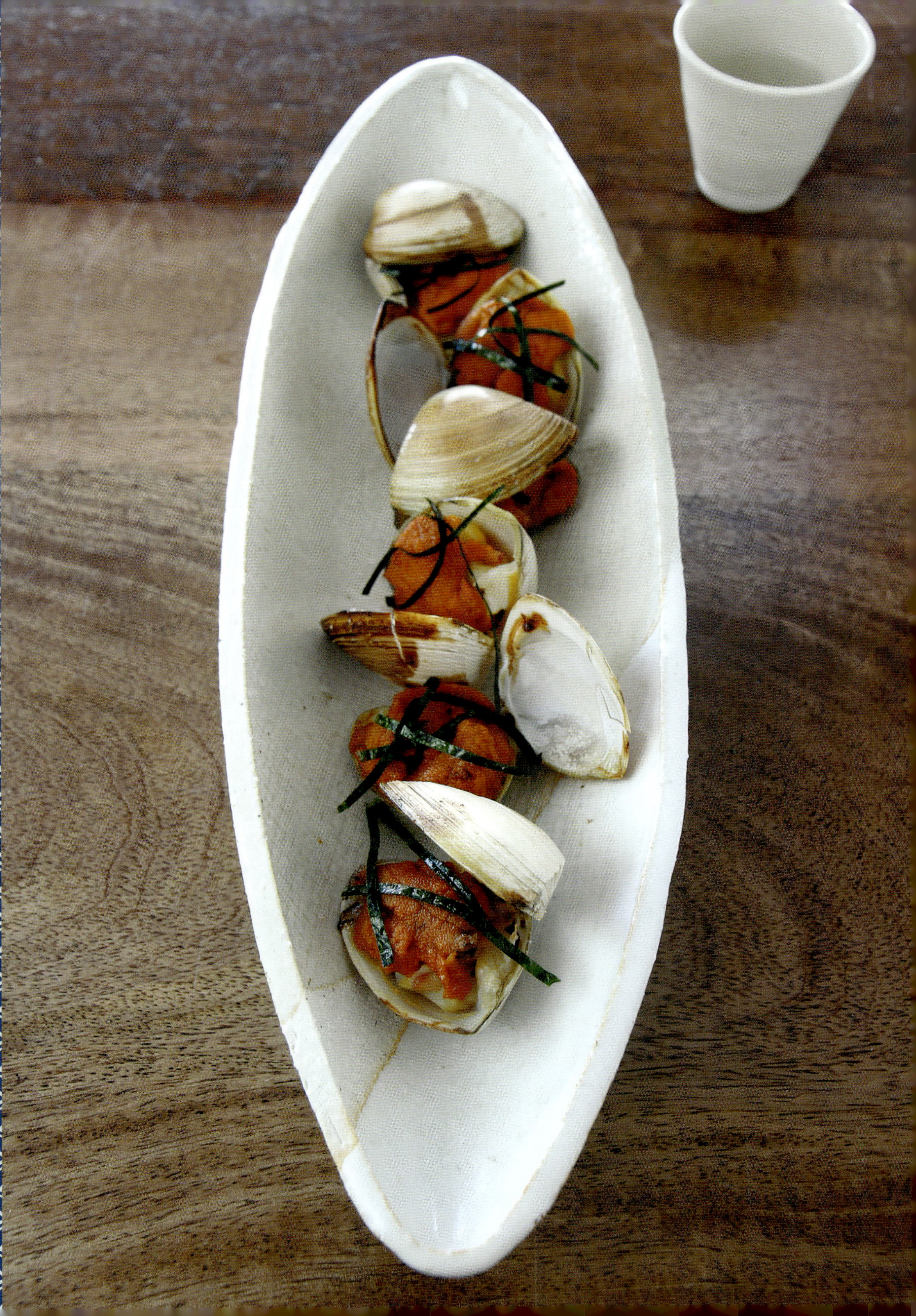

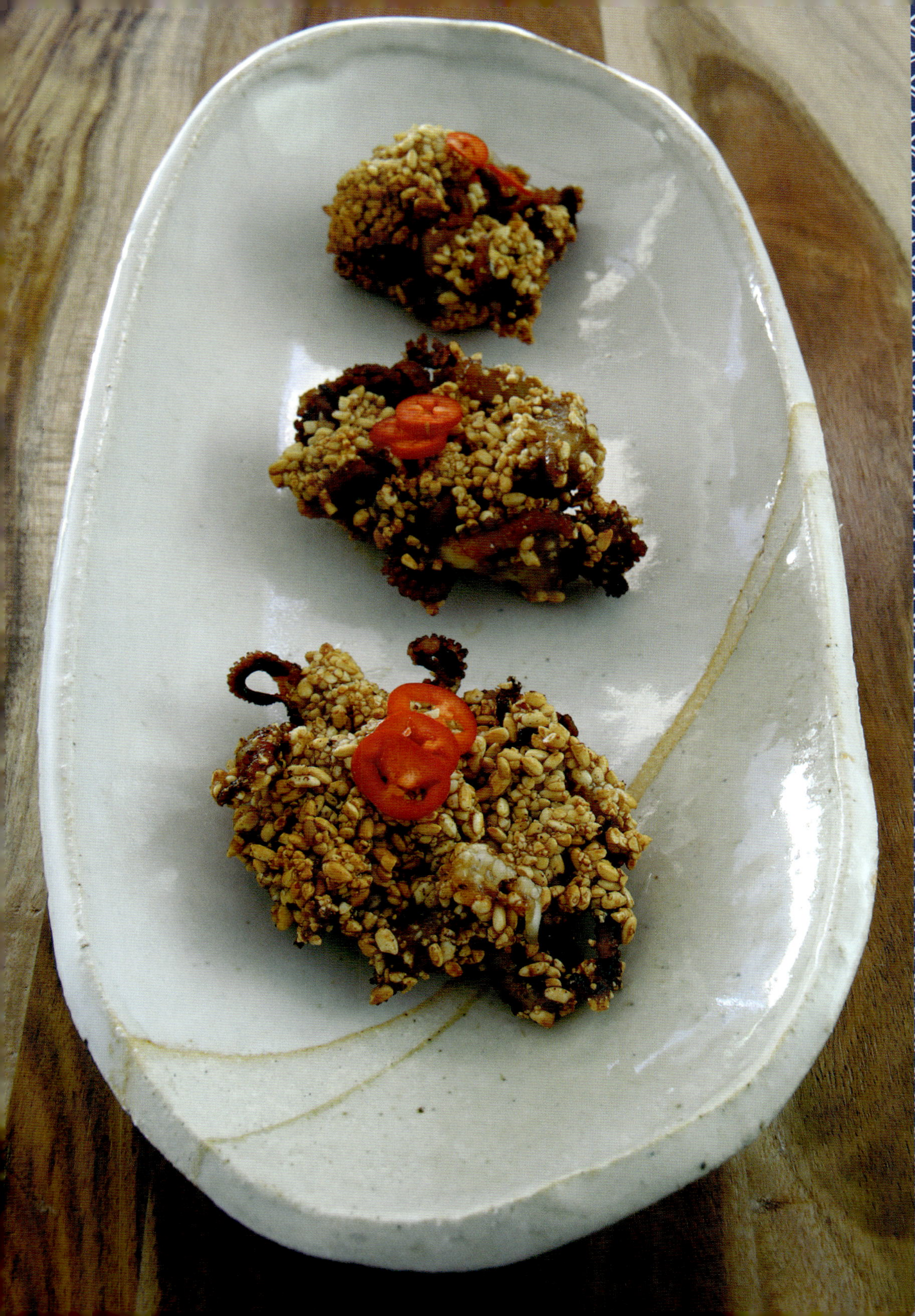

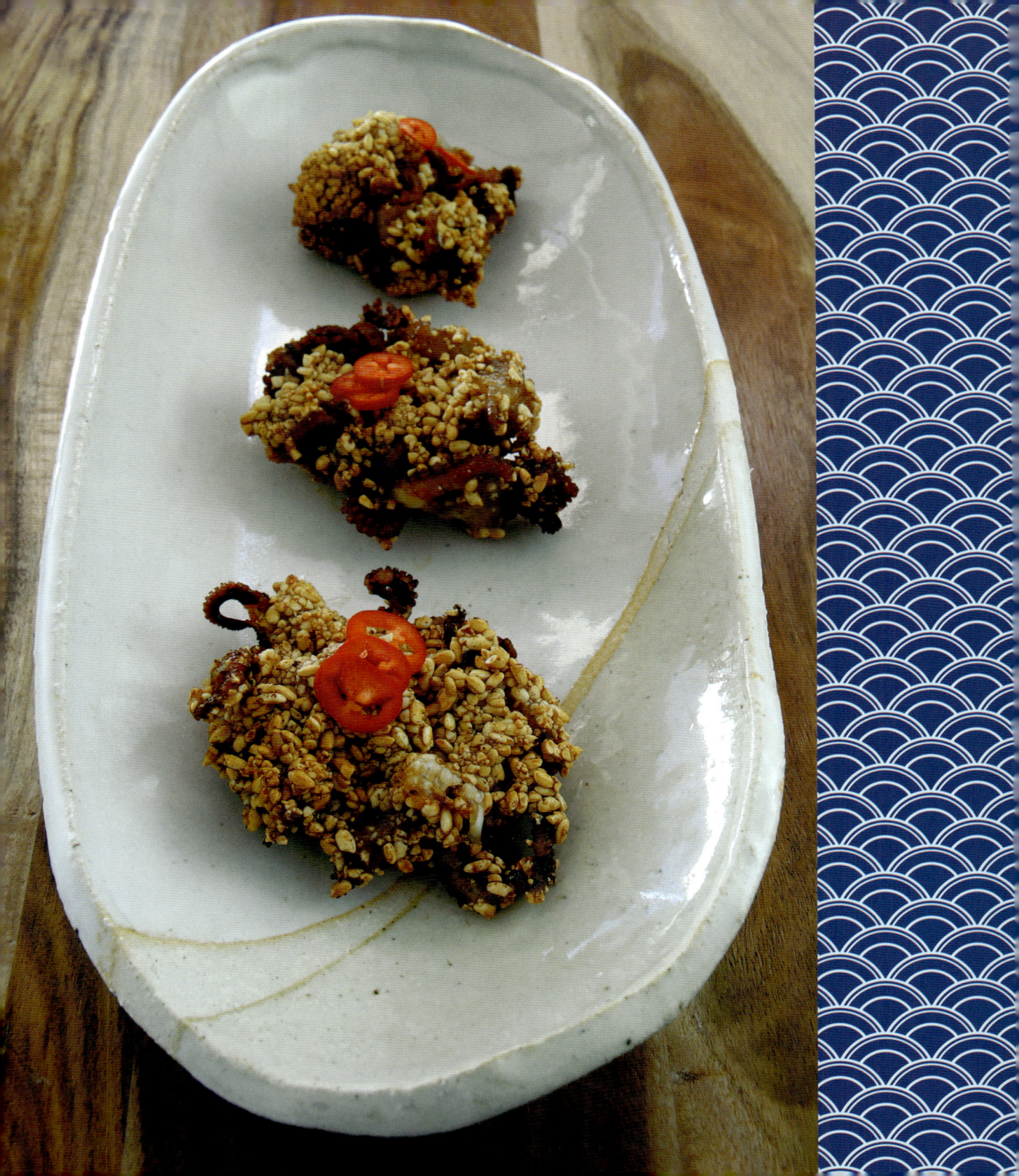

Baby octopus crackers

200g (7 oz) baby octopus
2 tbsp potato starch
4 tbsp awase-jyoyu (see Basics page)
100g (3½ oz) sticky rice, crushed
Vegetable oil for deep-fry
½ large red fresh chilli, sliced

一 With a rolling pin, bash octopus until flat.

二 Mix potato starch and awase-jyoyu in a bowl. Place octopus into the mixture.

三 Coat octopus with the sticky rice evenly and leave for 5 minutes to set.

四 Prepare oil and heat it to 180°C (355°F).

五 Deep-fry octopus until crispy.*

*When deep-frying octopus, please be careful of handling hot oil.

Steamed baby abalone

4 baby abalones
1 tsp salt
1 tbsp sake
1 tsp grated ginger
80g (2¾ oz) daikon, peeled and julienne
1 tsp potato starch, mixed with 1 tbsp water
2 tbsp awase-jyoyu

In this book, small bamboo steam baskets are used, but you may use a larger size.

一 Sprinkle salt and sake on the surface of the baby abalones and leave for 10 minutes.
二 Rinse the abalones.
三 Remove abalones from shells.
四 With a knife make slits on the surface of abalone.
五 Place each abalone in the steam baskets.
六 Arrange daikon and ginger on top of the abalone.
七 Prepare steamer and bring it to boil.
八 In the meantime, mix potato starch and awase-jyoyu.
九 Set abalone in the steamer and spoon sauce over each abalone.
十 Steam for about 5 minutes.

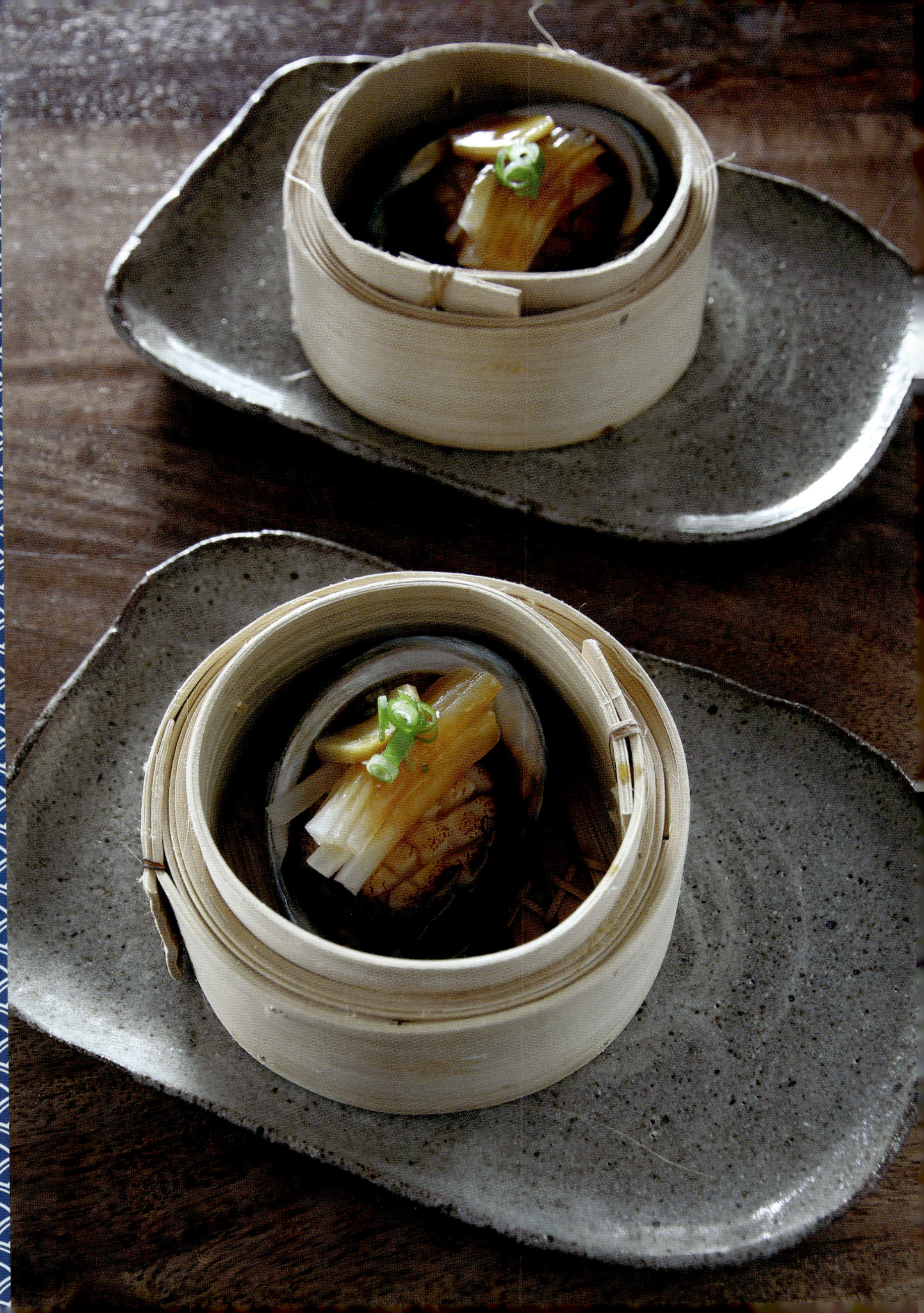

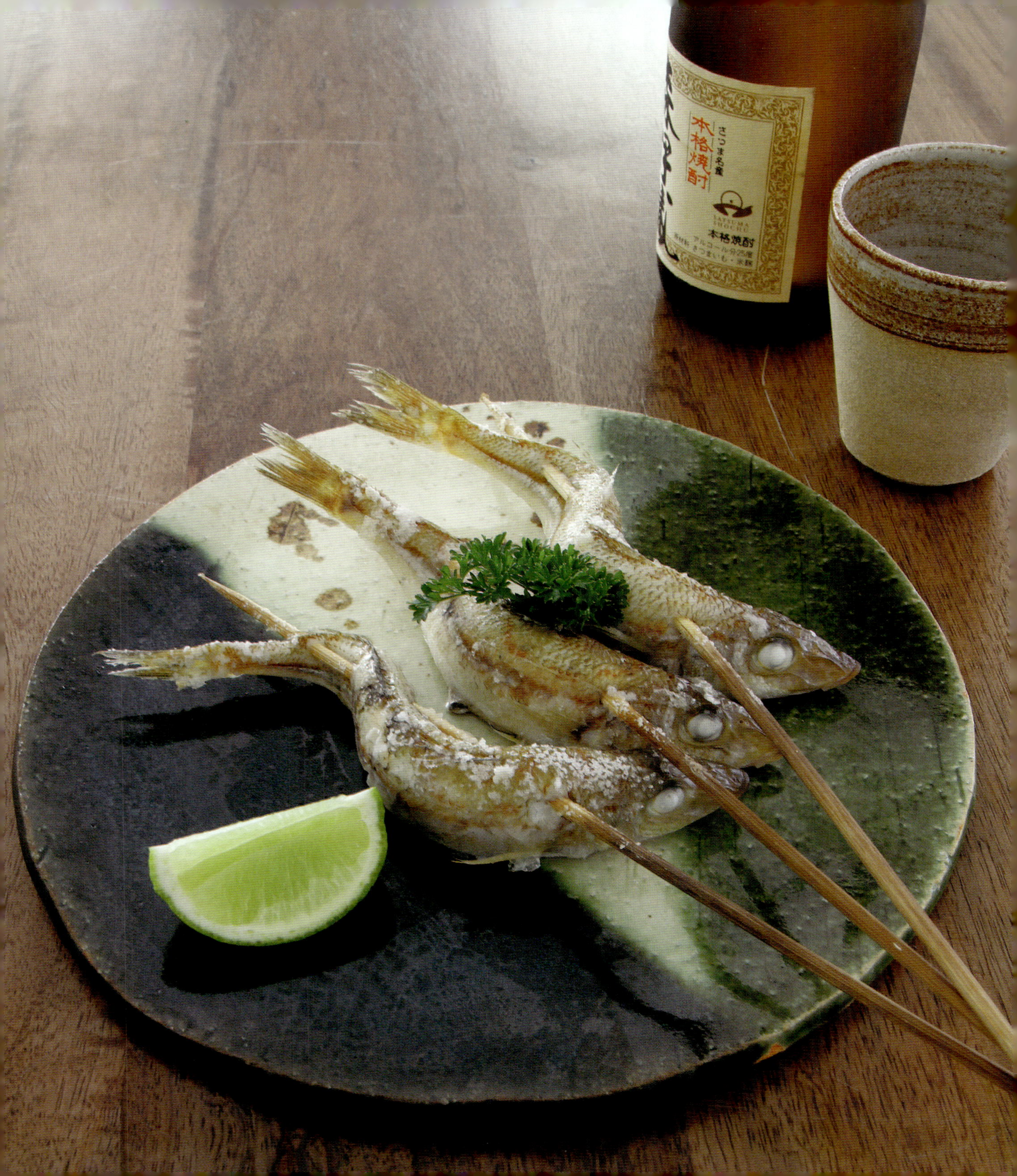
さつま名産
本格焼酎
本格焼酎

Grilled skewered whiting

SERVES 4
4 whiting (100-150g/3½–5¼ oz each)
1 tbsp sake
1 tbsp salt
4 lime or lemon wedges
Parsley for garnish
4 bamboo skewers

一 Preheat the oven to 190°C (375°F).

二 Remove scales form whiting using scalar or knife. Make a slit on belly side and remove guts and gills. Rinse under running water.

三 Insert bamboo skewer through the collar of each fish along the length of the body, coming out at the tail, using a weaving motion.

四 Sprinkle with sake and salt.

五 Place whiting in the oven and cook for 10 minutes or until cooked.

六 Serve on individual plates with lemon wedge and parsley for garnish.

Sardine tatsuta-age

4 sardines
1 tbsp soy sauce
1 tbsp mirin
Potato starch for coating
Vegetable oil
4 tbsp grated daikon
1 stem spring onion, trimmed and chopped

一 Cut head off sardine. Insert knife from shoulder toward the tail. With fingers, gut out and with a tip of knife remove the bone.

二 Add soy sauce and mirin in a tray and marinate sardine for 10 minutes.

三 Pat sardines with kitchen paper to remove excess liquid.

四 Coat with potato starch and set aside for 5 minutes.

五 Heat oil in pan to 170°C (340°F) and deep-fry sardines in oil until lightly browned.

六 Drain oil over a rack or kitchen paper.

七 Serve with grated daikon and top with spring onion.

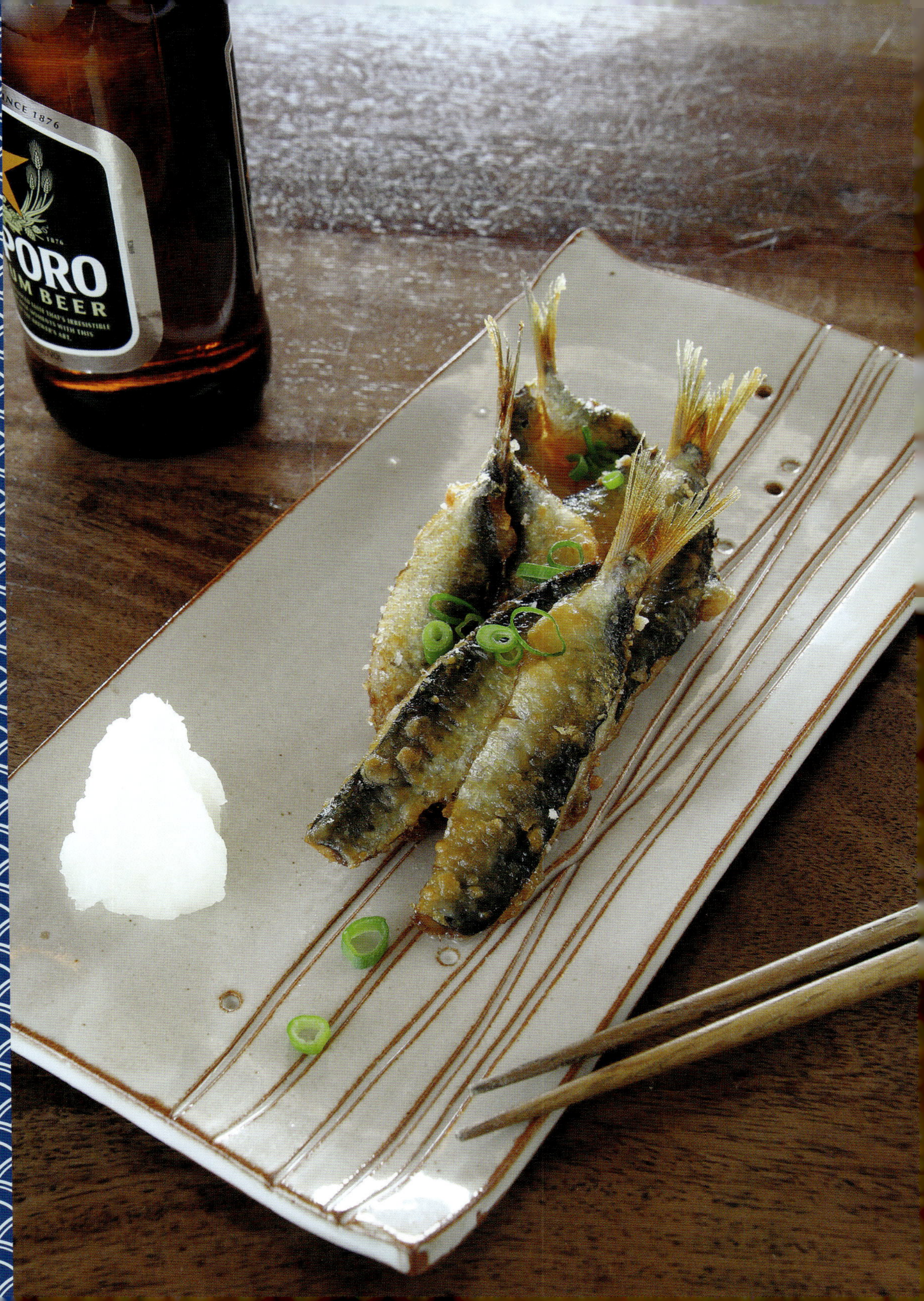
NCE 1876
PORO
UM BEER

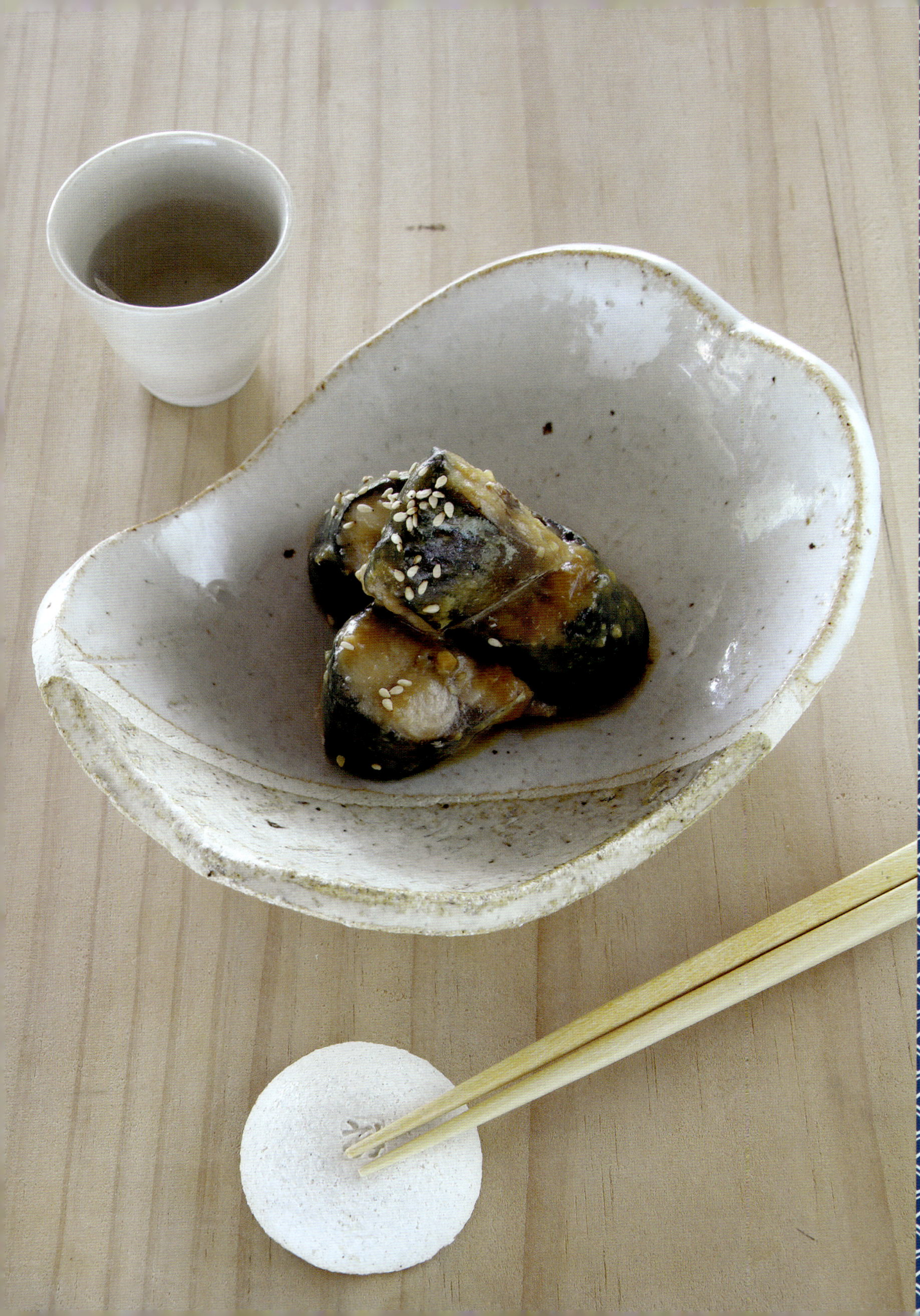

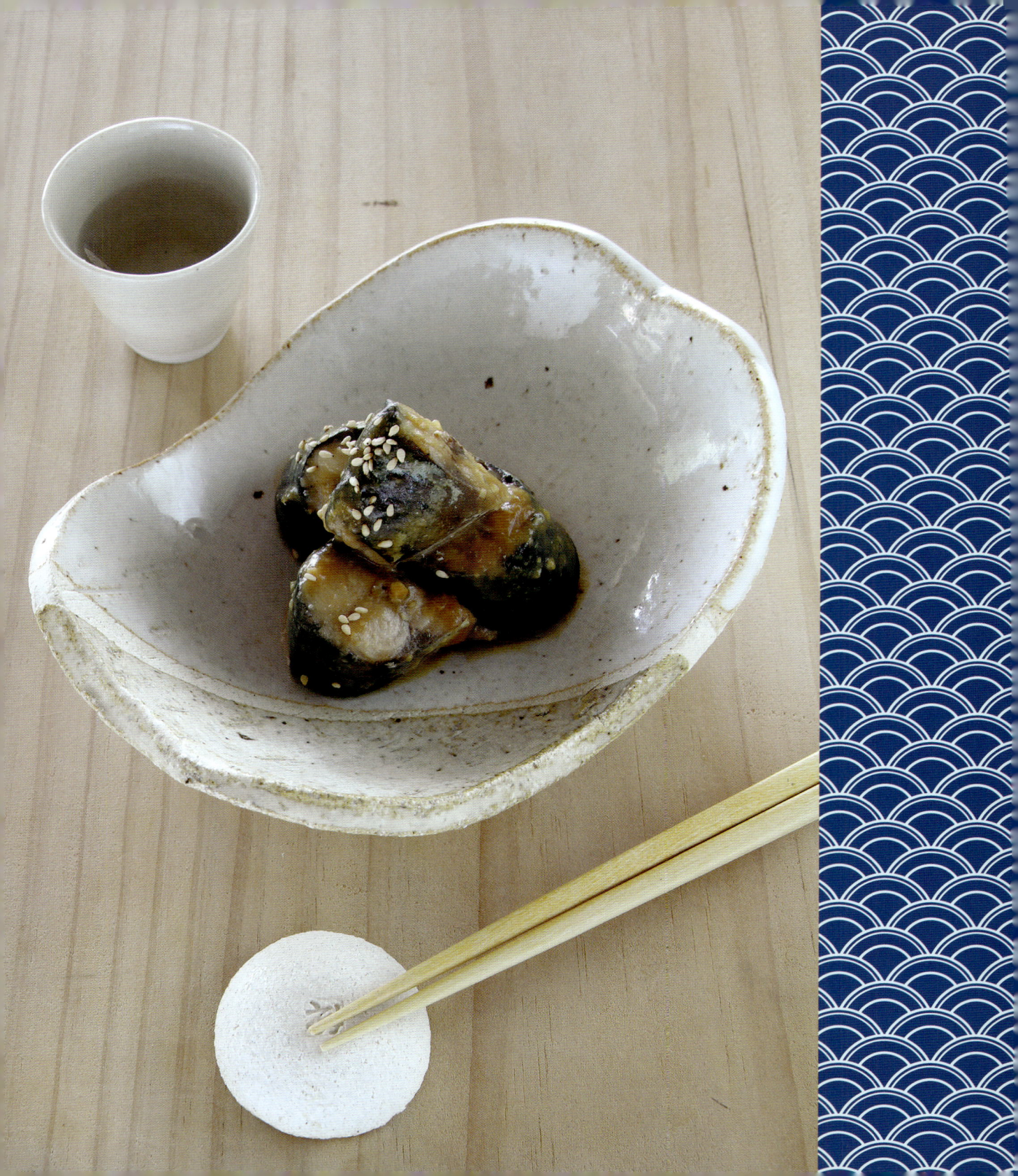

Mackerel cooked in miso

240g (8½ oz) mackerel fillet or about 500g (17½ oz) whole

½ cup water

1 tbsp sake

3 tbsp mirin

1 tbsp raw or caster sugar

40g (1½ oz) ginger, peeled and sliced

4 tbsp miso

1 tsp white roasted sesame seeds

A drop lid or use baking paper the size of a big pan as a dropping lid

一 Fillet mackerel in sanmai-oroshi (into 3 pieces, see page 156). Cut each fillet in half lengthways. With the tip of the knife, make a crisscross slit.

二 Add water in a pan and bring it to the boil.

三 Add 1 tbsp sake, mirin, sugar and ginger. Once it has boiled, arrange fillets in the pan skin side up without overlapping each other.

四 Bring to boil and spoon sauce over the fillet. Once the colour of the fish has changed, place a drop lid or baking paper on top of the fillet and simmer for 10 minutes.

五 Mix miso with some sauce in the pan until dissolved.

六 Pour miso over the fillet and simmer for another 5 minutes with a lid on.

Arrange mackerel in a shallow bowl and sprinkle sesame seeds.

Saikyo-style grilled cod

200g (7 oz) cod fillet
80g (2¾ oz) saikyo-miso
1 tbsp mirin
2 tbsp caster sugar
2 stems spring onion, (the white part), trimmed and sliced julienne lengthways

一 Cut the cod into two pieces.
二 Mix saikyo-miso, mirin and caster sugar and marinate cod in the paste overnight.
三 Lightly pat off miso from cod and grill until lightly brown.
四 Also grill spring onion stems.
五 Arrange cod with spring onion on side.

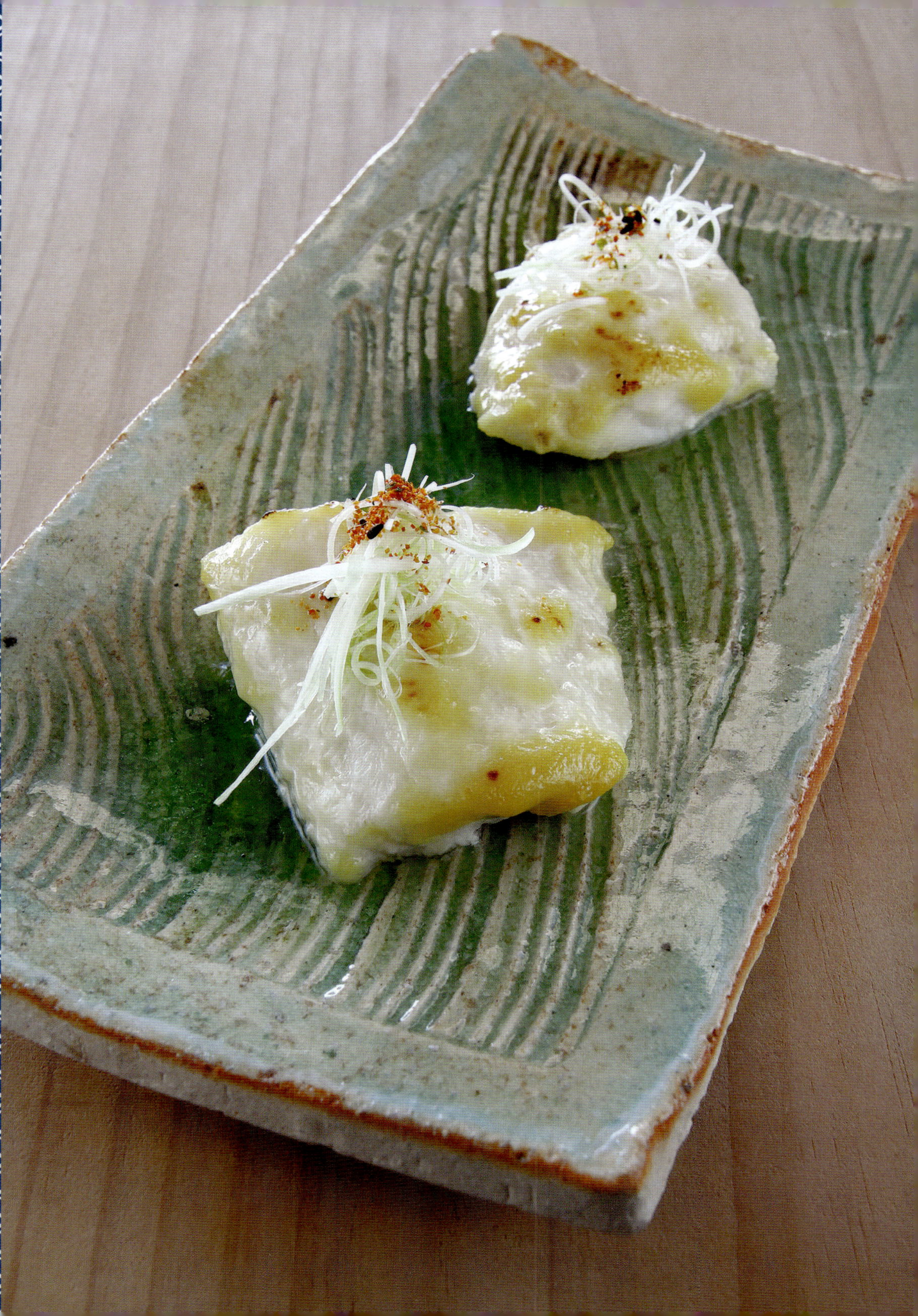

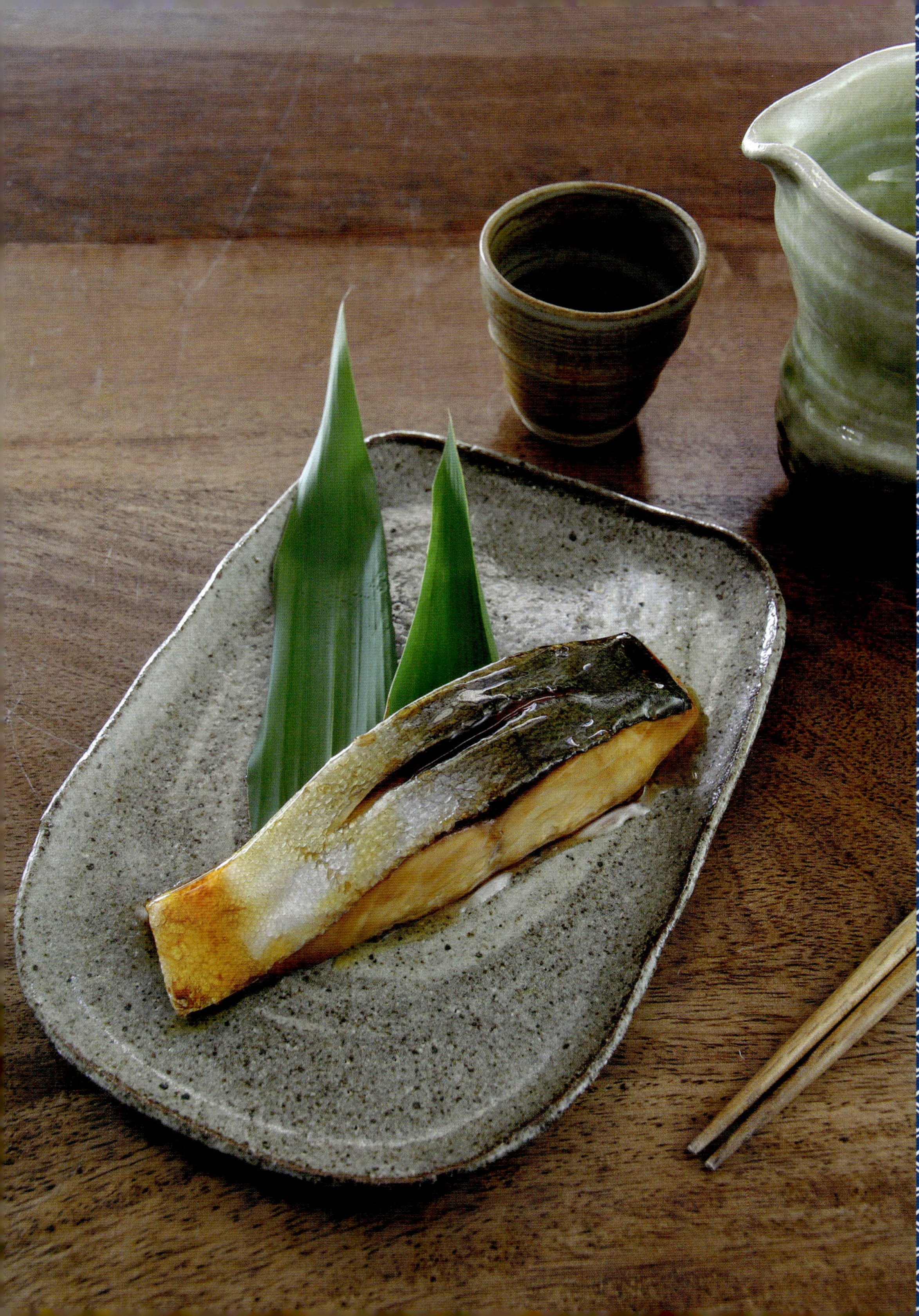

Teriyaki kingfish

SERVES 2

2 small king fish fillets, 45g (1½ oz) each
30g (1 oz) Teriyaki sauce, (see Basics page)

— Marinate kingfish in a teriyaki sauce for 1 hour.

二 Pat kingfish with kitchen paper.

三 Grill kingfish for 2 minutes and brush with teriyaki sauce, repeat a couple of times until cooked.

Hotate with soy sauce butter

SERVES 2

4 Hotate: scallops
Freshly grounded salt and pepper
1 tbsp of butter
1 tsp soy sauce
1 stem spring onion, trimmed and chopped

一 Crack salt and pepper over the scallops.

二 Place butter in a frying pan and heat the pan over moderate heat, and cook butter until slightly golden, swirling the pan continuously. Add scallops and cook both sides.

三 Add soy sauce and simmer for 2 minutes or until the sauce slightly thickens, spooning soy sauce butter over the scallops.

四 Serve onto the plate and sprinkle spring onion.

Saikyo style grilled scallops

4 sashimi quality scallops
1 tbsp olive oil
1 tbsp saikyo-miso
1 tbsp sake
2 kumquat, sliced

一 Sprinkle olive oil over the scallops.

二 Combine saikyo-miso and sake in a small container or bowl.

三 Marinate scallops in the miso mixture and keep it in refrigerator for half an hour.

四 Pat scallops with a kitchen paper.

五 Preheat grill and grill scallops until lightly brown.

六 Top with sliced kumquat and bring back to the griller and grill until lightly scorched.

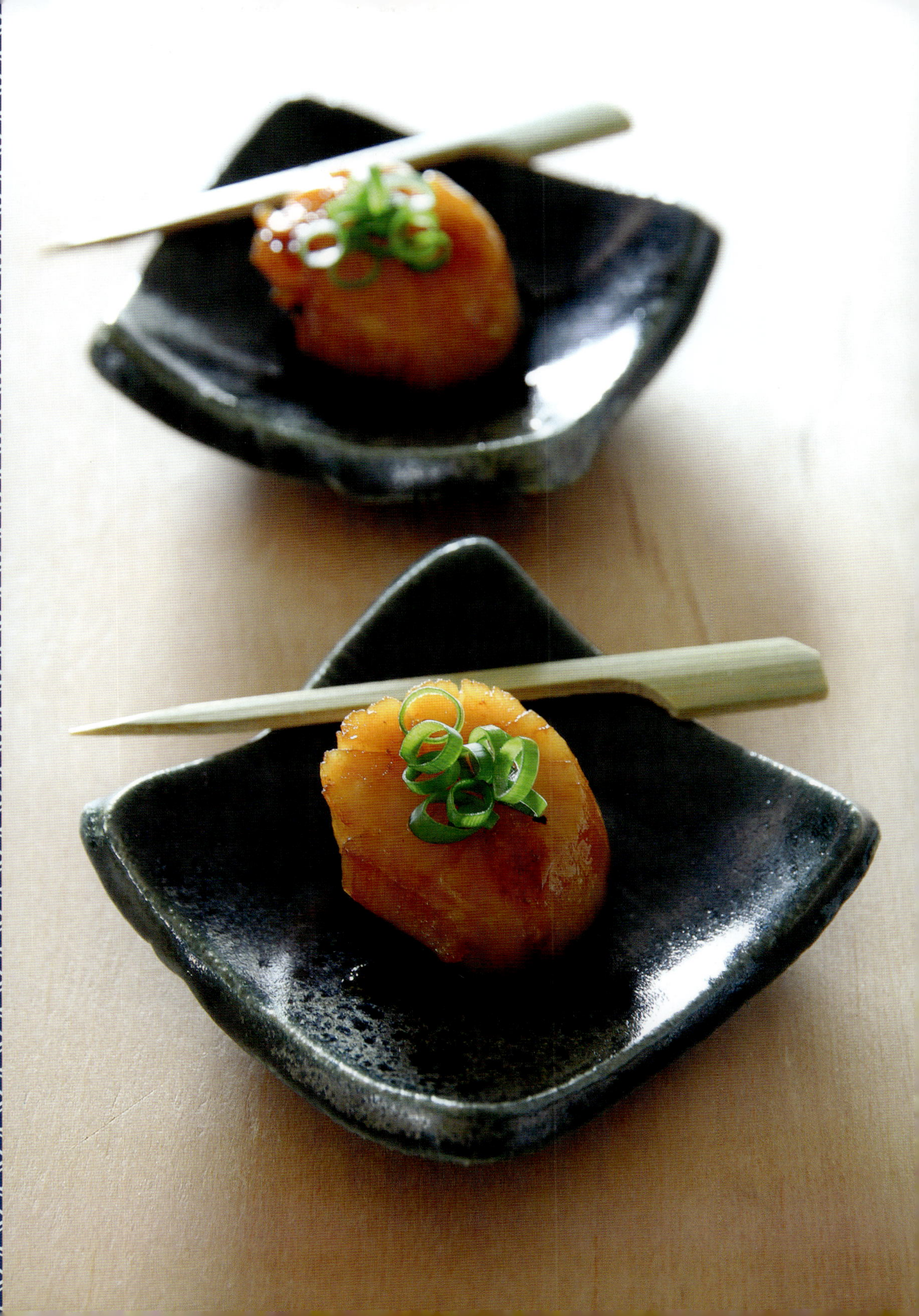

九デシリットル

Rice

Basics
    Preparing rice
        Preparing sushi rice

Sushi
    Mini ura-maki: Mini inside-out roll
    Hoso-maki
    Nigiri

Yaki-onigiri: Soy sauce flavoured grilled rice ball

Garlic rice

Ochazuke, rice in tea broth

Zosui: Egg and rice porridge

Kamameshi: Steamed rice with shiitake, enoki mushroom and oyster in a pot

BASICS
Preparing rice

3 cups short grain rice (japonica)
3 cups water

It is essential to have a rice cooker at home to cook rice.

一 Using the measuring cup provided with the rice cooker, measure 3 cups of rice into the bowl from the rice cooker.

二 Pour water into the cooking bowl until it just covers the rice. Holding the bowl with one hand, stir rice briskly for 10–15 seconds with the other hand.

三 Carefully tip the milky water out, covering rice with one hand.

四 For the second and third rinse, add ample water and stir for about 30 seconds to remove excess starch. Tip out the water.

五 Drain over a fine-mesh sieve and leave for 30 minutes.

六 Place rice and measured water into the rice cooker pan.

七 Wipe the underneath of the pan properly with a dry towel and set it in the rice cooker.

八 Leave for another 30 minutes then cook.

九 When cooked, leave for 20 minutes to steam.

十 Before serving, turn rice over gently with a moistened rice paddle to allow excess moisture to escape as steam.

Preparing sushi rice

Cooked sushi rice (see opposite for method)
½ cup rice vinegar
3 tbsp or ⅓ cup fine caster sugar
A small pinch of salt

Note: pre-made sushi vinegar (awase-zu) is also available, either liquid or powder.

一 To make the sushi vinaigrette, mix rice vinegar, sugar and salt in a bowl, until sugar has dissolved.

二 Moisten the wooden bowl.

三 Using a damp rice paddle, transfer the hot cooked rice into the bowl.

四 Spread rice evenly in the bowl. Gradually pour sushi vinaigrette over the rice.

五 Mix the rice evenly around the bowl with a slicing action.

六 While mixing, cool the rice with a hand fan so that the rice absorbs the vinegar mixture and becomes glossy.

七 Cover with a muslin cloth and let it cool down until slightly warm.

IZAKAYA • RICE

SUSHI
Mini ura-maki: Mini inside-out roll

TO MAKE 2 ROLLS
160g (5½ oz) sushi rice
1 nori sheet, half
Choose filling as preference
Soy sauce and wasabi to serve

一 Place nori on the bamboo mat. With wet fingers spread rice all over the nori. Spread a piece of plastic wrap over the rice.

二 Place one hand on top of the plastic wrap, one hand underneath the mat and gently turn up side down.

三 Remove the mat and place it underneath. The resulting arrangement is now the bamboo mat on the bottom, then the plastic wrap, rice and nori on top.

四 With your finger draw a thin line of wasabi and mayonnaise along the nori. Place fillings along the entre of the nori. Using both dry hands, roll up and two thirds of the way.

五 Lift the mat and pull free the edge of the plastic wrap so it doesn't get caught in the roll. Roll the last bit, and remove the mat but not the plastic.

六 With a sharp wet knife, cut in half and cut both rolls twice to give 6 pieces.

七 Remove the plastic wrap. Decorate with some toppings such as Tobbiko, roasted sesame seeds, etc.

八 Repeat with another nori sheet.

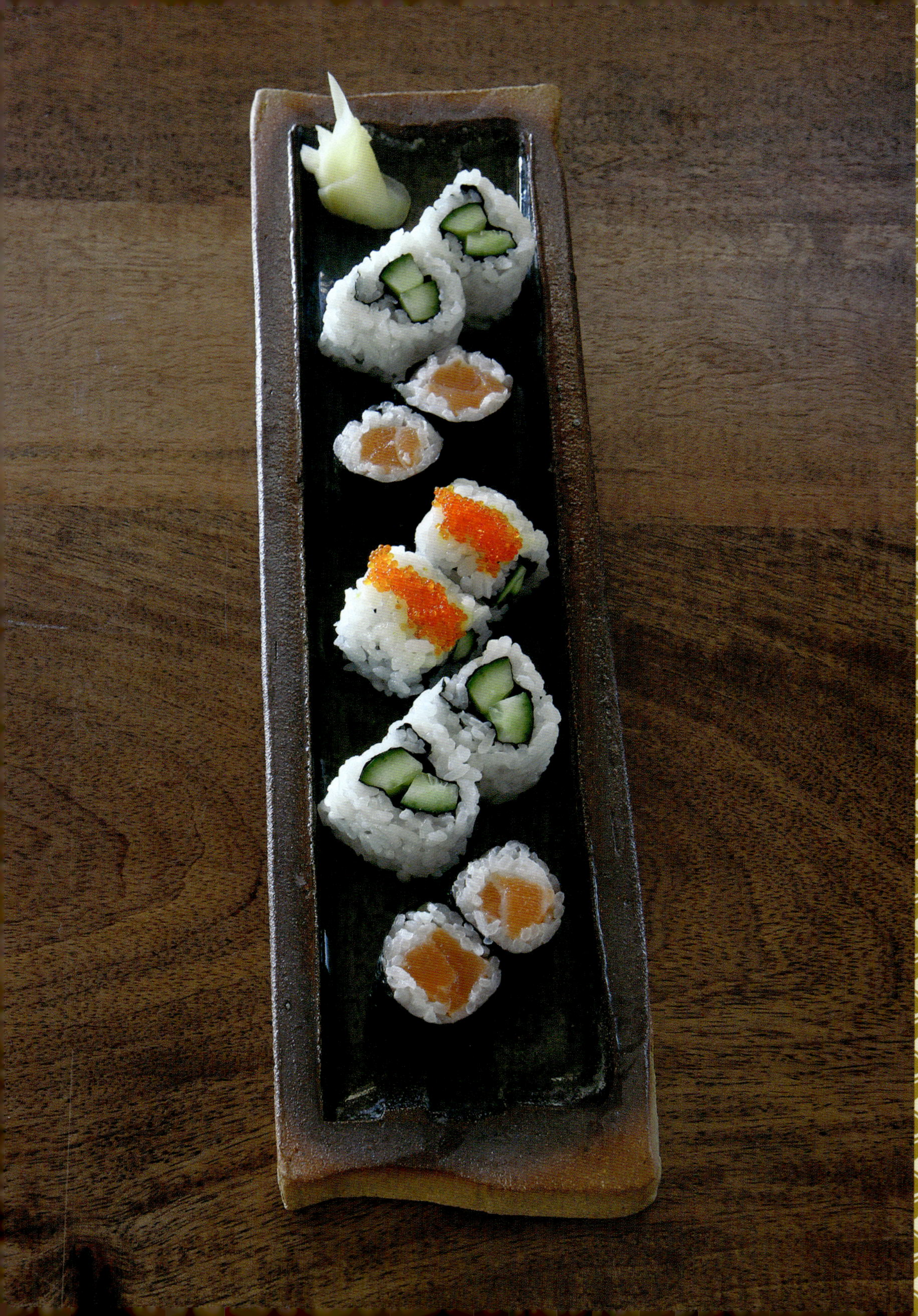

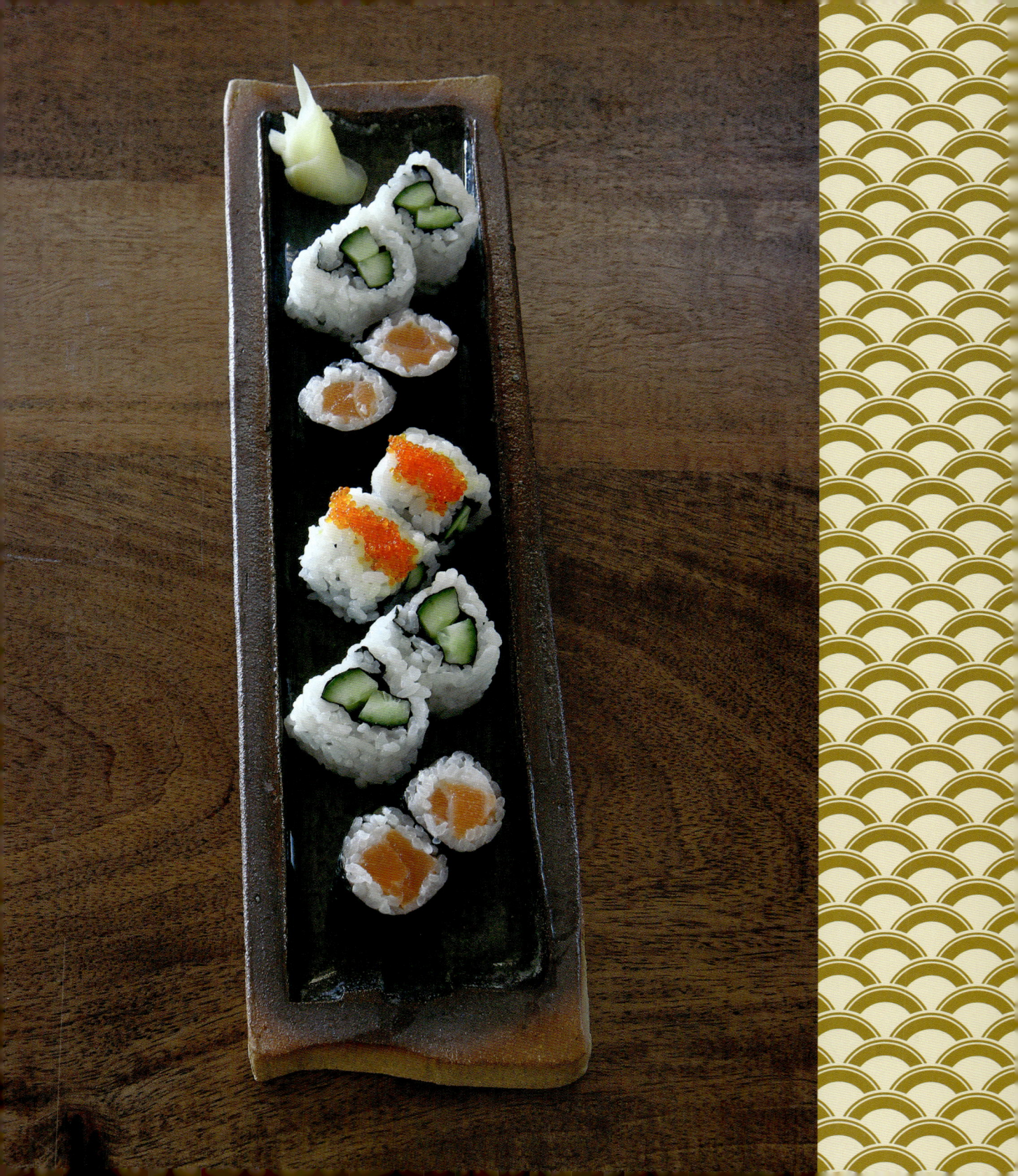

Hoso-maki

TO MAKE 1 THIN ROLL
80g (2¾ oz) of sushi rice
1 nori sheet, half
Fillings, such as
VEGETABLES: cucumber, carrot, asparagus, avocado
FISH: such as sashimi (raw fish) slices, imitation crab stick, can of fish
Chicken, beef or pork in teriyaki, sausages
OTHERS: cheese stick
UTENSILS: bamboo sushi mat, tezu (bowl of water or vinegar water)

一 Cover a sushi bamboo mat with a sheet of plastic wrap, folding it over the edges to attach it to the back of the mat.

二 Place the half nori sheet on the mat.

三 Dip right fingers in water.

四 With moistened fingers, spread rice over the nori, covering the entire sheet.

五 Carefully pick up rice-covered nori by the corners and quickly turn it over and place upside down on the mat.

六 Arrange fillings along centre of nori.

七 Roll rice and nori on the mat, pressing in on ingredients with your fingertips, stopping 2cm (¾ inch) short of the end.

八 Lift up mat, roll back a little, then roll forward to join the edges.

九 Use gentle pressure to shape, either round, oval or square.

十 Transfer the roll onto a dry board and with a moistened knife cut each roll in half, then cut both rolls twice to give 6 equal-sized pieces.

十一 Repeat with another nori sheet.

IZAKAYA • RICE

Nigiri

TO MAKE 8 PIECES
About 160g (5½ oz) sushi rice
8 pieces toppings, such as kingfish, salmon and cuttlefish
About 1 tsp of wasabi paste in a bowl
Soy sauce for serving
UTENSILS: Tezu (bowl of water or vinegar water)

一 Prepare all of the toppings.

二 Moisten hand with the vinegar water and pick up about 1 tbsp of rice. Form into an oval shape, pressing gently with the hand, but do not squeeze too tightly.

三 Place one topping in the palm of your other hand. Spread on a dab of wasabi with one finger.

五 Place rice on the topping and with index and middle fingers press firmly to form a mounded shape.

六 Roll sushi over and press again with two fingers against the topping.

七 Rotate sushi 360-degrees and press again with two fingers against the topping.

八 Arrange on a platter. Garnish with pickled ginger and serve with soy sauce.

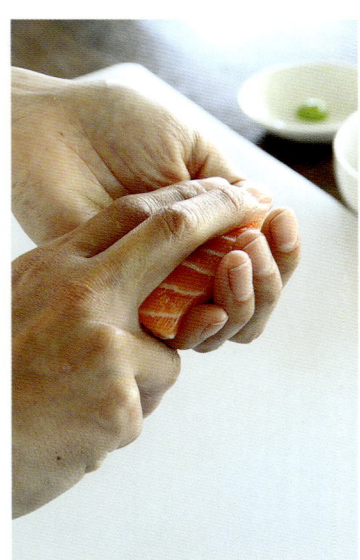

RICE • IZAKAYA

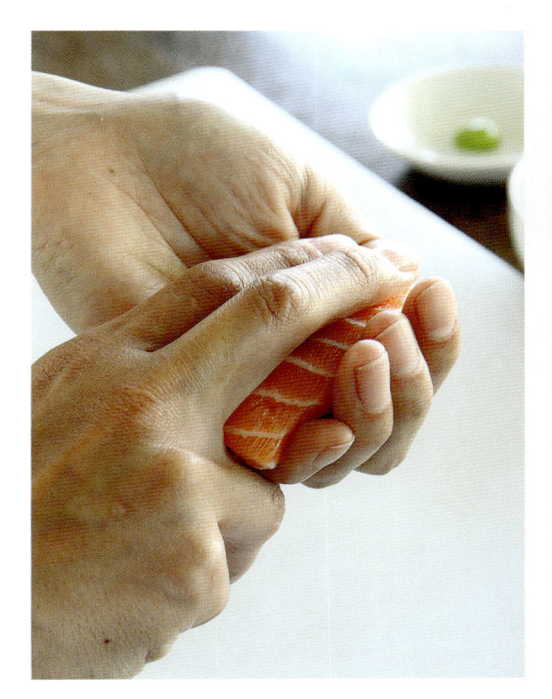

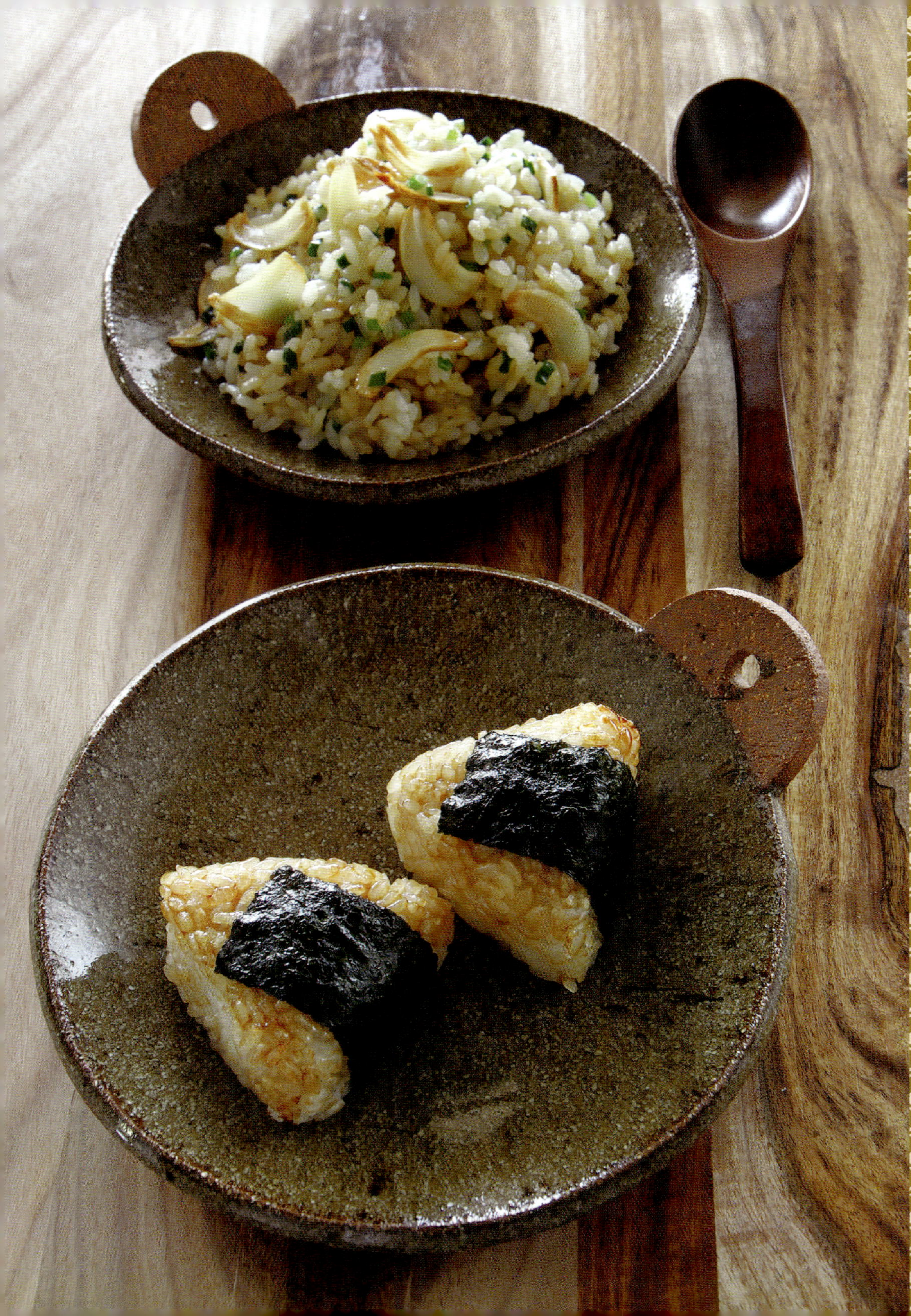

Yaki-onigiri: soy sauce flavoured grilled rice ball

TO MAKE 4 RICE BALLS

Approx. 4 cups hot cooked rice

Awase-jyoyu (see Basics page) for brushing

4 roasted nori strips

一 Prepare a bowl of water with a pinch of salt.

二 Dip hands into salty water to moisten.

三 Transfer a cup of rice into the palm of your hand. Using both hands, mould the rice into a triangular shape. Press the rice only just hard enough to keep the rice firmly together.

四 Brush awase-jyoyu over the onigiri and grill or cook in a non-stick pan with a little oil until lightly scorched.

五 Wrap a strip of nori around the edge.

Garlic rice

SERVES 2

4 cloves garlic, peeled and sliced

1 tbsp vegetable oil

2 cups cooked rice

1 tbsp chopped garlic chives

1 tbsp butter

½ tbsp soy sauce

Salt and pepper to taste

一 Place garlic, oil and butter in a frying pan.

二 Over low heat, gradually heat the oil and cook garlic until lightly brown.

三 Transfer garlic to a plate.

四 Place rice in a frying pan and over moderate heat stir for 3 minutes or until cooked through.

五 Add chopped garlic chives and stir for about 30 seconds.

六 Return the garlic to the rice and add butter, and stir well.

七 Add soy sauce and to taste with salt and pepper.

八 Serve onto a bowl or plate.

Ochazuke: rice in tea broth

SERVES 2

2 cups cooked rice

200g (7 oz) salmon fillet, salted and grilled

2 tsp roasted white sesame seeds

2 pinches Nori flakes, cut ½ whole sushi nori into julienne or tear into small pieces

Wasabi for serving

Green tea, such as genmai-cha, hoji-cha, ban-cha

一 Flake grilled salmon.

二 Serve cooked rice in a slightly bigger rice bowl.

三 Top salmon and sprinkle sesame seeds and nori.

四 Put wasabi on the edge of the bowl.

五 Pour over green tea before eating.

This is a simple dish with rice. A bowl of rice eaten with green tea, served with pickled vegetables on top or as a side dish. Ochazuke is likely eaten at the end of a meal.

Other accompaniments are, mentaiko (salted pollack roe), umeboshi (pickled plum), or nori flakes.

Zosui: Egg and rice porridge

SERVES 4

200g (7 oz) cooked rice

3 cups dashi or chicken stock

1 tsp salt or 1 tbsp soy sauce

1 egg

Shredded nori or chopped shallots for topping

Roasted white sesame seeds for topping

一 Place cooked rice in a strainer and rinse to loosen grains. Drain well.

二 Add dashi in a pan, flavour with salt or soy sauce. Add rice and lightly mix.

三 Cook over low heat for 5 minutes.

四 Whisk egg and pour egg over the rice.

五 With a spoon, gently stir through and cover with a lid. Remove from heat and steam for 3 minutes.

六 Serve in a bowl, with the addition of nori or shallots and sesame seeds.

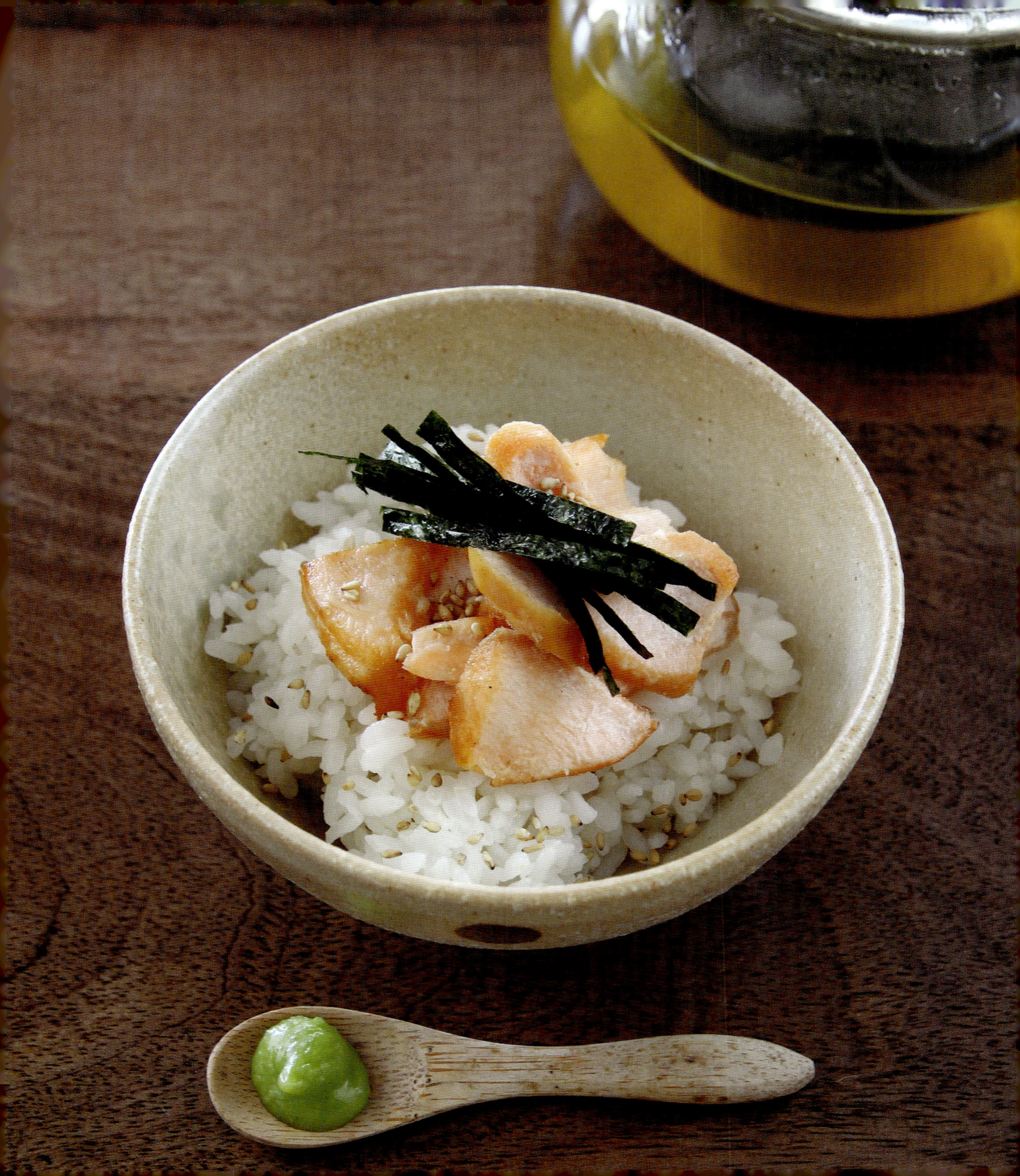

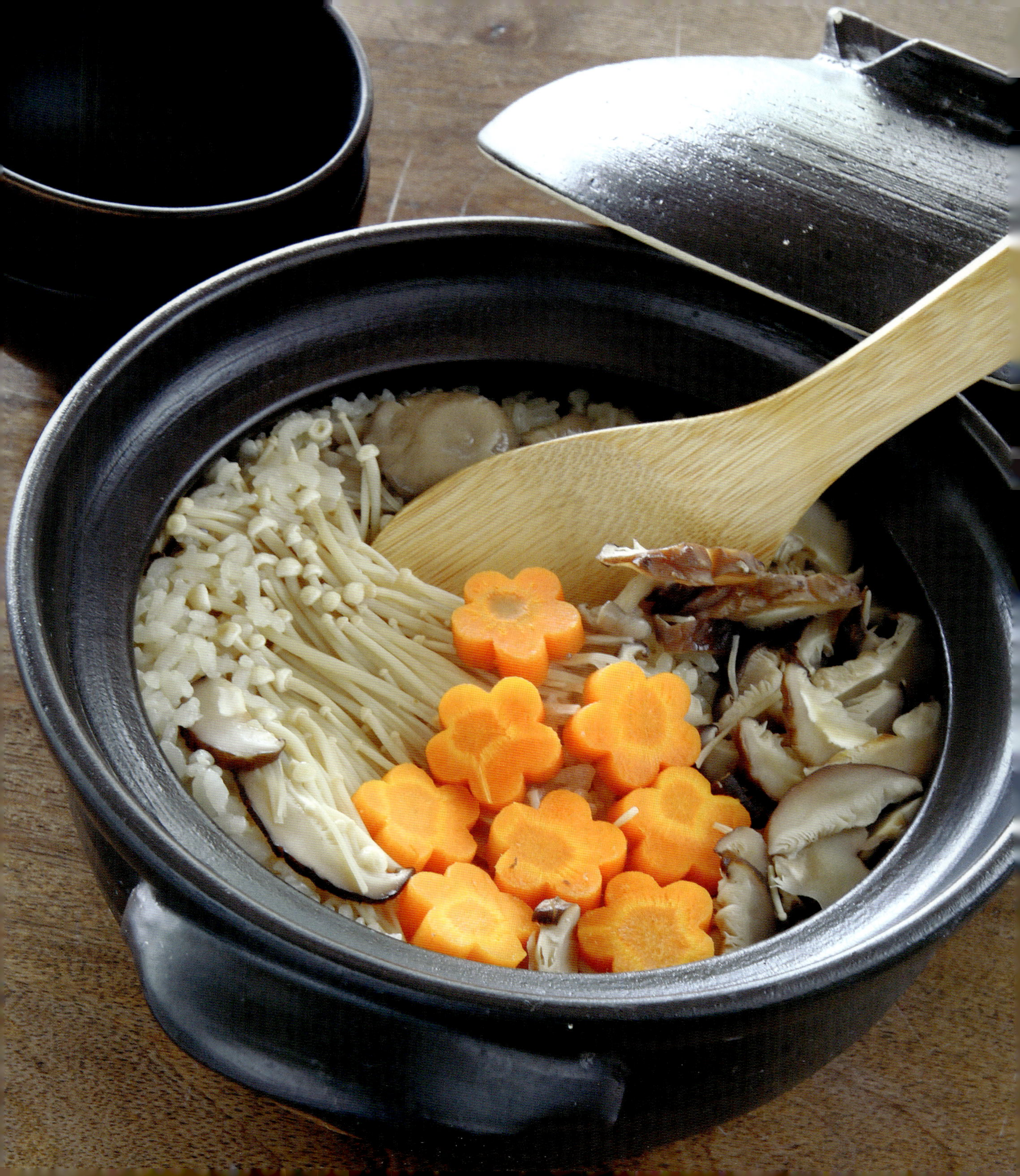

Kamameshi: Steamed rice with shiitake, enoki mushroom and oyster in a pot

SERVES 4

2 cups short grain rice

8 pieces flower-shaped carrot

4 dried shiitake mushrooms, soaked in water, discard the stem, and slice

¼ bunch enoki mushroom, discard the dark bottom parts

1 tsp sake

2 cups dashi (see Basics page)

1 tsp mirin

1 tsp soy sauce

A pinch salt

4 oysters

一 Rinse and drain rice.

二 Place rice in an earthen pot and add shiitake and enoki.

三 Add sake, stock, mirin, soy sauce and salt.

四 Put a lid on and bring it to the boil over low heat and cook for about 10 minutes.

六 Add oyster and cook for 5 minutes, then steam for 5 minutes.

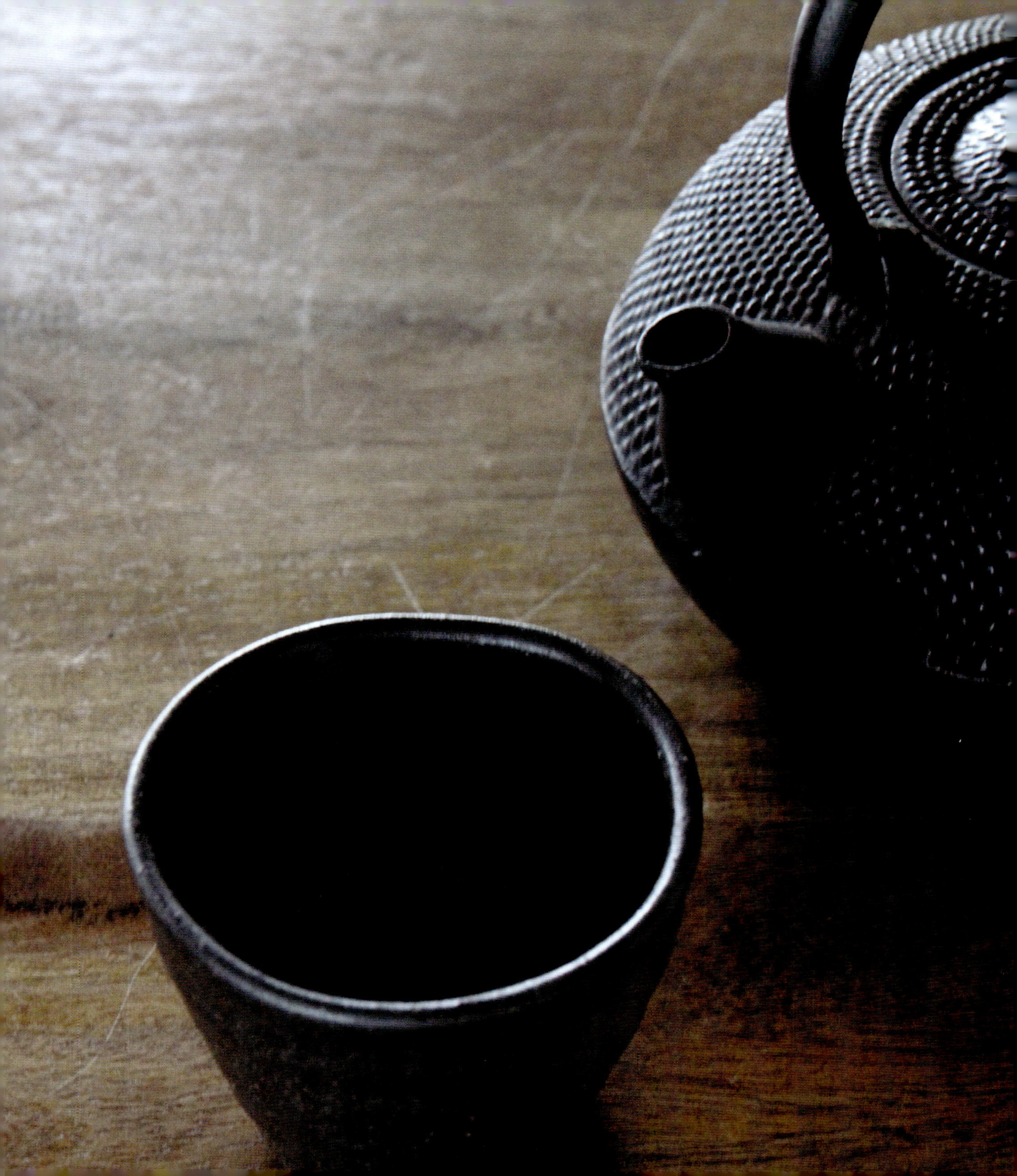

Dessert

Hojicha ice cream

Mattcha ice cream with sweet red beans

Wafu Danish

Green tea roll cake

Black sugar creme brulee

Black sesame seed ice cream

Black sesame cake

Umeshu jelly

Sake and peach sorbet

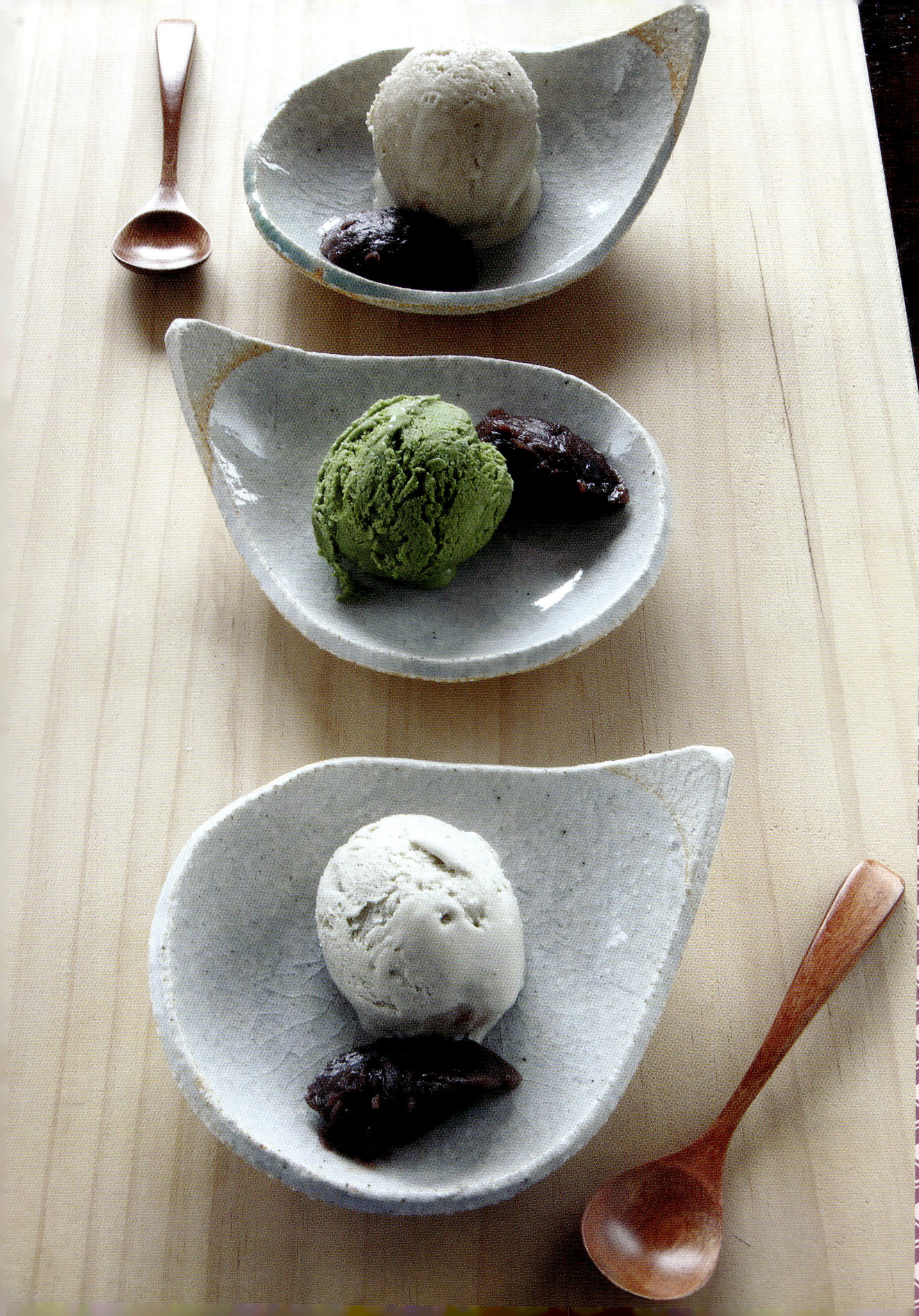

Hojicha ice cream

120ml (4 fl oz) water
10g (⅓ oz) hojicha: roasted green tea
160ml (5½ fl oz) milk
2 egg yolks
90g (3 oz) raw or caster sugar
150ml (5 fl oz) thickened cream

一 Bring the water to boil in a pan and add the hojicha, and infuse over low heat to extract flavour of tea for 1 minute and rest for 5 minutes with a lid on.

二 Add the milk to tea and bring it to boil.

三 Remove from heat and steam for 5 minutes.

四 In the meantime, place the egg yolk and sugar and whisk until it becomes pale.

五 Strain milk tea into another pan and bring it to the boil.

六 Gradually pour the hot milk mixture into the egg, stirring with a wooden spoon.

七 Make the mixture into custard by cooking over a double boiler or low heat to the ribbon stage, stirring continuously with a wooden spoon. Set aside and cool it down.

八 Whip thickened cream until it forms stiff peaks.

九 Mix cream and egg custard and churn mixture in an ice cream machine.

Mattcha ice cream with sweet red beans

¼ cup caster sugar
3 egg yolks
150ml (5 fl oz) cream
200ml (6¾ oz) milk
3 tbsp of green tea powder mixed with
    3 tbsp of hot water

一 In a bowl, whisk the sugar and egg yolks together until pale.

二 Place the milk in a pan and bring it to boil.

三 Gradually pour the hot milk into the mixture, stirring with a wooden spoon.

四 Transfer the mixture into a pan.

五 Make the mixture into custard by cooking over a double boiler or over low heat to the ribbon stage, stirring continuously with a wooden spoon.

六 Add green tea mixture and combine well.

七 Transfer the mixture into a bowl and churn mixture in an ice cream machine.

TO PREPARE SWEET RED BEANS:

Makes about 700g (24½ oz)
300g (3½ oz) azuki beans: red beans
270g (9½ oz) caster sugar
A pinch of salt
Water to cook

一 Place azuki beans in the sieve and rinse under running water.

二 Transfer azuki to a pan and add water up to 5cm (2 inches) above the beans and soak in water for more than 4 hours or overnight.

三 Bring it to boil and add a glass of cold water, this makes the beans soften evenly inside. Bring it to boil again, sieve and rinse lightly.

四 Transfer the beans back to a pot and add water, bring it to boil.

五 Simmer for 40 minutes or until the beans soften, occasionally add water to cover the beans. When cooked, drain over a strainer and transfer back to the pot. Add sugar and salt and cook over low heat, stirring gently with a wooden spoon for about 10 minutes or the paste thickens. Remove from the heat and cool it down.

Wafu Danish

1 pastry sheet, cut into 12 strips
250g (8¾ oz) sweet red bean paste
½ pear, sliced into 12

一 Preheat the oven to 180°C (355°F).

二 Lay baking paper over a baking tray.

三 Cut one pastry into 6 rectangular shapes.

四 Arrange the pastries on the tray evenly.

五 Spoon red beans on the centre.

六 Bake for 20 minutes or until slightly golden.

七 Take out of the oven and cool down on a rack.

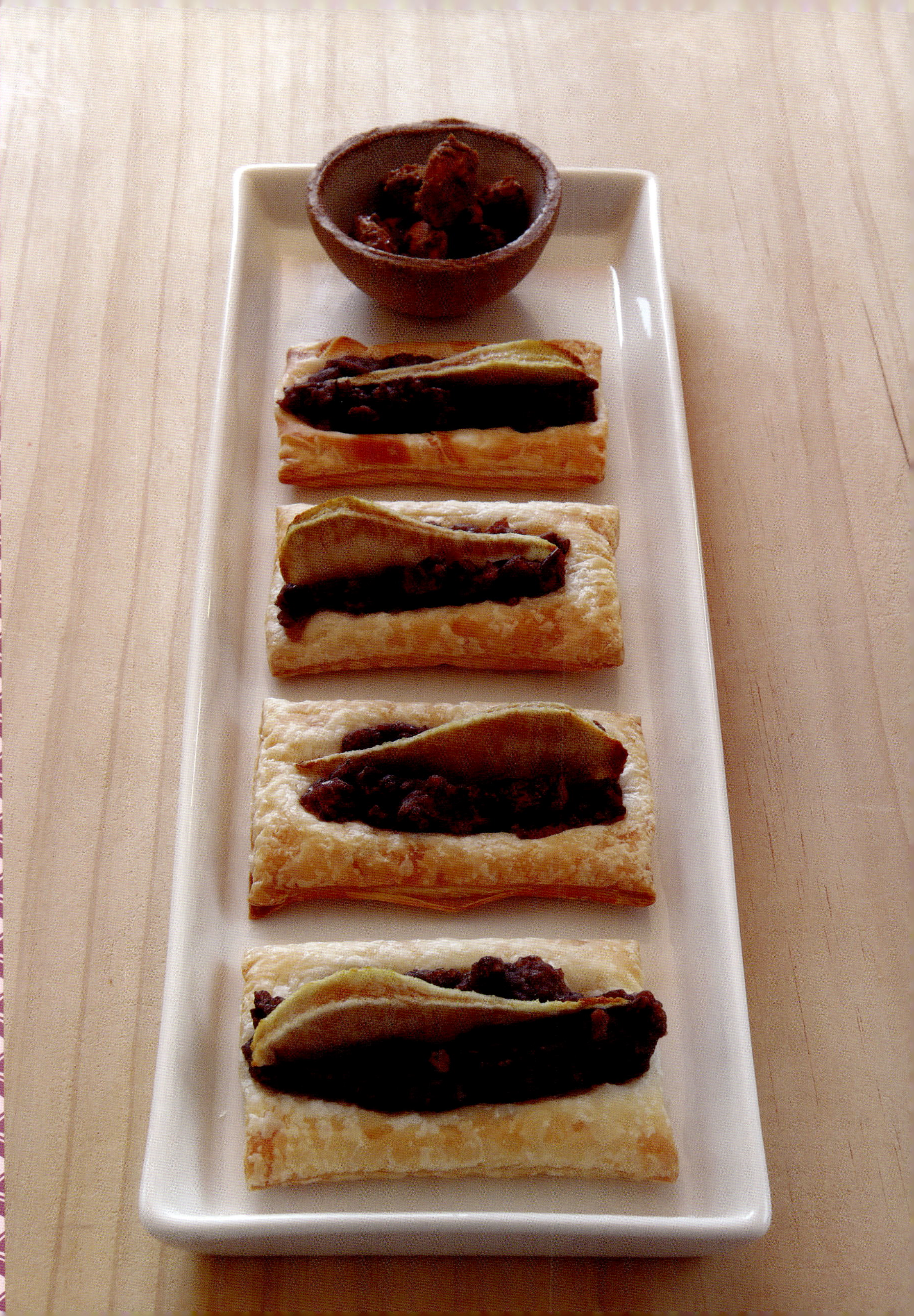

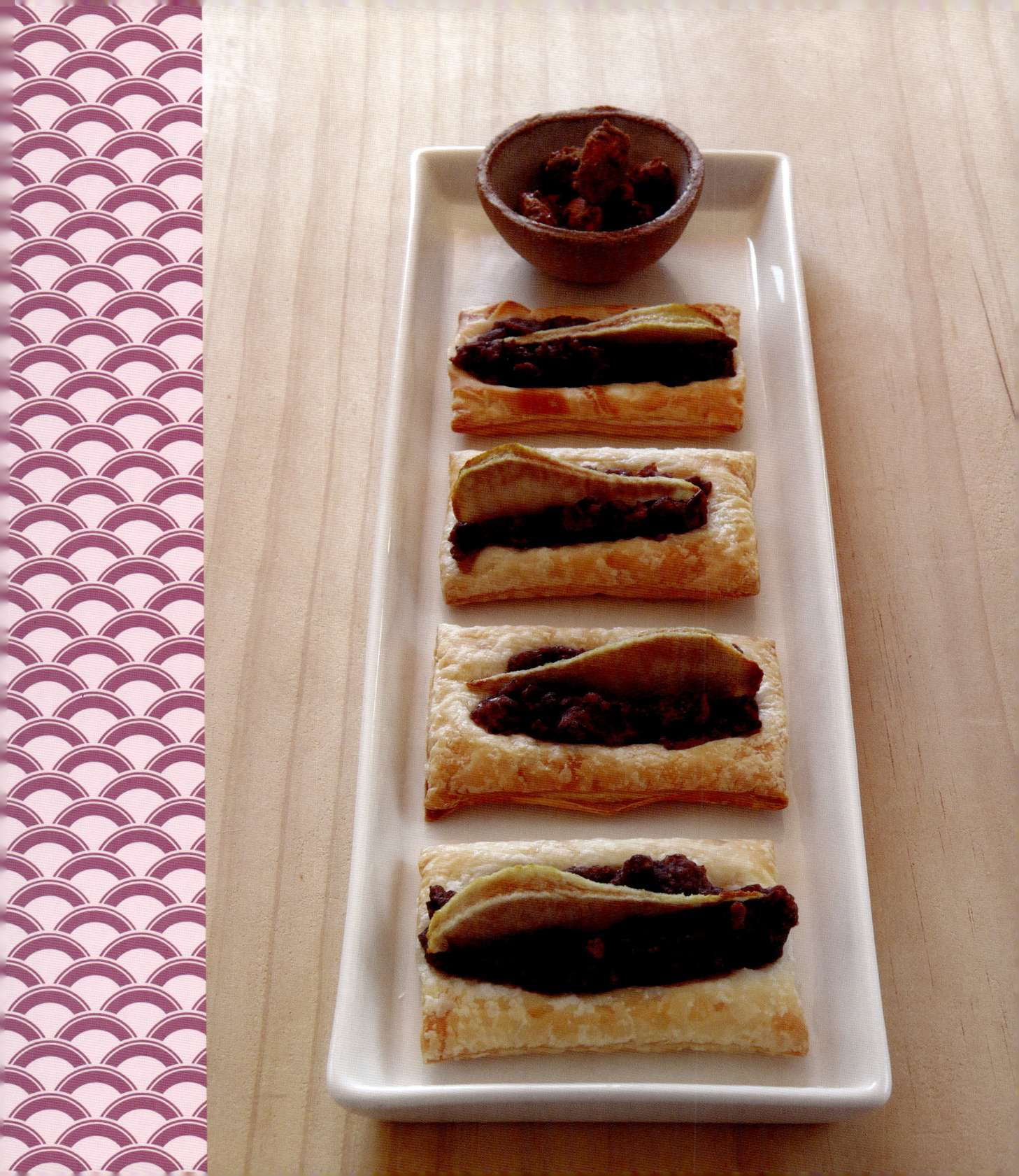

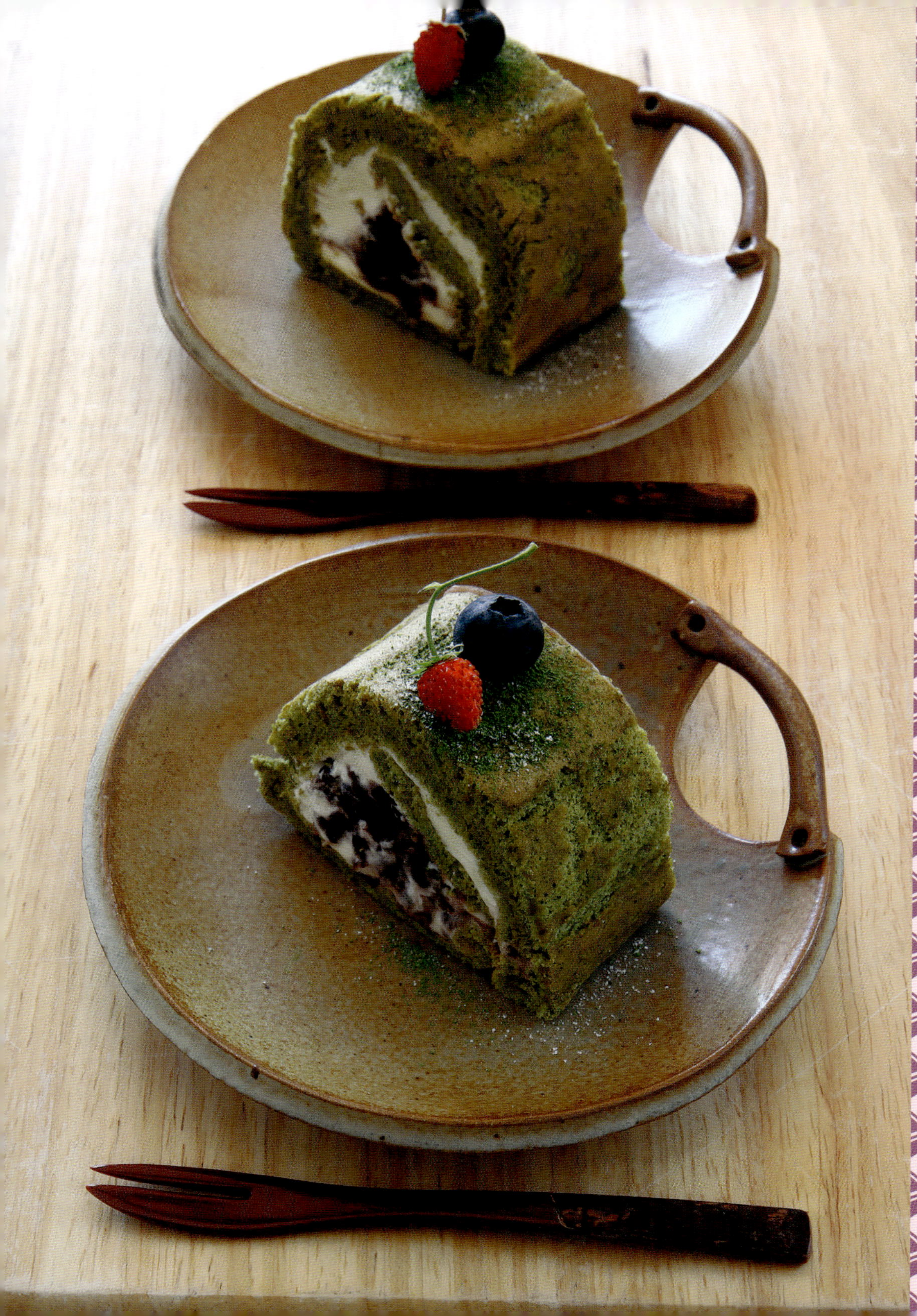

Green tea roll cake

25cm x 35cm (10 x 14 inch) baking tray
4 egg yolks
30g (1 oz) caster sugar
30ml (1 fl oz) vegetable oil
60ml (2 fl oz) water
80g (2¾ oz) weak flour, sieve with 10g (⅓ oz) of green tea powder

MERINGUE
4 egg whites
40g (1½ oz) caster sugar

GREEN TEA CREAM
4 tbsp green tea powder
1 tbsp caster sugar
1 tbsp hot water

SWEET BEAN PASTE
150ml (5 fl oz) thickened cream
2 tbsp caster sugar
100g (3½ oz) sweet red beans paste

一 Lay baking sheet on the baking tray.
二 Preheat the oven to 190°C (375°F).
三 Add egg yolks and sugar and whisk well until pale.
四 Add oil and water and whisk until smooth.
五 Add flour to the egg mixture, and with a wooden spoon fold to combine well.
六 To make the meringue, add egg white into a clean bowl, whisk the egg white and gradually add sugar while beating until it becomes thick and glossy with stiff peaks.
七 Add one third of the meringue into the green tea mixture and whisk to combine well. Repeat this two times, with one third of meringue.
八 With a rubber spatula, transfer the mixture into the baking tray.
九 Smooth the surface.
十 Bake for 13 minutes or until cooked.
十一 Cool it down.
十二 In the meantime, mix the green tea powder and sugar with hot water until dissolved in a bowl then add cream. Whisk until stiff peaks.
十三 Spread sweet bean paste over the cake, leaving 2cm (¾ inch) of cake empty on the far end.
十四 Spread cream over the sweet beans.
十五 Roll up the cake using baking paper and rest for an hour in a refrigerator.

Black sugar creme brulee

MAKES 4 CUPS

1½ tbsp brown sugar or 2 tbsp matcha (green tea) powder, dissolved with 1 tbsp of hot water
1 cup thickened cream
125ml (4¼ fl oz) soy milk or milk
3 tbsp caster sugar
3 egg yolks
6 tbsp Demerara or caster sugar for caramelising

一 Preheat the oven to 150°C (300°F).
二 Fill hot water in a deep oven tray.
三 Place cream and milk in a pan and cook over low heat, turn off the heat just before boiling.
四 In a large bowl add egg yolks and sugar and combine well. Add brown sugar or matcha and mix well.
五 Gently add cream and milk into the mixture, little by little, whisking without making bubbles until combined well.
六 Prepare a sieve over a bowl, sieve the mixture, then pour the mixture into 4 heatproof bowls.
七 Arrange the bowls in the oven tray.
八 Transfer the tray to the oven and steam for about 20 minutes or until cooked.
九 Once cooled down to room temperature, refrigerate.
十 Before serving sprinkle each brulee with 1 tbspful of sugar and caramelise using a blowtorch scorch or under a griller.

Black sesame seed ice cream

150g (5¼ oz) cream
200ml (6¾ fl oz) milk
¼ cup of caster sugar
3 egg yolks
2 tbsp black sesame seeds, ground

一 Make custard following the recipe for Mattcha ice cream.
二 Add black sesame seeds in the custard and combine.
三 Cool in an ice bath until cold and churn in an ice-cream machine.

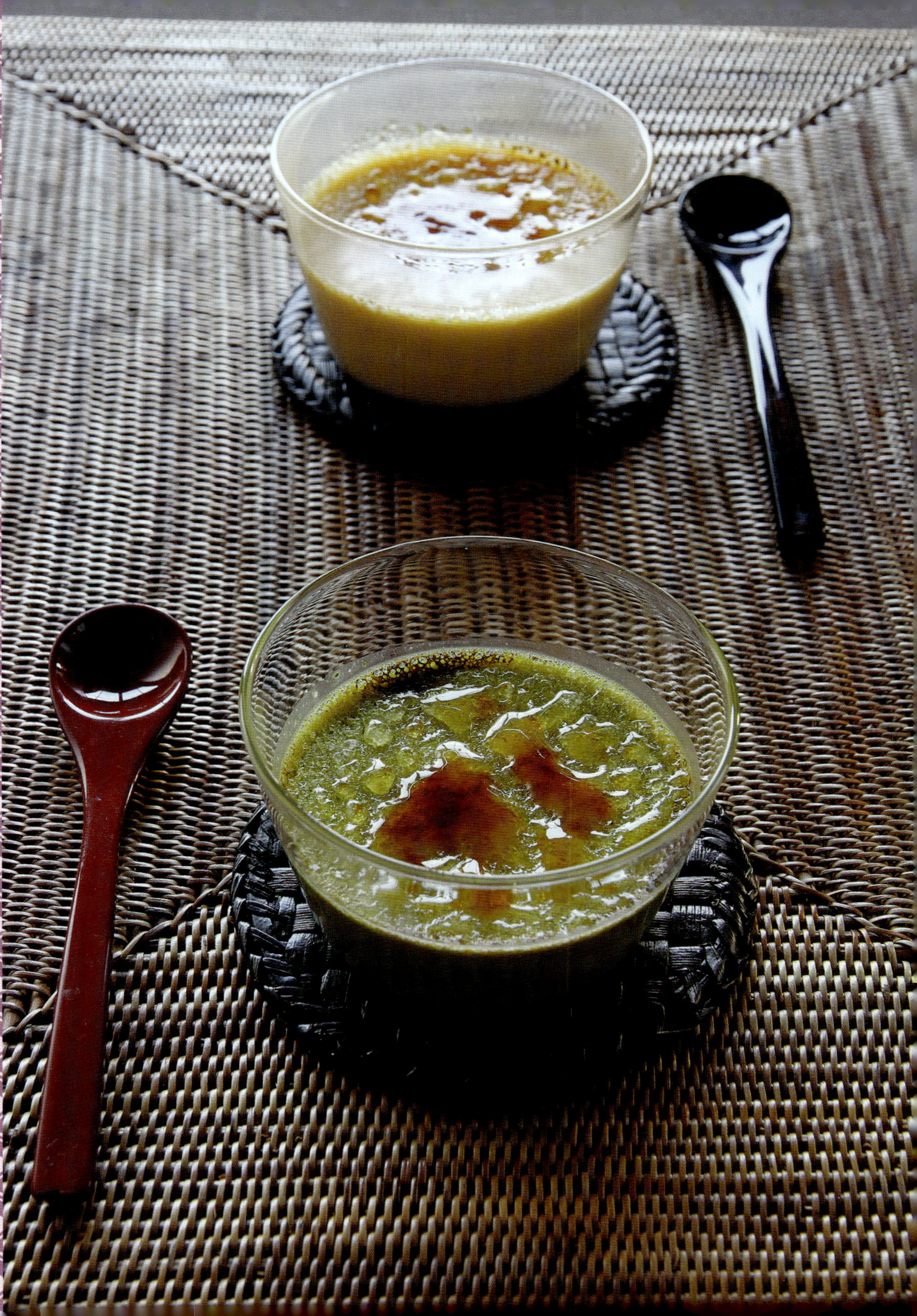

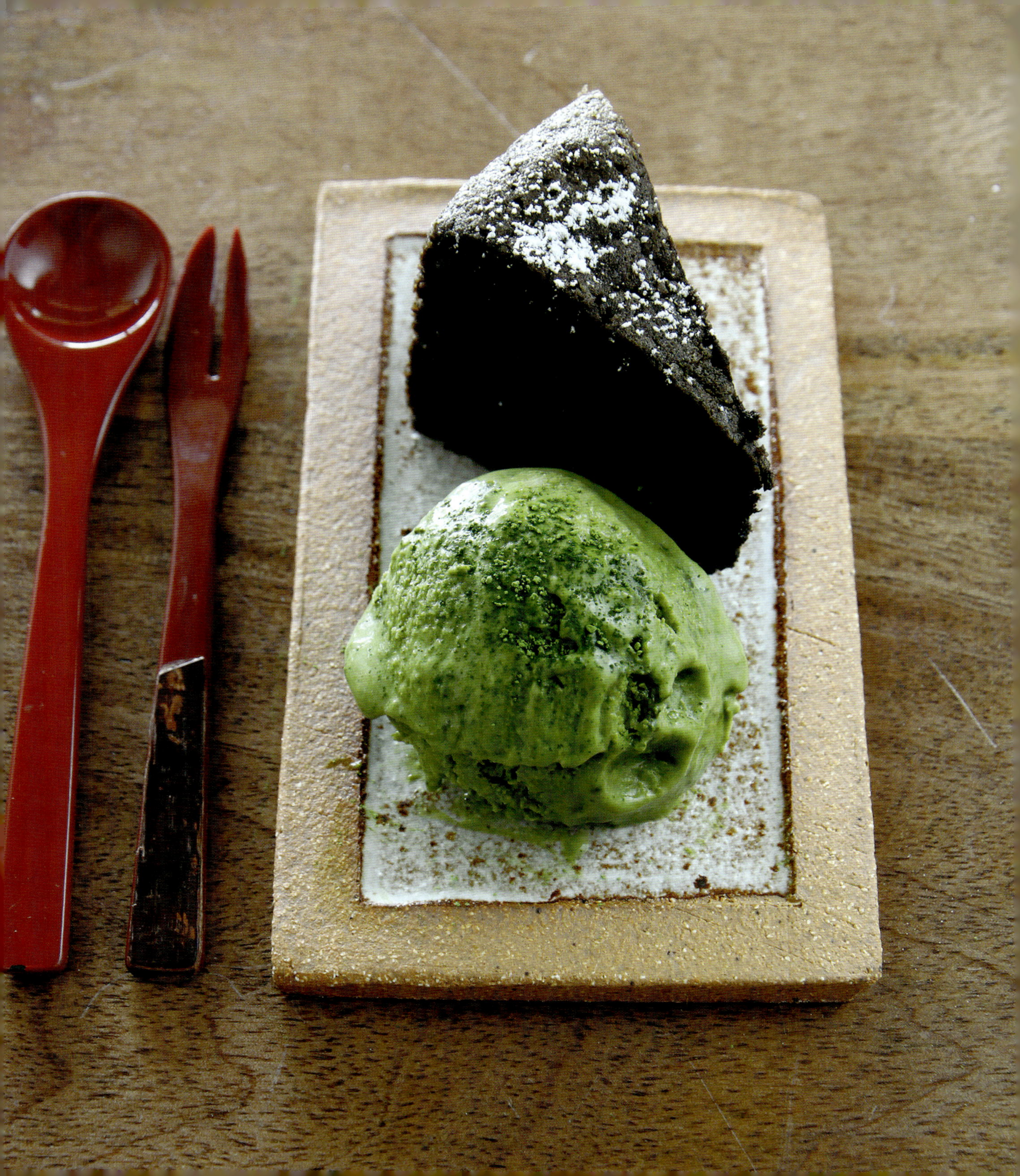

Black sesame cake

20cm (8 inch) round cake tin
150g (5¼ oz) unsalted butter, leave it at room temperature to soften
100g (3½ oz) caster sugar
3 egg yolks
140g (5 oz) black sesame paste
1 tbsp milk

MERINGUE
3 egg whites
50g (1¾ oz) caster sugar

50g (1¾ oz) weak flour, sieved

一 Prepare baking paper around the cake tin.

二 Preheat oven to 200°C (390°F).

三 Using a hand mixer or mixer, whip the butter until pale, then add sugar (1¾ oz) at a time and mix.

四 Add egg yolks and mix. Then add black sesame paste and combine. Add milk and mix.

五 To make meringue, whisk egg white and gradually add sugar and beat until thick and glossy with stiff peaks.

六 Add half the quantity of meringue into the butter mixture and combine using a rubber spatula. Add sieved flour and mix well. Then add the rest of the meringue into the mixture and combine.

七 Transfer the mixture into the cake tin and flatten the surface.

八 Bake for 10 minutes at 200°C (390°F) then reduce to 170°C (340°F) and bake for 25 minutes.

九 Transfer the cake onto the cooling wire and once slightly cooled down, remove cake from tin.

十 Serve with green tea ice cream.

IZAKAYA • DESSERT

Umeshu jelly

4 tall glasses
120ml (4 fl oz) water
4 tbsp caster sugar
10g (⅓ oz) gelatine sheet or powder, soaked in water
120 ml (4 fl oz) umeshu: Japanese sweet plum wine

SEASONAL FRUITS FOR TOPPING:
Seasonal berries
1 tsp of sugar
Juice of ½ orange

一 Place water and sugar in a pan and bring it to boil.

二 Add gelatine to the pan and dissolve.

三 Transfer the mixture into a bowl over ice. Gently stir with a rubber spatula to cool it down.

四 Add umeshu to the mixture and mix well.

五 Transfer the mixture into the container with a lid. Refrigerate until set.

六 In the meantime, mix fruits in a bowl with sugar and orange juice, and then rest in the refrigerator.

七 Serve jelly in a glass topped with fruits or alternatively spoon jelly and fruit into a tall glass.

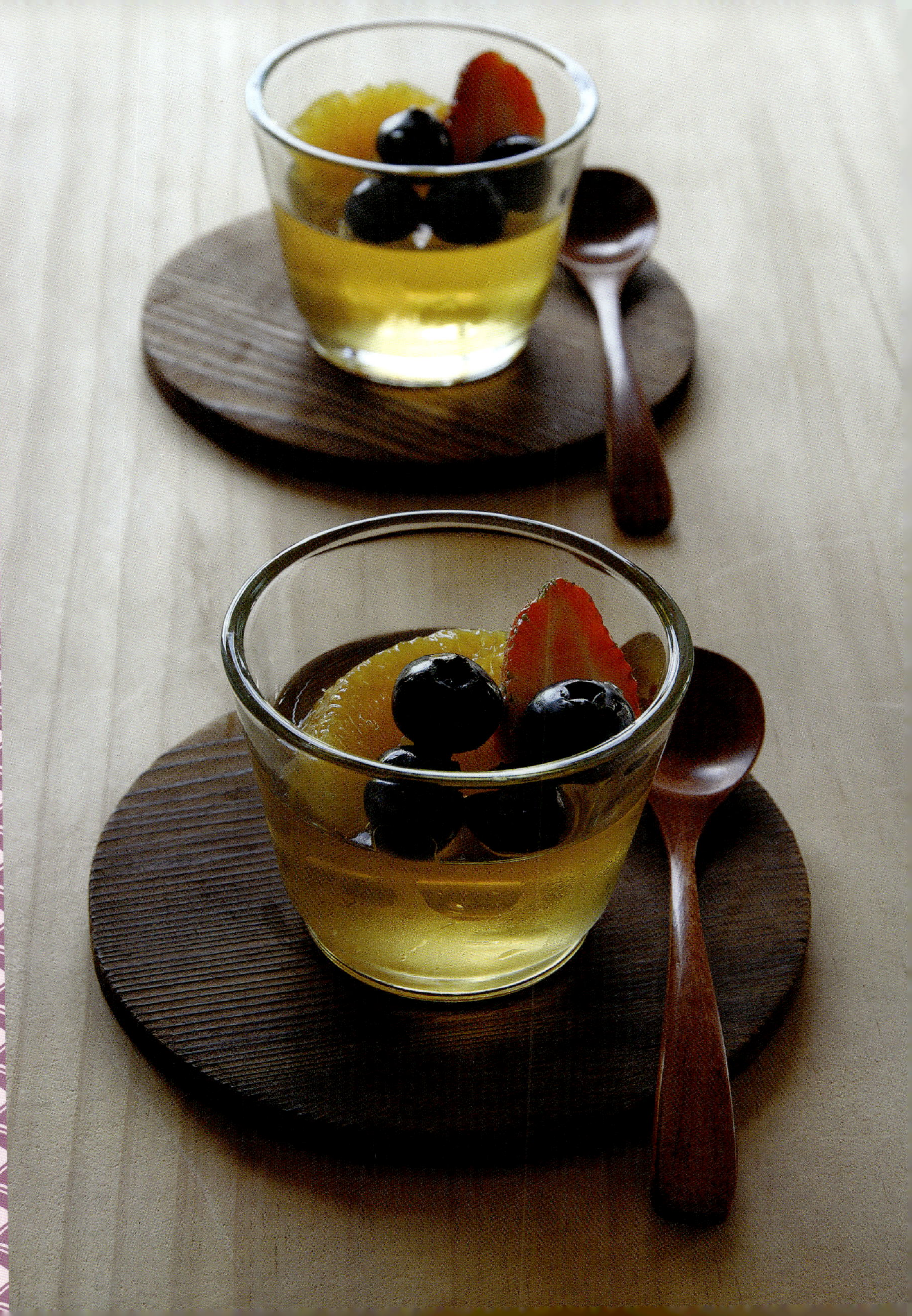

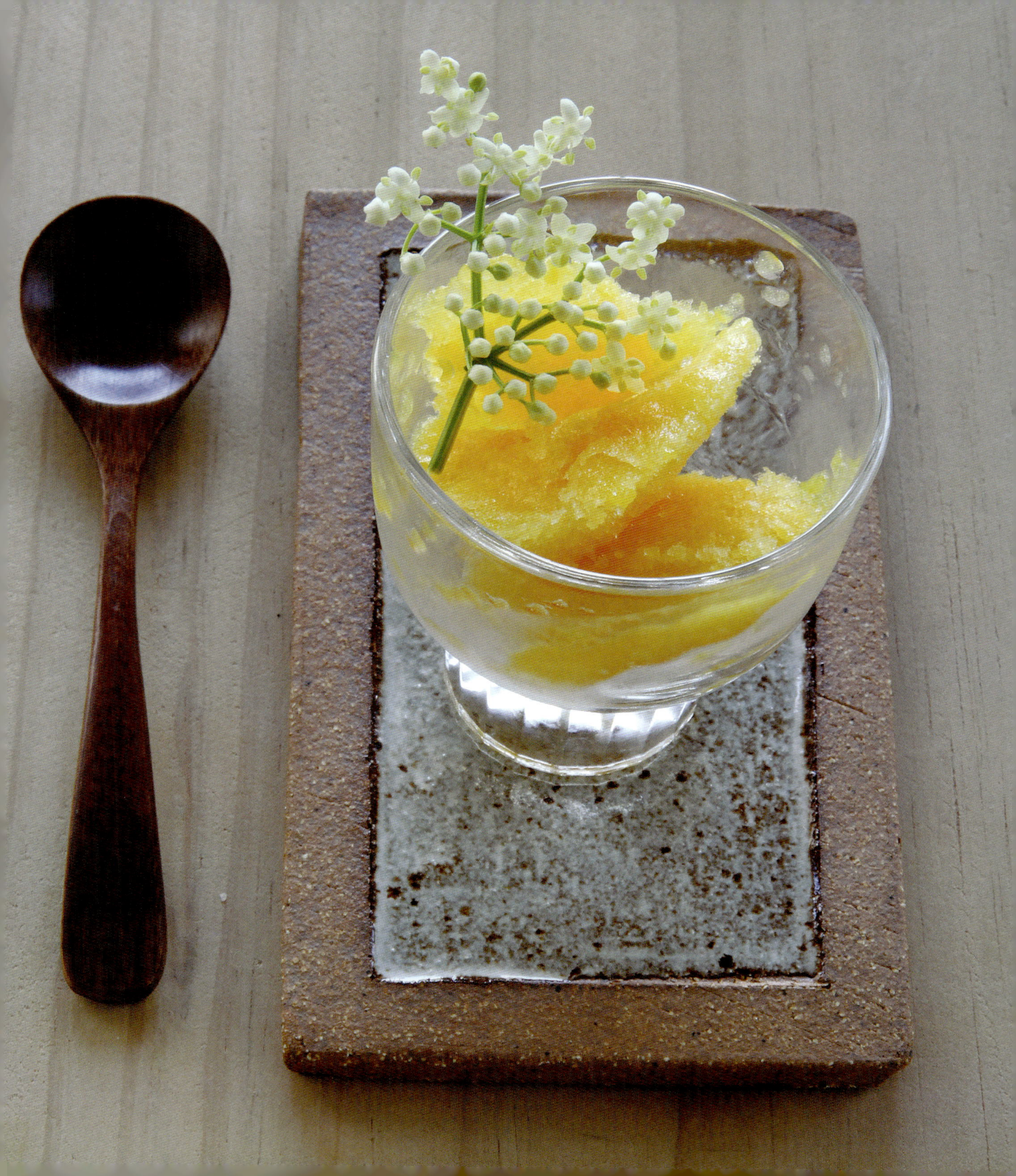

Sake and peach sorbet

SERVES 4–5

250g (8¾ oz) can of peach
50ml (2 fl oz) syrup from peach can
2 tbsp caster sugar
1 tbsp lemon juice
3 tbsp sake
5g (⅕ oz) powder gelatine, soaked with 2 tbsp of water
150g (5¼ oz) can of peach
Elder flower for garnish

一 Soak gelatine in water.

二 Add peach, peach syrup, caster sugar, lemon juice and sake in a mixer and smooth. Transfer them into a container.

三 Cook gelatine until dissolved.

四 Add gelatine to the peach mix and combine well.

五 Freeze for 2 hours, mix with a fork every hour.

六 Chop 150g (5¼ oz) of peach and add to the sorbet, then combine well.

七 Freeze until frozen, mix with a fork every hour to make the sorbet creamy.

八 Serve in individual glass.

Japanese groceries

Abura-age: thin deep-fried sliced tofu
Ao-nori: green seaweed flakes
Bainiku: pickled salted plum puree
Chikuwa: cylinder-shape fish cake tube
Edamame: green soy beans
Eringe: eringe-mushroom
Enoki: enoki-mushroom
Daikon: daikon radish
Gobo-ten: deep-fried fish paste with burdock stick
Goma: sesame seeds: shiro-goma (white sesame seeds); Kuro-goma (black sesame seeds)
Harusame: thin rice noodle
Hijiki: dried hijiki seaweed
Hoji-cha: roasted green tea
Kamaboko: kamaboko fish cake
Katsuo-bushi: bonito flakes
Kinome: Japanese mountain pepper leave
Kombu: kelp
Konnyaku: konnyaku-potato hard jelly
Matcha: green tea powder
Mentaiko: salted pollack roe
Mirin: sweet cooking sake
Miso: fermented soy bean paste
Shinshu-miso: common light brown colour
Saikyo-miso or Shiro-miso: white sweet miso
Aka-miso or Haccho-miso: dark brown miso with rich flavour
Mochi: Japanese sticky rice cake
Myoga: miyoga ginger
Nasu: Japanese eggplant
Natto: fermented cooked soy beans
Nori: nori-sheet
Renkon: lotus root
Ponzu: citrus vinaigrette

Ryori-shu: sake for cooking
Sansho: Japanese mountain pepper
Satsuma-imo: Japanese sweet potato
Shichimi: Japanese seven spices
Shiitake: shiitake mushroom, fresh and dried are available
Shimeji: shimeji mushroom
Shiso: Japanese green basil
Shio-kombu: dried salted kelp strips
Shoyu: soy sauce
Koikuchi-shoyu: common soy sauce
Usukuchi Shoyu: light colour soy sacue
Tamari-jyoyu: sashimi soy sauce
Soba: buckwheat noodle
Su: vinegar
Komezu: rice vinegar
Yuzu-su or ponzu: citrus vinegar
Akajiso-zu: red shiso vinegar
Tofu: Soybean curd: kinugoshi-dofu is soft tofu and Momen-dofu is a bit firm tofu. Other products with tofu are Abura-age (thin deep-fried sliced tofu) and Atsu-age (thick deep-fired tofu).
Tonkatsu-sauce: thicken sauce with a flavour like Worcester sauce, it is often used for breadcrumbed deep-fries
Ume-boshi: salted pickled plum
Wakame: seaweed
Wafu: means Japanese style
Wasabi: wasabi mustard
Wagarashi: Japanese hot mustard
Yukari: yukari is a product name, but it is a dried salted red shiso flakes
Yuzu: yuzu citrus; Yuzu-su: yuzu flavoured vinegar; Yuzu-kosho: Yuzu flavoured paste

Afterword, Andre Bishop

To label an izakaya as just another form of restaurant would be doing this style of dining institution a great injustice. It is so much more, and the place it holds in Japanese culture is a testament to its enduring appeal.

It's heritage it closely tied to the serving of beverages first and foremost, but as we all know drinking excites the appetite and food to accompany those drinks closely followed. Therefore, the styles of dishes found at an izakaya are well suited to be enjoyed with drinks, sake and beer in particular.

Traditionally, small neighbourhood drinking and eating sanctuaries where Japanese would gather to digest the day's trials and tribulations, izakaya now present themselves in many forms. Tiny, cosy establishments share the landscape with large chains and price points ranging from "cheap and cheerful" to upmarket.

Izakaya provide the environment where deals are made, business relationships are forged, friendships formed, strengthened and renewed, problems shared and forgotten, love found and lost. Izakaya perform an important social service, they provide a window into the tapestry of daily life.

The food is intended to be shared, many small dishes, many tastes that ebb and flow with the mood and the fancy of the diners. There is a loose format that is generally followed. Light cold, dishes to start, such as sashimi or beef tataki moving on to heartier, richer dishes as the palette warms and the discussion deepens.

My relationship with izakaya has been a long and enjoyable one. My first experience was Izakaya Chuji in Melbourne, the old dame of Australian izakaya, celebrating its 25th anniversary in 2014. After my first trip to Japan in 1996 I became so enraptured with this style of Japanese eatery that in a strange twist of fate I purchased Izakaya Chuji in 2003 to save it from closure.

The importance of the classic izakaya, its food and the influence it has had on the world dining stage cannot be underestimated. It and its close relatives above have changed the modern dining landscape. Where degustation dining is generally associated to special signature dishes showing a chefs prowess with the associated price tag, izakaya fare offers this experience as a common daily occurrence.

Hideo Dekura knows the place that izakaya and izakaya food holds in the heart of the Japanese people. He brings his skill, knowledge and love of this food to bear in the pages of this book. You will be inspired by these recipes to create food that is intended to be shared and bring a little of that izakaya vibe to your dinning table. Enjoy with friends! (Oh, and don't forget the sake).

Andre Bishop is a Melbourne based Sake Professional and is recognised as Australia's leading authority on sake.

Index

A
Aburi-style marinated pork with miso 151
Agedashi mochi: Deep-fried rice cake in broth 60
Agedashi-dofu 54
Avocado tofu dip 33
Awase-jyoyu (kaeshi) 20

B
Baby octopus crackers 185
Barbecued chicken yakitori 84
Bari-Bari salad 79
Basic dashi: kelp and bonito stock 20
Beer 15
Black sesame cake 227
Black sesame seed ice cream 224
Black sugar creme brulee 224
Blanched beef in rice vinaigrette 140
Boiled egg in miso 38
Braised chicken soft bone with garlic, sesame and soy sauce 116
Braised sliced eggplant topped with red miso 75

C
Cabbage and bacon with soy sauce butter 64
Carrot and daikon in shio-kombu 29
Celery sticks in salt and kelp 29
Chicken ball 91
Chicken giblet with rocket leaves in earthenware pot 116
Chicken kara-age 112
Chicken tsukune: Skewered minced chicken 115
Chucai 17
Cream cheese with bainiku (pickled plum puree) or yukari (salted red shiso flakes) 33
Cream cheese with miso or saikyo miso 33
Cream cheese with wasabi 33
Crispy nori 38
Cuttle fish with mentaiko and green salad leaves 169

D
Daikon salad 76
Dashimaki-tamago: Japanese egg omelette 120
Deep-fried Brussels sprouts 63
Deep-fried diced pork with umeboshi 151
Deep-fried garlic 38
Deep-fried gyoza sheet with cheese and nori sheet 71
Deep-fried lotus roots in olive oil, grilled with parmesan cheese 68
Deep-fried mochi cubes 49
Deep-fried white fish paste in shiso-leave 102
Deep-fried zucchini with miso-mayo 99
Diced avocado and julienned cucumber tossed with wasabi mayonnaise 76
Diced rice cake with sweet soy sauce 49
Dressed up king prawn 99

E
Edamame harumaki: Edamame spring roll 63
Edamame: Young green soy beans 30
Eggplant marinated in lemon vinaigrette 71

F
Filleting (shima-aji in sanmai oroshi, three pieces filleting) 156
Fishcake with lotus root and carrot garnished with lemon wedge 102
Fresh pacific oyster combined with plum and soy sauce 170
Furofuki daikon: Simmered caikon with miso paste 75

G
Garlic rice 211
Grated daikon salad with Shimeji and enoki mushrooms 68
Green tea roll cake 223
Grilled abura-age 53
Grilled clam stuffed with sea urchin 182
Grilled eggplant with various sauce 72
Grilled skewered whiting 189
Grilled squid tube with shichimi 177
Grilled sundried whiting with mirin 181
Grilled tiger prawn stuffed with mango and chilli 178
Gyoza dumpling with stamina sauce 152

H
Hachimitsu-dare: honey dressing 23
Harumaki: Spring roll with king prawn and asparagus 101
Hijiki-seaweed and soy bean salad 63
Hiyayakko: Tofu with toppings 45
Hojicha ice cream 219
Hoso-maki 207
Hotate with soy sauce butter 198

I
Ika-somen 166

J
Japanese croquette in sukiyaki flavour 106
Japanese egg omelette with scallops 122

K
Kaki-age 96
Kaki-furai: Deep-fried oyster with breadcrumbs 105
Kamameshi: Steamed rice with shiitake, enoki mushroom and oyster in a pot 215
Kara-age: Deep fried flounder with shiitake glazing sauce 174
Karashi miso 34
Kushi-age, Skewered pork in breadcrumbs 87
Kyuri no Ume-ae: Cucumber ume salad 67

L
Lamb chop or pork soft rib in chilli miso 148
Lightly braised thinly sliced beef tongue 135

M
Mackerel cooked in miso 193
Mattcha ice cream with sweet red beans 219
Mentaiko (salted Pollack roe) dressing 22
Mini ura-maki: Mini inside-out roll 204
Minudaru: Steamed pork in black sesame 147
Mizore-nabe: Hot pot with grated daikon with tofu 57
Mizuna salad with onion dressing 112

IZAKAYA · INDEX

Motsu-nabe: soy sauce flavoured slow-cooked beef with fresh spring onion 127
Motsu-ni with chicken offal 131
Motsu-ni: Miso flavoured slow-cooked brisket with daikon 128

N
Namban miso 34
Negi miso cream cheese 34
Nigiri 208
Nikujyaga: Beef and vegetable sweet soy sauce stew 143
Ninniku dare: garlic dressing 23
Nori ribbon 46

O
Ochazuke, rice in tea broth 212
Octopus in vinaigrette 173
Octopus with daikon and bainiku sauce 173
Oden 90
Onion dressing 22

P
Pickle cabbage in salt 29
Ponzu: citrus dipping sauce 21
Pork Shabu-Shabu salad 132
Potato salad 107
Preparing daikon-tsuma 159
Preparing rice 202
Preparing sushi rice 203

Q
Quick tsumami spicy sardines in a can 41

R
Renkon chips: Lotus roots chips 41
Renkon senbei karikari chips with sweet soy sauce: Lotus root chips with sweet soy sauce 107
Rice noodle salad drizzled with lemon dressing 60
Rolled cabbage 91

S
saikyo-style grilled cod 194
Saikyo-style grilled scallops 198
Sake 15
Sake and peach sorbet 231
Sake-miso dare: sake and red miso dressing 23
Sardine cream cheese dip 33
Sardine tatsuta-age 190
Sashimi 161
Sashimi slicing techniques 158
Satsuma-imo (Japanese sweet potato) chips with sweet soy sauce 41
Sawa-Sour 17
Sesame miso 34
Shiro-ae: Tofu salad 50
Shoga dare: ginger dressing 22
Sliced lotus roots and mandarin orange pickeld in sweet rice vinegar 30
Snapper carpaccio 165
Soba age: Crispy buck wheat noodle 38
Sochu 16
Spicy konnyaku 42
Steamed baby abalone 186
Steamed chicken tenderloin tossed with plum puree 115
Steamed chicken, Yuan style 119
Steamed iceberg lettuce 64
Steamed vegetables with ponzu and sesame dip 67
Stir-fried lamb liver 143
Stirred potato and carrot with salt and shichimi 71
Summer salad with plum gellée 80
Suri-goma dare: ground sesame seed dressing 22
Sweet and hot Julianne beef skirt 136

T
Tama-miso mustard vinaigrette 24
Tama-miso vinaigrette 24
Tama-miso: Miso with egg dressing 24
Teba to ninniku age: Deep fried chicken wing and garlic 111
Tempura 95
Teriyaki kingfish 197
Teriyaki sauce 21
Tofu in hot pot 57
Tofu salad 51
Tofu steak 50
Tofu-cream dip 34
Tofu-dengaku with sansho miso 53
Tomato salad with red onion 68
Topside cubed steak 139
Tossed chrysanthemum and enoki mushrooms with Japanese mustard 76
Tuna sashimi combined with natto 162
Tuna sashimi with avocado 162
Umeboshi-dare: pickled plum dressing 22

U
Umeshu jelly 228

V
Vegetable pickles in soy sauce 30

W
Wafu carpaccio 144
Wafu Danish 220
Wafu-marinating sauce 21
Wasabi soy sauce dressing 22
White sesame dressing 22

Y
Yaki miso: Grilled miso on wooden rice spoon 37
Yaki shiitake: Grilled shiitake tossed with bonito flakes and soy sauce 72
Yaki-edamame: Scorched edamame served with shichimi 30
Yaki-onigiri: Soy sauce flavoured grilled rice ball 211

Z
Zosui: Egg and rice porridge 212